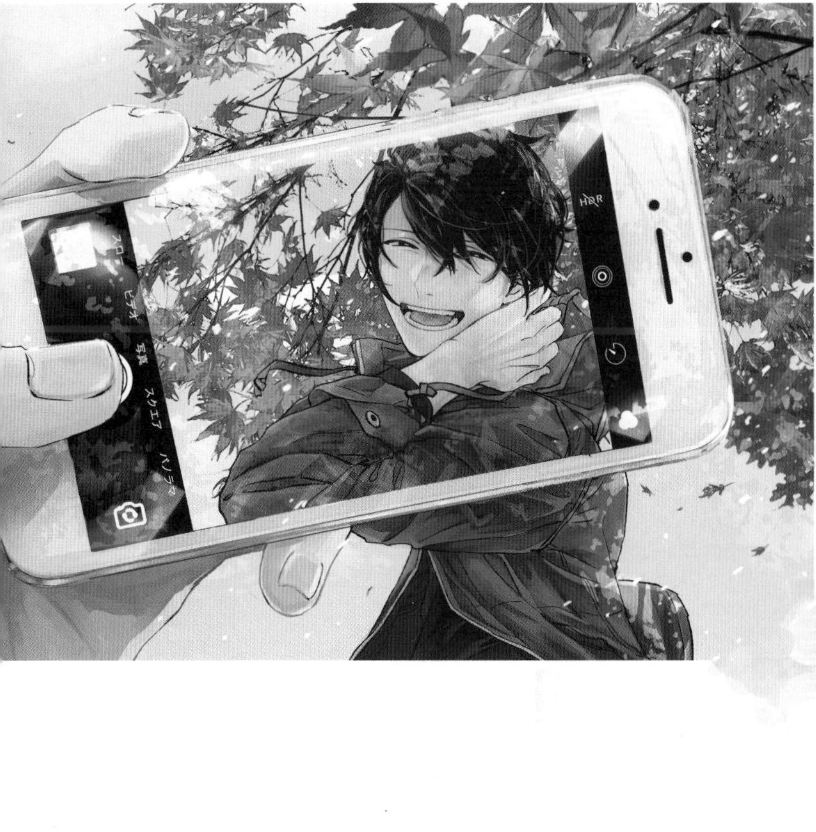
HDR
ビデオ
写真
スクエア
パノラマ

Given

Story and Art by **Natsuki Kizu**

volume **3**

CONTENTS

SUBLIME
SuBLime Manga Edition

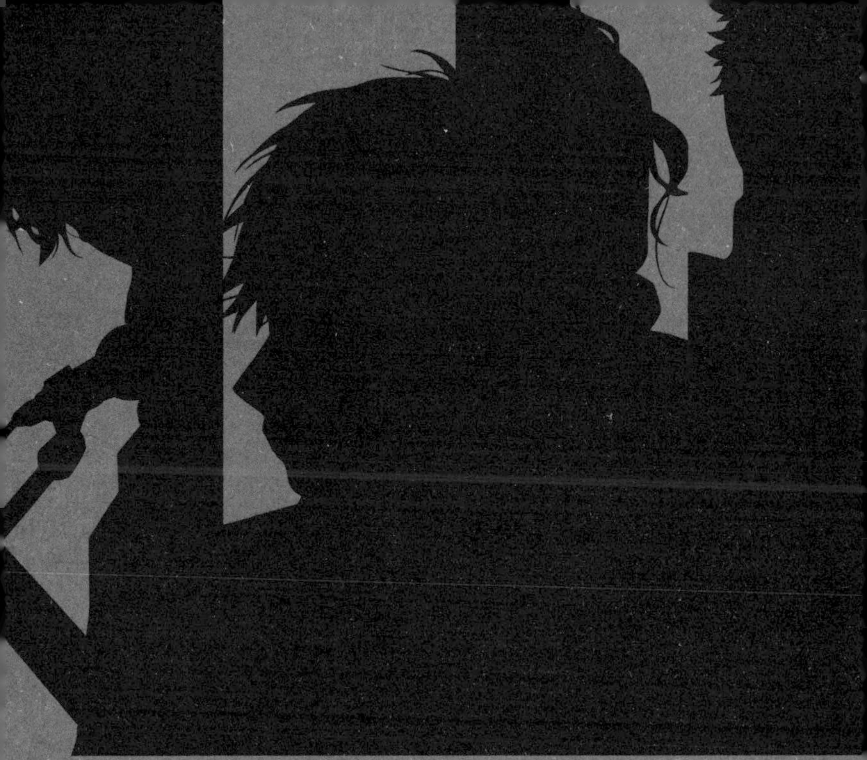

given

VOLUME 3

NATSUKI KIZU

STORY

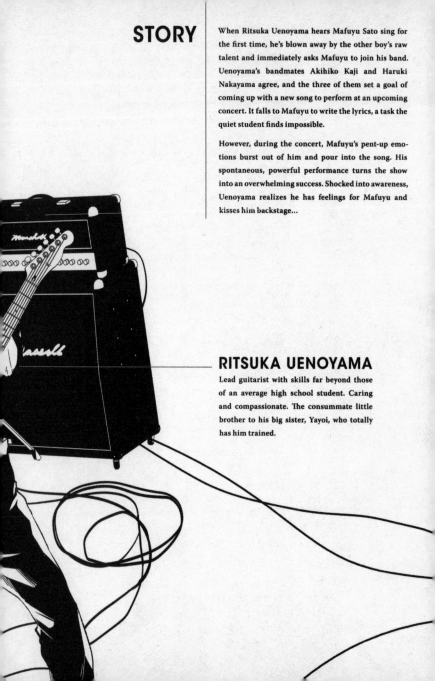

When Ritsuka Uenoyama hears Mafuyu Sato sing for the first time, he's blown away by the other boy's raw talent and immediately asks Mafuyu to join his band. Uenoyama's bandmates Akihiko Kaji and Haruki Nakayama agree, and the three of them set a goal of coming up with a new song to perform at an upcoming concert. It falls to Mafuyu to write the lyrics, a task the quiet student finds impossible.

However, during the concert, Mafuyu's pent-up emotions burst out of him and pour into the song. His spontaneous, powerful performance turns the show into an overwhelming success. Shocked into awareness, Uenoyama realizes he has feelings for Mafuyu and kisses him backstage...

RITSUKA UENOYAMA

Lead guitarist with skills far beyond those of an average high school student. Caring and compassionate. The consummate little brother to his big sister, Yayoi, who totally has him trained.

MAFUYU SATO

High school classmate of Uenoyama's. Has an impressive singing voice. Attached to Uenoyama ever since he fixed Mafuyu's broken guitar.

HARUKI NAKAYAMA

Graduate student. The band's bassist. He's extremely good-natured and kind.

AKIHIKO KAJI

University student. The band's drummer. A bit of a playboy who's popular without ever trying.

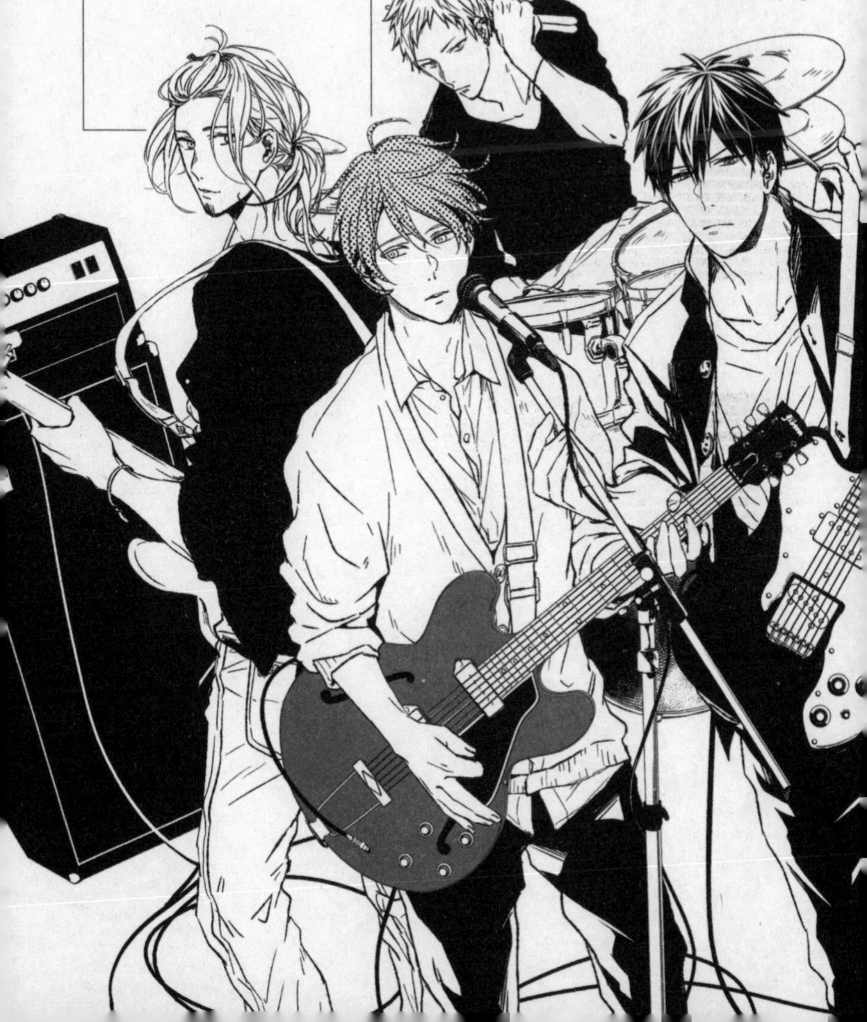

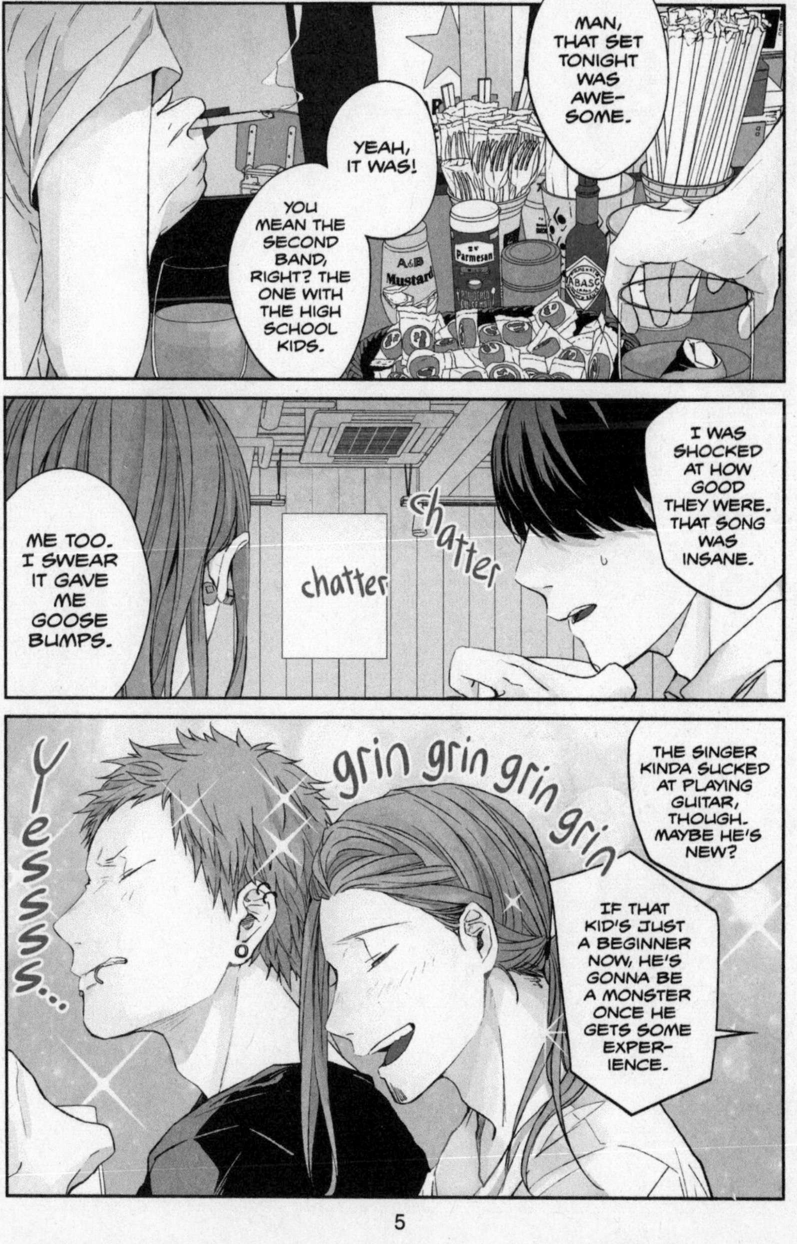
MAN, THAT SET TONIGHT WAS AWESOME.
YEAH, IT WAS!
YOU MEAN THE SECOND BAND, RIGHT? THE ONE WITH THE HIGH SCHOOL KIDS.
I WAS SHOCKED AT HOW GOOD THEY WERE. THAT SONG WAS INSANE.
chatter
chatter
ME TOO. I SWEAR IT GAVE ME GOOSE BUMPS.
THE SINGER KINDA SUCKED AT PLAYING GUITAR, THOUGH. MAYBE HE'S NEW?
IF THAT KID'S JUST A BEGINNER NOW, HE'S GONNA BE A MONSTER ONCE HE GETS SOME EXPERIENCE.
grin grin grin grin
Yessss...

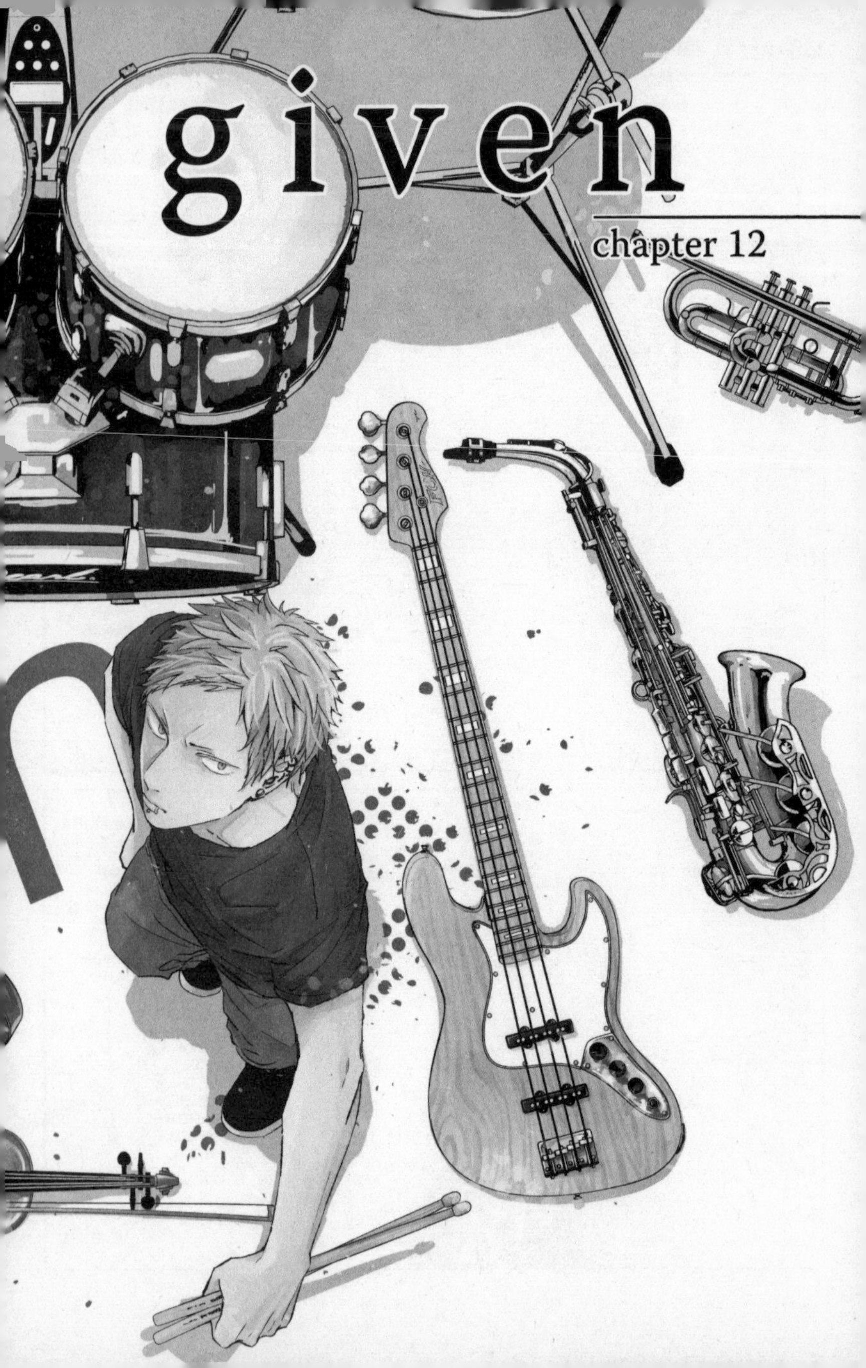
given
chapter 12

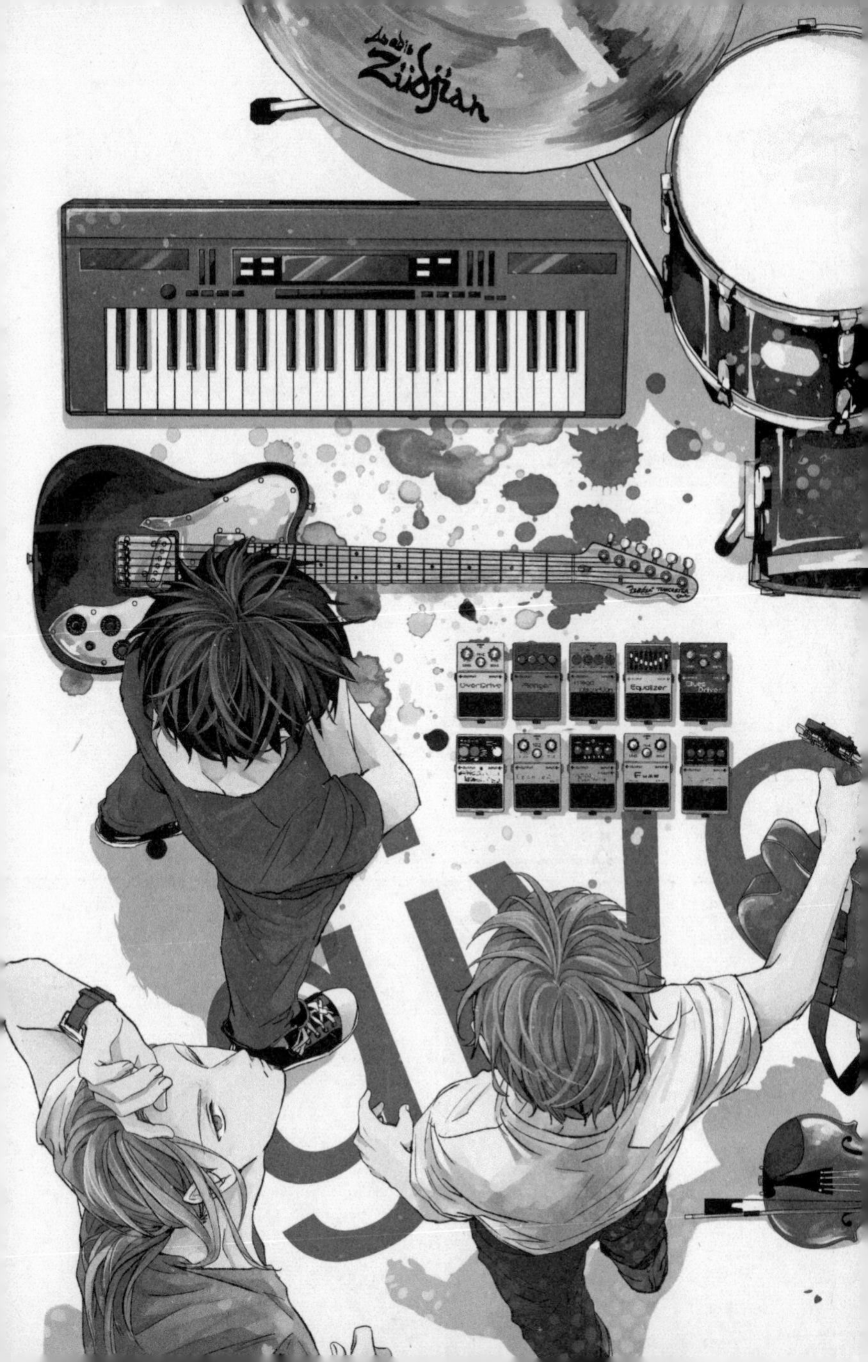
Zildjian
OverDrive
Equalizer
Blues Driver
Fuzz

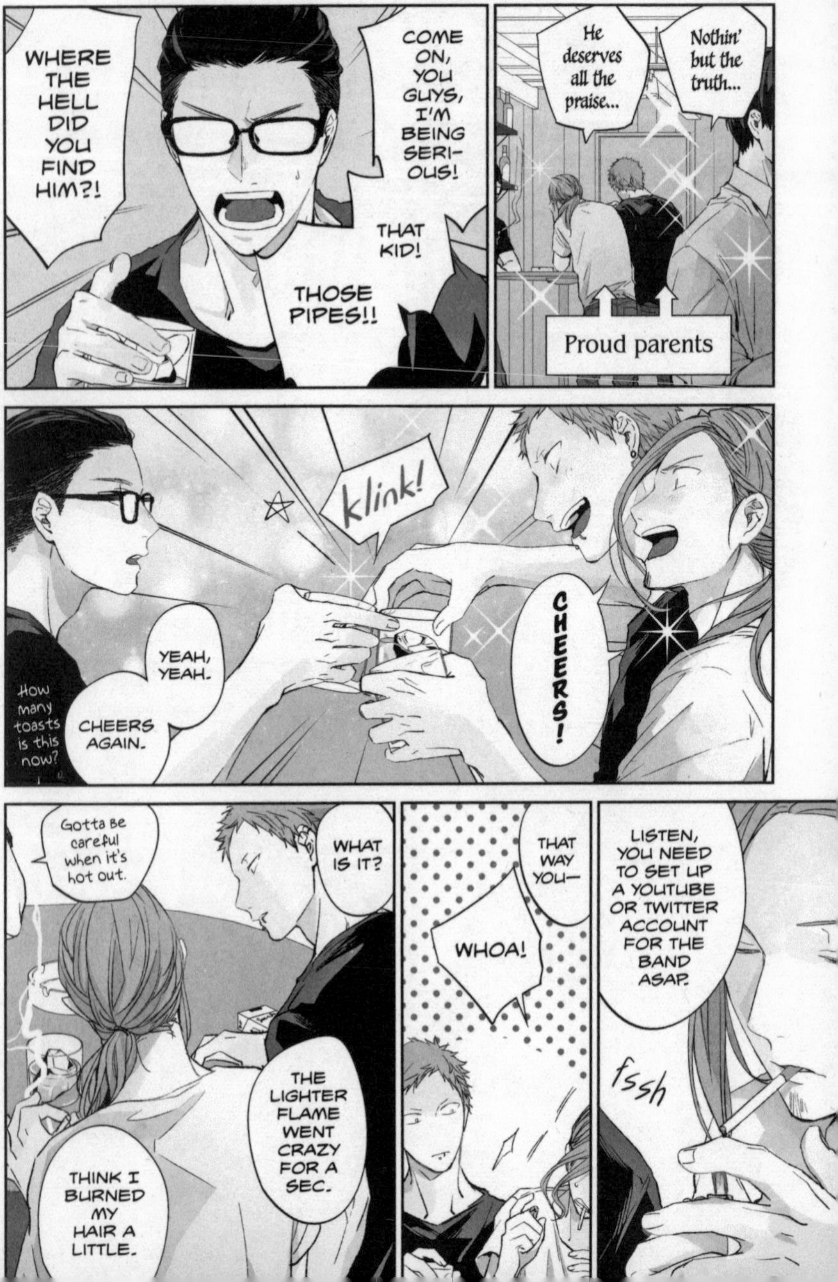
Nothin' but the truth...
He deserves all the praise...
Proud parents
COME ON, YOU GUYS, I'M BEING SERI-OUS!
WHERE THE HELL DID YOU FIND HIM?!
THAT KID!
THOSE PIPES!!
CHEERS!
klink!
YEAH, YEAH.
CHEERS AGAIN.
How many toasts is this now?
LISTEN, YOU NEED TO SET UP A YOUTUBE OR TWITTER ACCOUNT FOR THE BAND ASAP.
fssh
THAT WAY YOU—
WHOA!
WHAT IS IT?
Gotta be careful when it's hot out.
THE LIGHTER FLAME WENT CRAZY FOR A SEC.
THINK I BURNED MY HAIR A LITTLE.

SWf

YOU'VE LET IT GET SO LONG IT'S DANGEROUS.

Ha ha ha!

I'VE GOTTA GET IT CUT SOON.

ZOOM

AH HA HA!

RIGHT! SO!

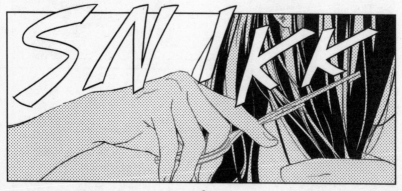

SNIKK

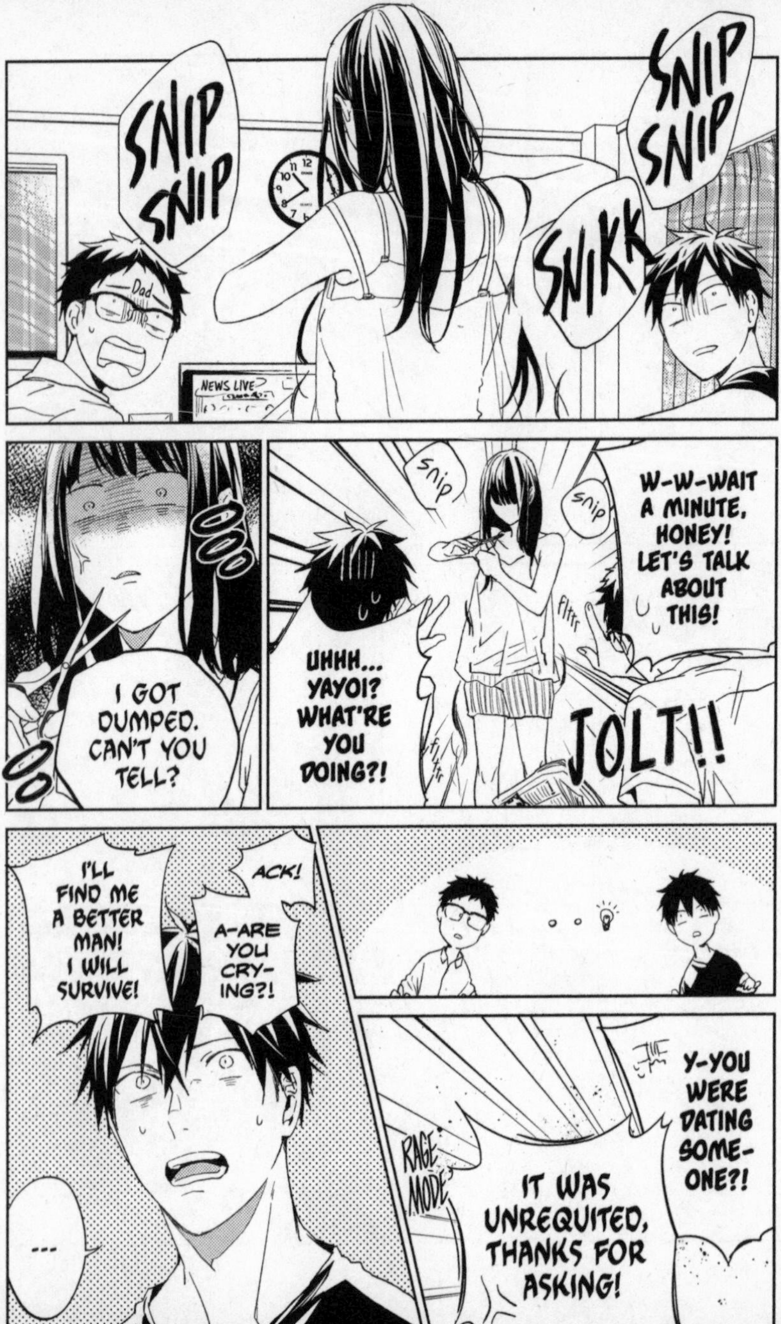
SNIP SNIP
SNIKK
SNIP SNIP
Dad
NEWS LIVE
snip
snip
W-W-WAIT A MINUTE, HONEY! LET'S TALK ABOUT THIS!
JOLT!!
UHHH... YAYOI? WHAT'RE YOU DOING?!
I GOT DUMPED. CAN'T YOU TELL?
. . .
Y-YOU WERE DATING SOME-ONE?!
IT WAS UNREQUITED, THANKS FOR ASKING!
RAGE MODE
ACK!
A-ARE YOU CRY-ING?!
I'LL FIND ME A BETTER MAN! I WILL SURVIVE!
...

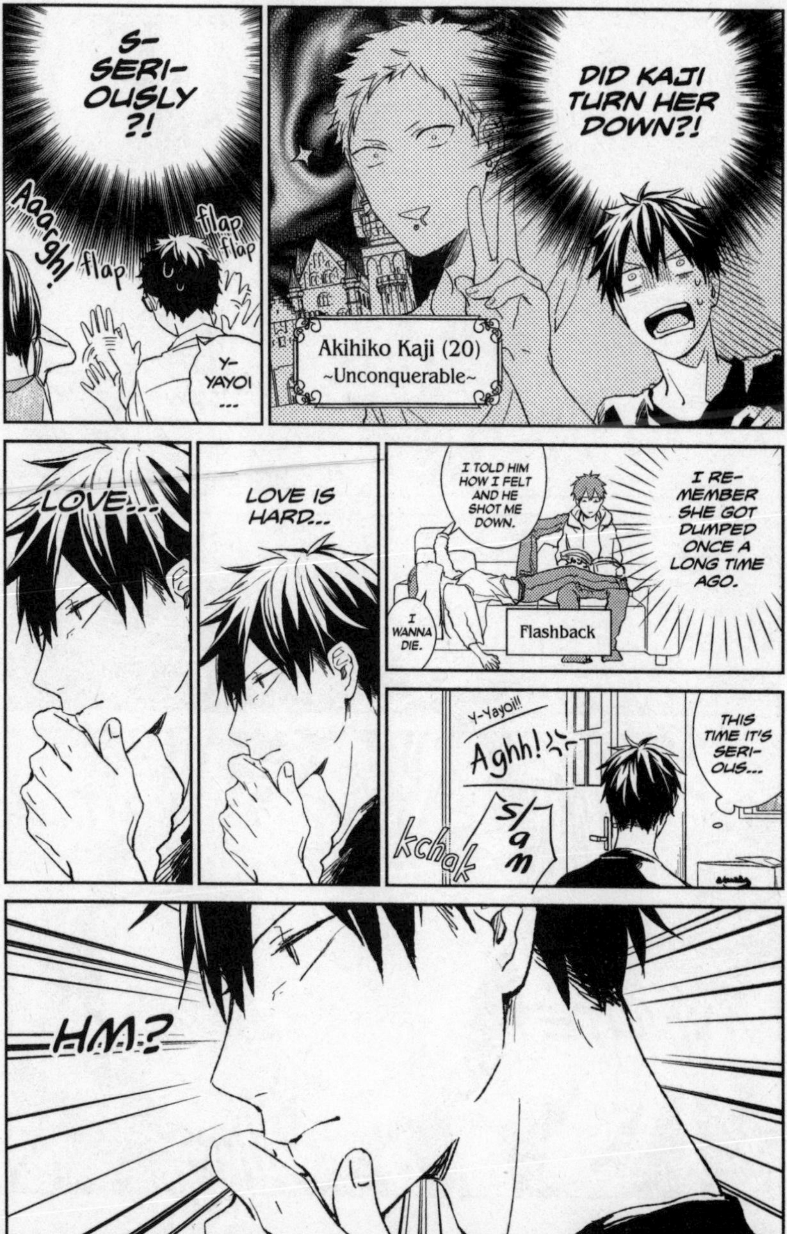
DID KAJI TURN HER DOWN?!
Akihiko Kaji (20)
~Unconquerable~
S-SERI-OUSLY?!
flap flap
Aaargh!
flap
Y-YAYOI ...
I RE-MEMBER SHE GOT DUMPED ONCE A LONG TIME AGO.
I TOLD HIM HOW I FELT AND HE SHOT ME DOWN.
I WANNA DIE.
Flashback
THIS TIME IT'S SERI-OUS...
Y-Yayoi!!
Aghh!
slam
kchak
LOVE IS HARD...
LOVE...
HM?

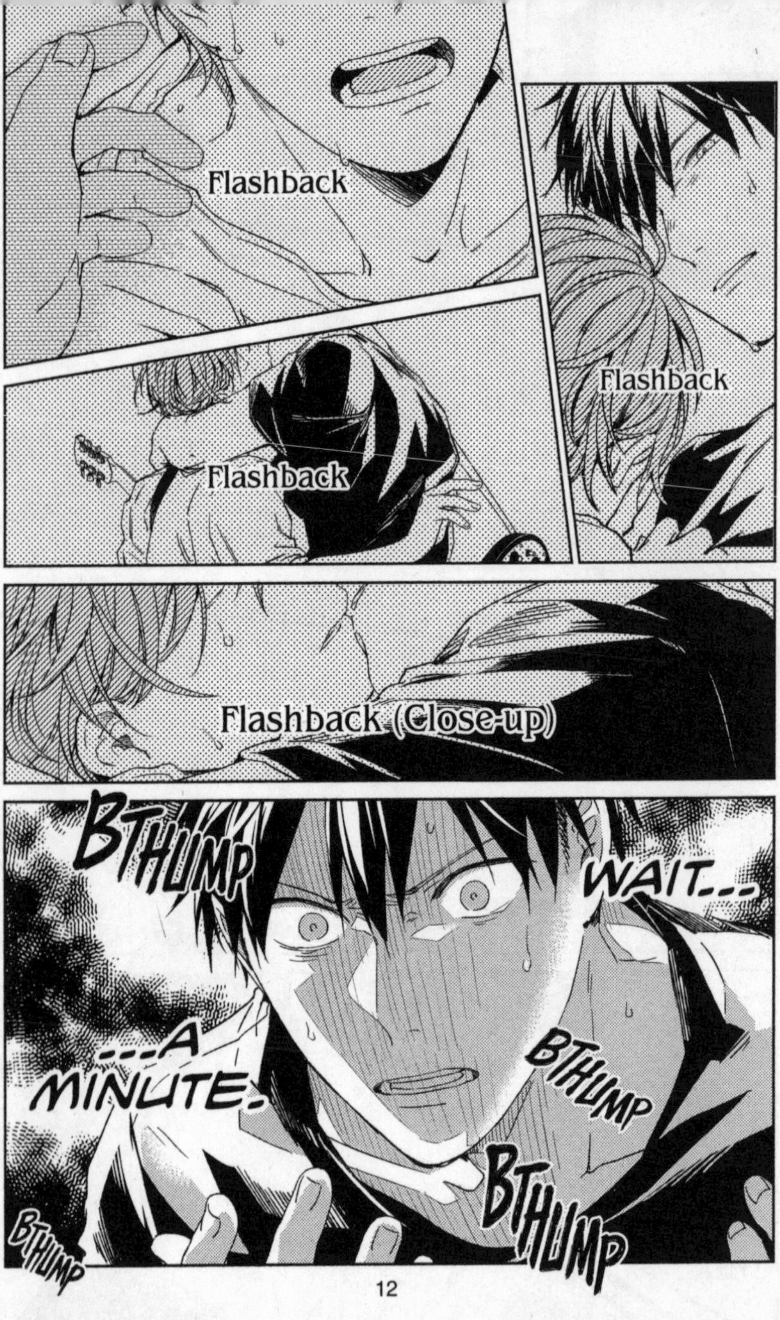
Flashback
Flashback
Flashback
Flashback (Close-up)
WAIT...
BTHUMP
BTHUMP
...A MINUTE.
BTHUMP
BTHUMP

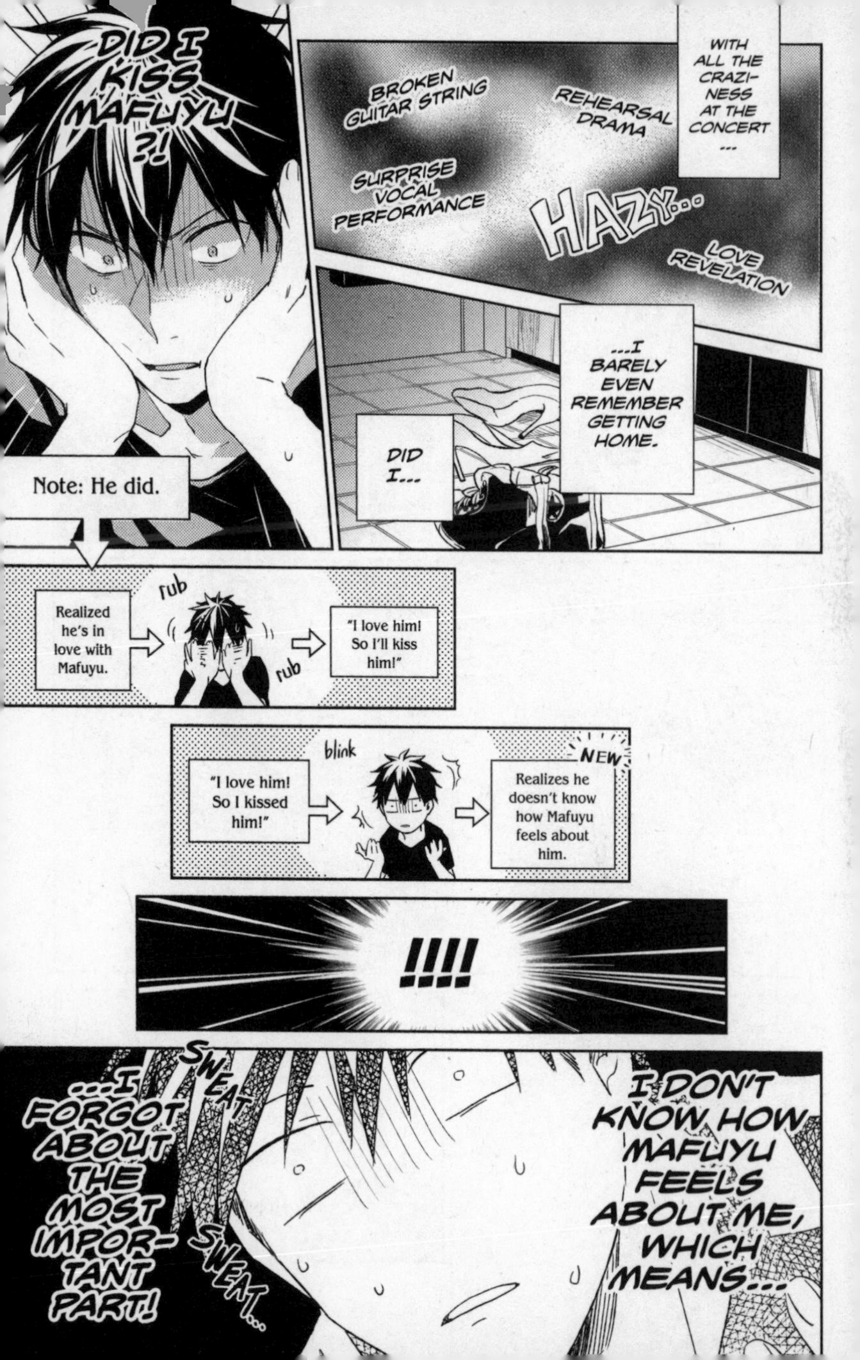
WITH ALL THE CRAZINESS AT THE CONCERT...
REHEARSAL DRAMA
BROKEN GUITAR STRING
SURPRISE VOCAL PERFORMANCE
HAZY...
LOVE REVELATION
...I BARELY EVEN REMEMBER GETTING HOME.
DID I...
DID I KISS MAFUYU?!
Note: He did.
Realized he's in love with Mafuyu.
rub
rub
"I love him! So I'll kiss him!"
"I love him! So I kissed him!"
blink
NEW
Realizes he doesn't know how Mafuyu feels about him.
!!!!
I DON'T KNOW HOW MAFUYU FEELS ABOUT ME, WHICH MEANS...
SWEAT
SWEAT...
...I FORGOT ABOUT THE MOST IMPOR-TANT PART!

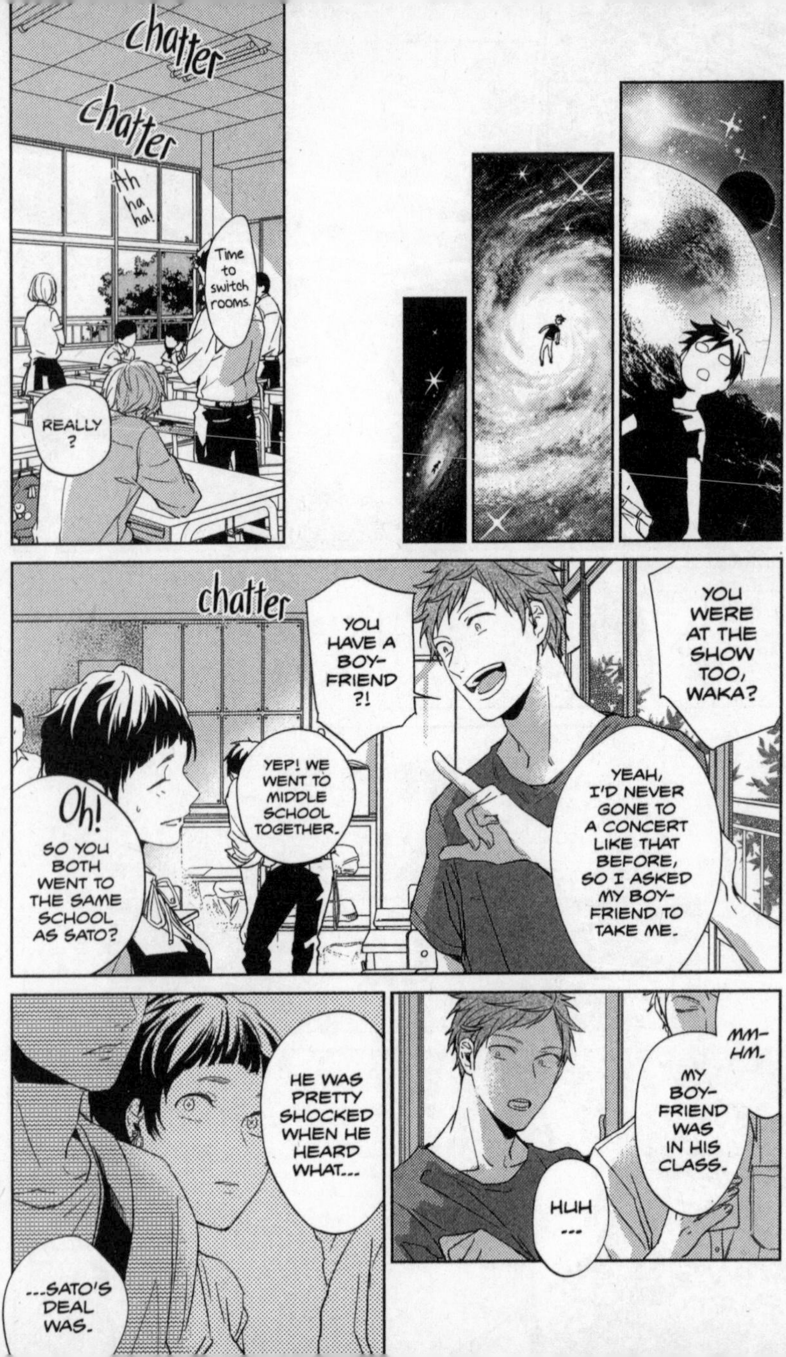
chatter
chatter
Ah ha ha!
Time to switch rooms.
REALLY?
YOU WERE AT THE SHOW TOO, WAKA?
YEAH, I'D NEVER GONE TO A CONCERT LIKE THAT BEFORE, SO I ASKED MY BOY-FRIEND TO TAKE ME.
YOU HAVE A BOY-FRIEND?!
chatter
YEP! WE WENT TO MIDDLE SCHOOL TOGETHER.
Oh!
SO YOU BOTH WENT TO THE SAME SCHOOL AS SATO?
MM-HM.
MY BOY-FRIEND WAS IN HIS CLASS.
HUH...
HE WAS PRETTY SHOCKED WHEN HE HEARD WHAT...
...SATO'S DEAL WAS.

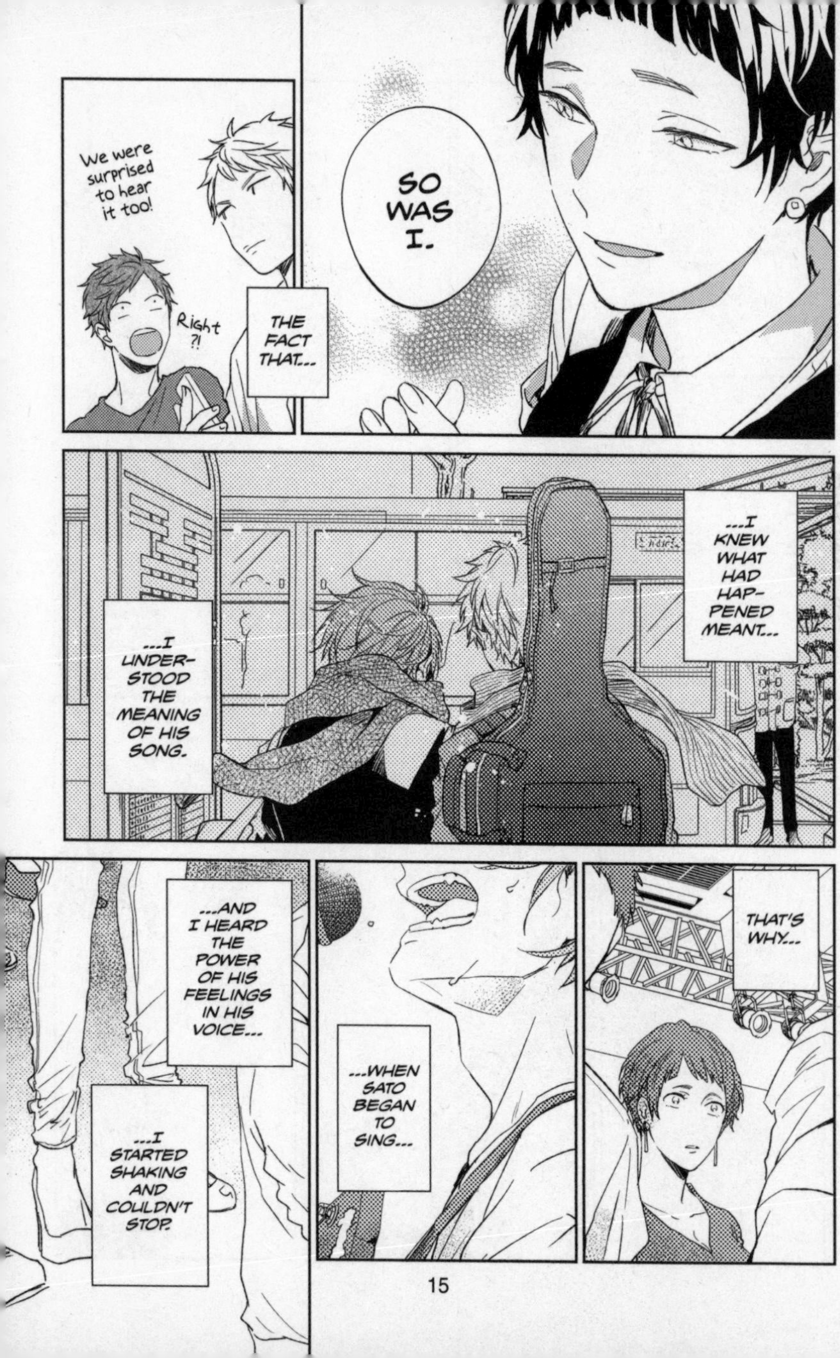
SO WAS I.
We were surprised to hear it too!
Right?!
THE FACT THAT...
...I KNEW WHAT HAD HAP-PENED MEANT...
...I UNDER-STOOD THE MEANING OF HIS SONG.
THAT'S WHY...
...WHEN SATO BEGAN TO SING...
...AND I HEARD THE POWER OF HIS FEELINGS IN HIS VOICE...
...I STARTED SHAKING AND COULDN'T STOP.

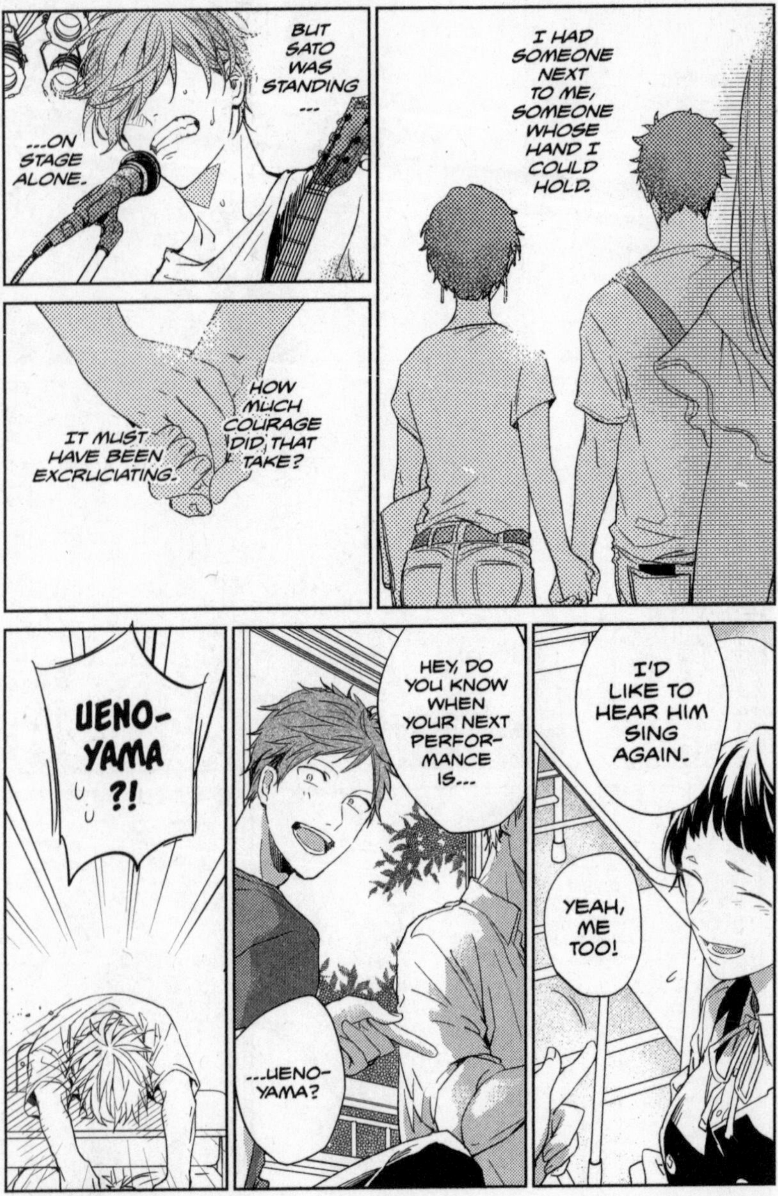
I HAD SOMEONE NEXT TO ME, SOMEONE WHOSE HAND I COULD HOLD.
BUT SATO WAS STANDING ...
...ON STAGE ALONE.
HOW MUCH COURAGE DID THAT TAKE?
IT MUST HAVE BEEN EXCRUCIATING.
I'D LIKE TO HEAR HIM SING AGAIN.
YEAH, ME TOO!
HEY, DO YOU KNOW WHEN YOUR NEXT PERFOR-MANCE IS...
...UENO-YAMA?
UENO-YAMA ?!

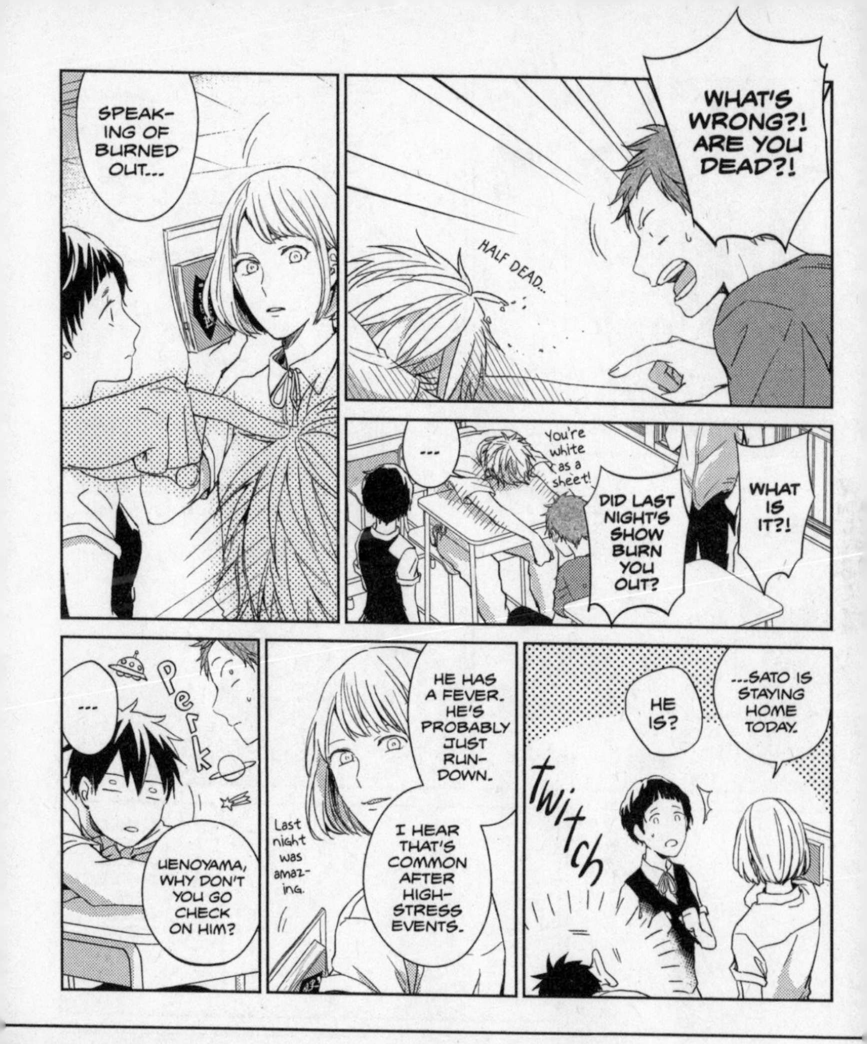
WHAT'S WRONG?! ARE YOU DEAD?!
HALF DEAD...
WHAT IS IT?!
DID LAST NIGHT'S SHOW BURN YOU OUT?
You're white as a sheet!
...
SPEAK-ING OF BURNED OUT...
...SATO IS STAYING HOME TODAY.
HE IS?
twitch
HE HAS A FEVER. HE'S PROBABLY JUST RUN-DOWN.
I HEAR THAT'S COMMON AFTER HIGH-STRESS EVENTS.
Last night was amaz-ing.
perk
...
UENOYAMA, WHY DON'T YOU GO CHECK ON HIM?
OOF...
Seems like Mafuyu is down with a fever.
I'm gonna look in on him, so I'll see you guys later.

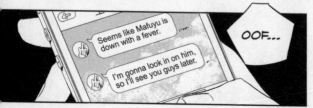

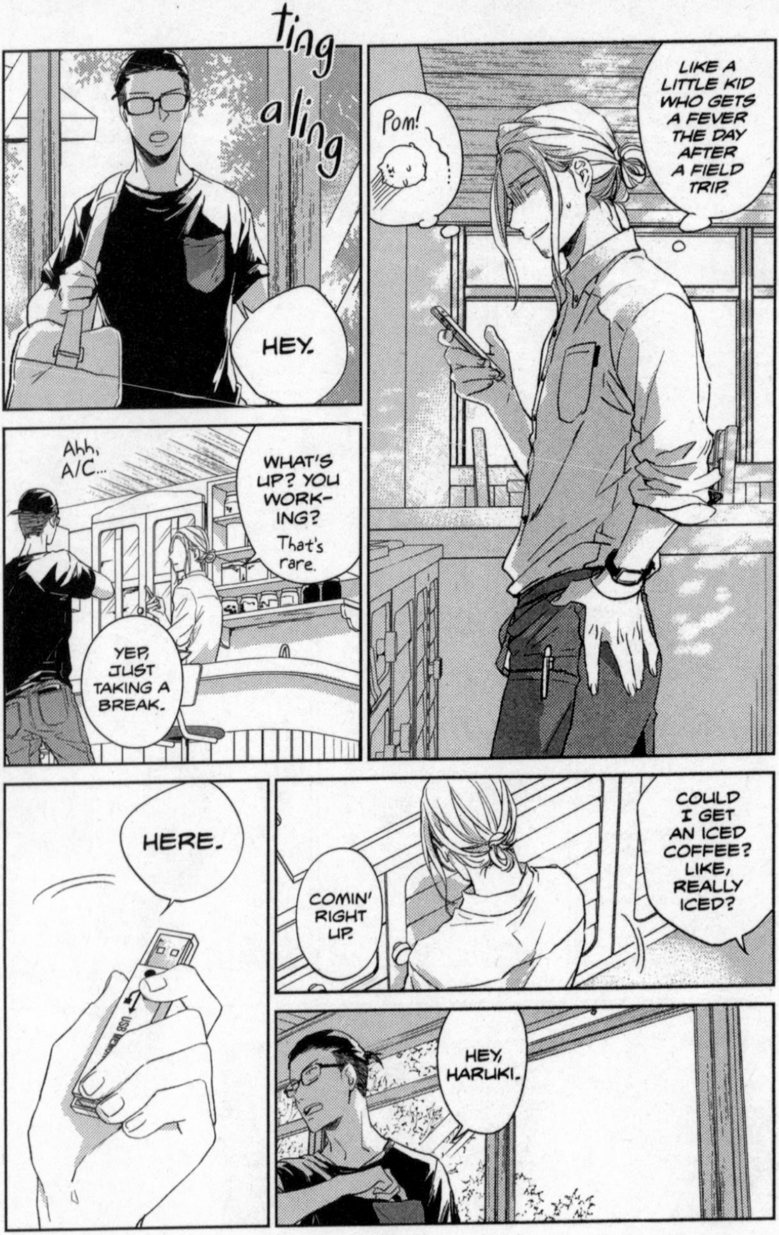
LIKE A LITTLE KID WHO GETS A FEVER THE DAY AFTER A FIELD TRIP.
Pom!
ting a ling
HEY.
WHAT'S UP? YOU WORKING?
That's rare.
Ahh, A/C...
YEP, JUST TAKING A BREAK.
COULD I GET AN ICED COFFEE? LIKE, REALLY ICED?
COMIN' RIGHT UP.
HEY, HARUKI.
HERE.

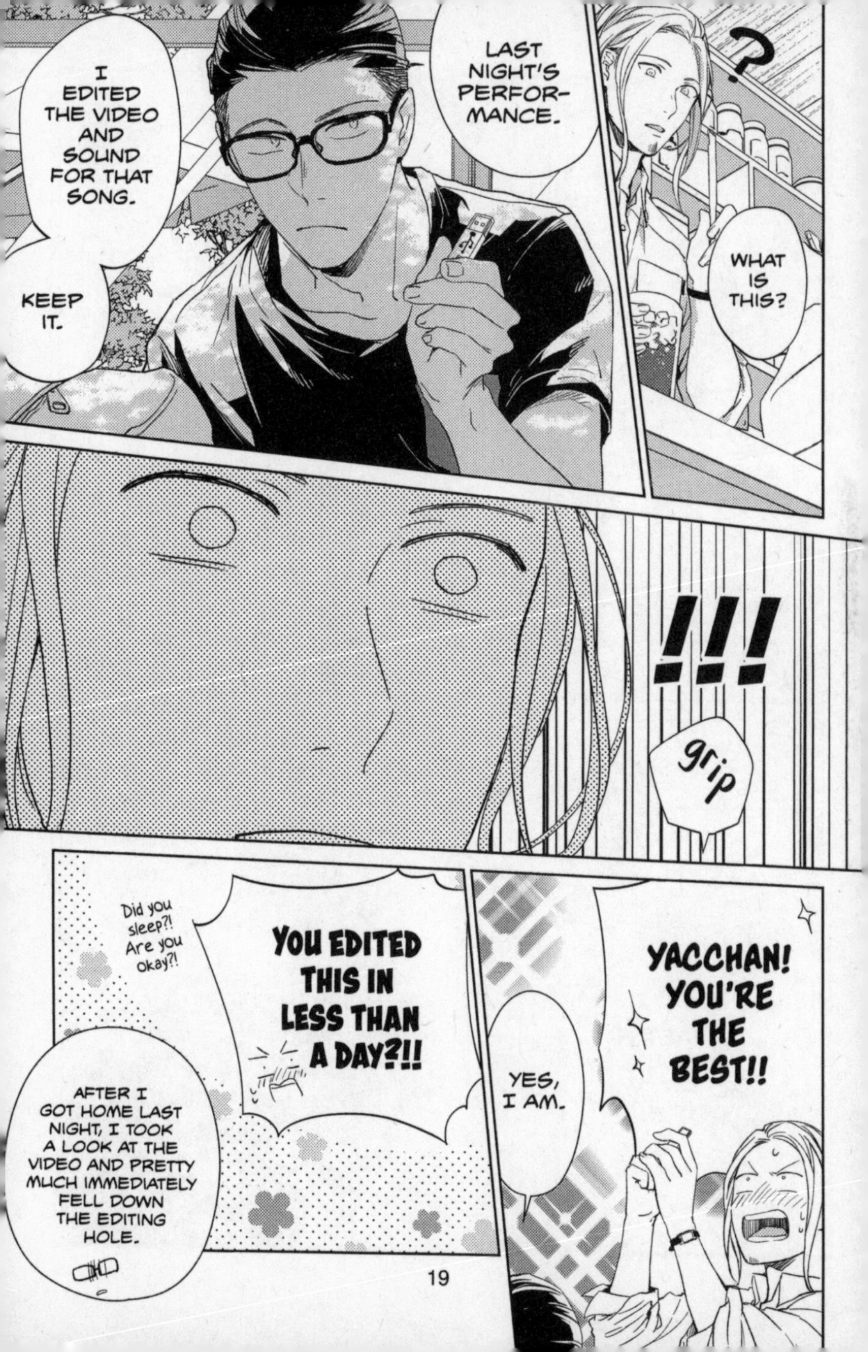
?
WHAT IS THIS?
LAST NIGHT'S PERFORMANCE.
I EDITED THE VIDEO AND SOUND FOR THAT SONG.
KEEP IT.
!!!
grip
YACCHAN! YOU'RE THE BEST!!
YES, I AM.
YOU EDITED THIS IN LESS THAN A DAY?!!
Did you sleep?! Are you okay?!
AFTER I GOT HOME LAST NIGHT, I TOOK A LOOK AT THE VIDEO AND PRETTY MUCH IMMEDIATELY FELL DOWN THE EDITING HOLE.

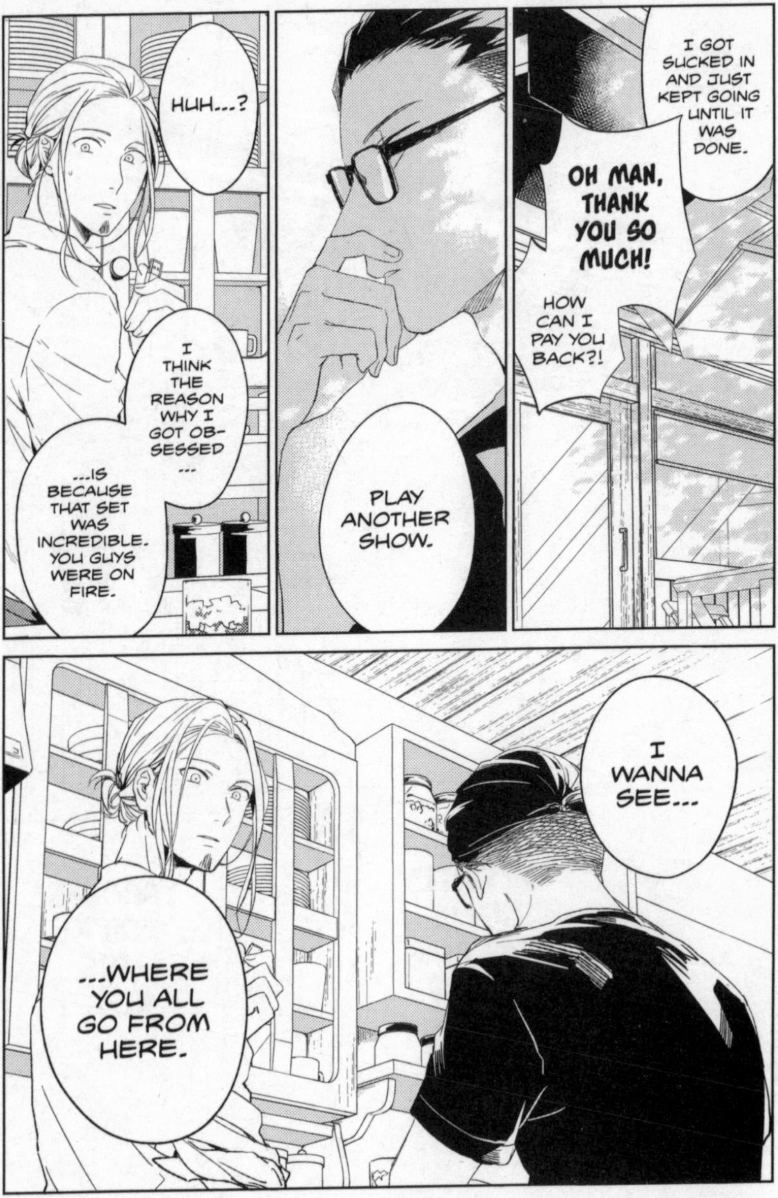
I GOT SUCKED IN AND JUST KEPT GOING UNTIL IT WAS DONE.
OH MAN, THANK YOU SO MUCH!
HOW CAN I PAY YOU BACK?!
PLAY ANOTHER SHOW.
HUH...?
I THINK THE REASON WHY I GOT OB-SESSED...
...IS BECAUSE THAT SET WAS INCREDIBLE. YOU GUYS WERE ON FIRE.
I WANNA SEE...
...WHERE YOU ALL GO FROM HERE.

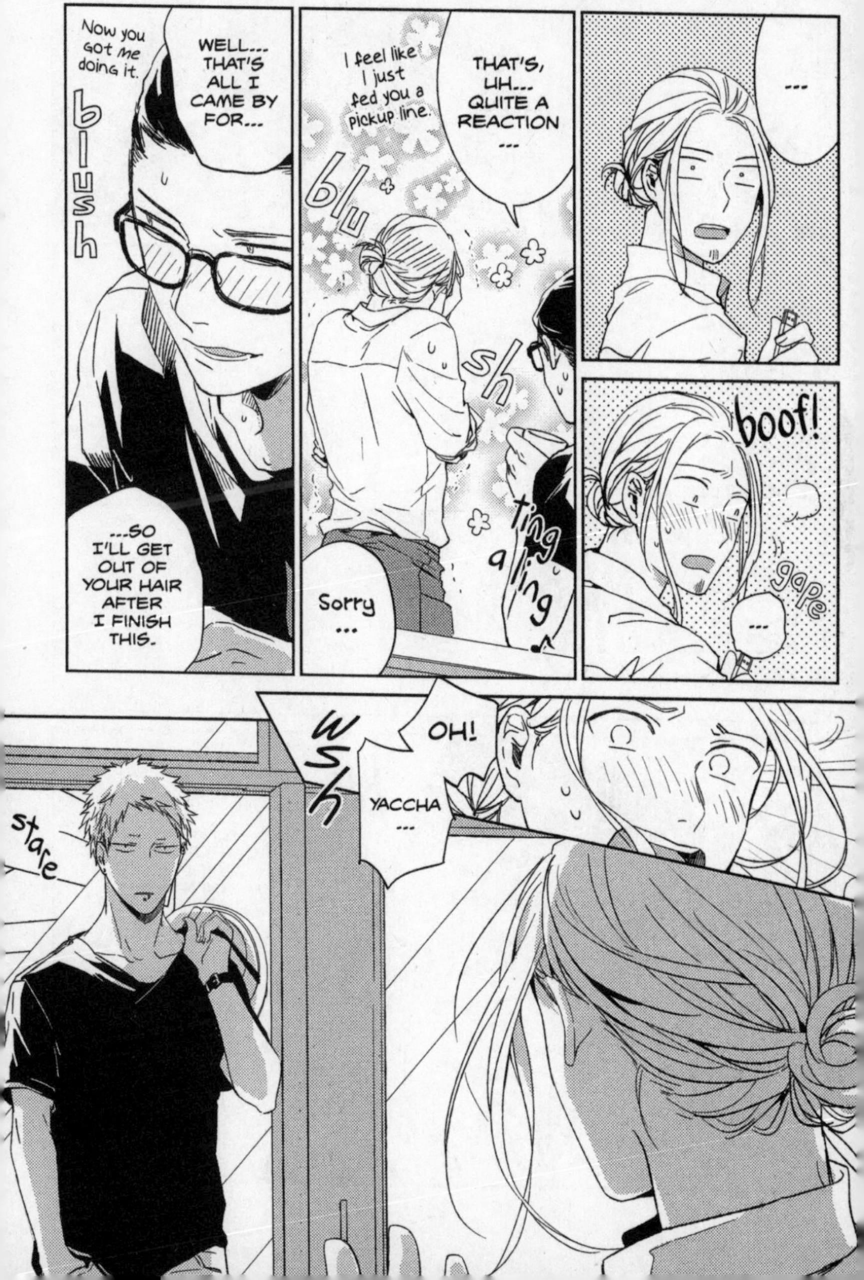
...
boof!
gape
...
THAT'S, UH... QUITE A REACTION ...
I feel like I just fed you a pickup line.
blu
sh
ting a ling ♪
Sorry ...
WELL... THAT'S ALL I CAME BY FOR...
Now you got me doing it.
blush
...SO I'LL GET OUT OF YOUR HAIR AFTER I FINISH THIS.
OH!
YACCHA ...
wsh
stare

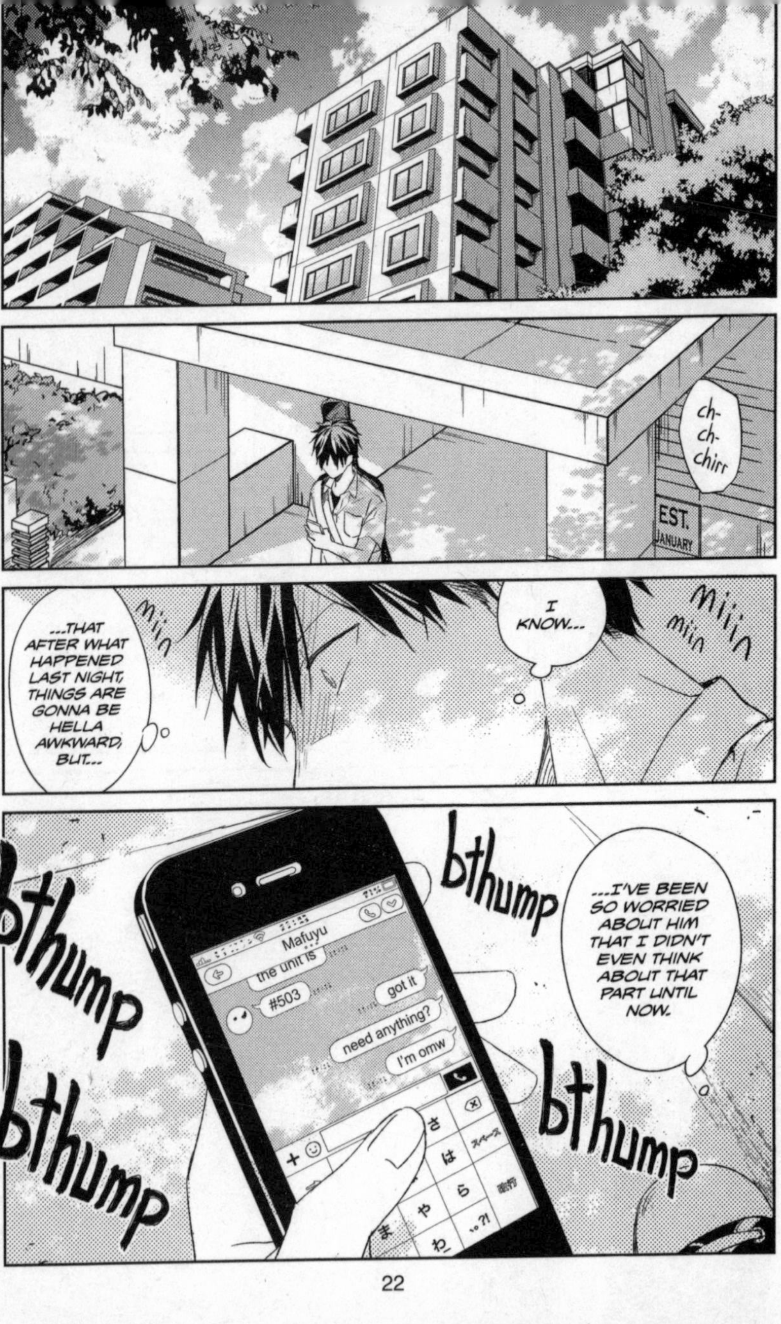
ch-ch-chirr
EST.
JANUARY
miiin miiin
I KNOW...
miin
...THAT AFTER WHAT HAPPENED LAST NIGHT, THINGS ARE GONNA BE HELLA AWKWARD, BUT...
...I'VE BEEN SO WORRIED ABOUT HIM THAT I DIDN'T EVEN THINK ABOUT THAT PART UNTIL NOW.
bthump
bthump
bthump
bthump
Mafuyu
the unit is
#503
got it
need anything?
I'm omw

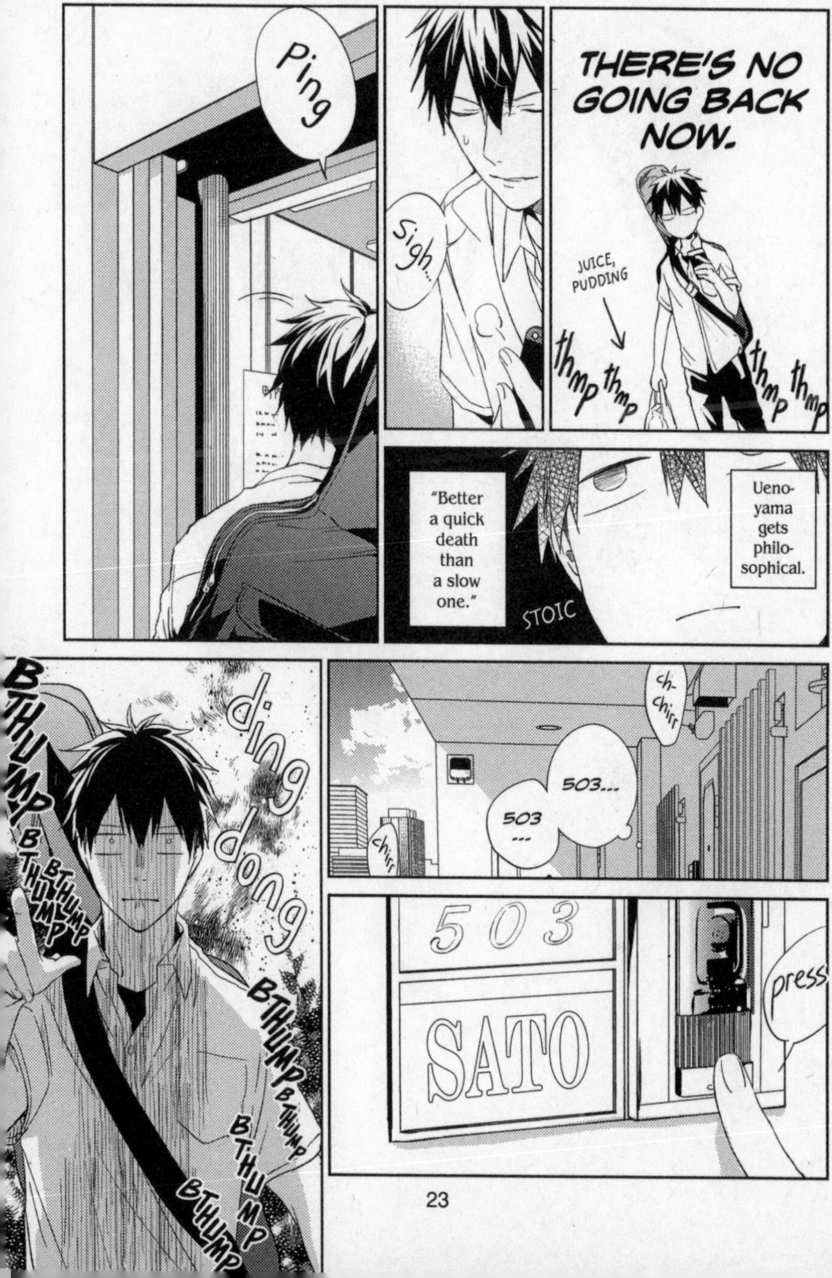
THERE'S NO GOING BACK NOW.
JUICE, PUDDING
thmp thmp
thmp thmp
Sigh...
Uenoyama gets philosophical.
"Better a quick death than a slow one."
STOIC
Ping
ch-chirr
503...
503 ...
chirr
503
SATO
press
ding dong
BTHUMP BTHUMP
BTHUMP BTHUMP
BTHUMP BTHUMP
BTHUMP BTHUMP

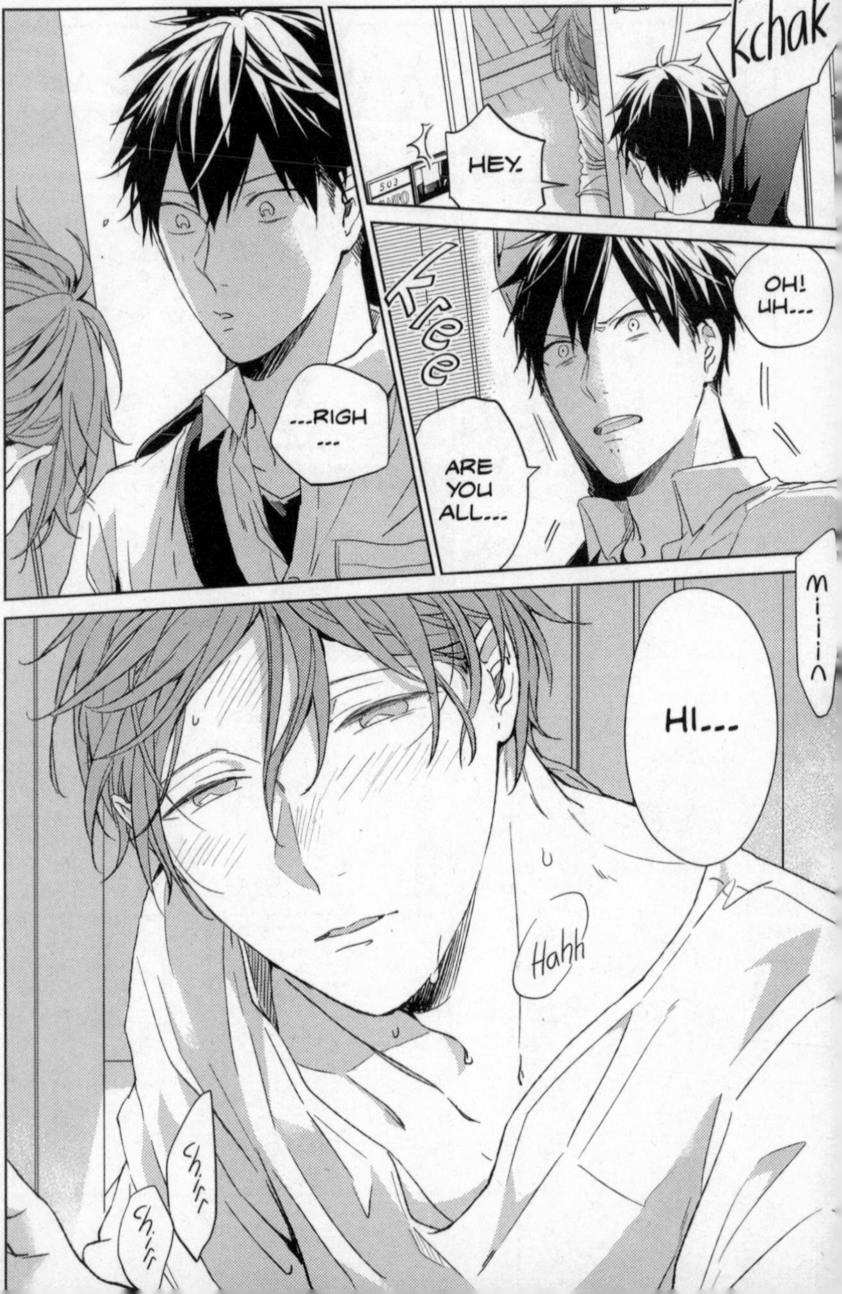

kchak
HEY.
OH! UH...
Kree
ARE YOU ALL...
...RIGH ---
Miin
HI...
Hahh
Chirr
Chirr

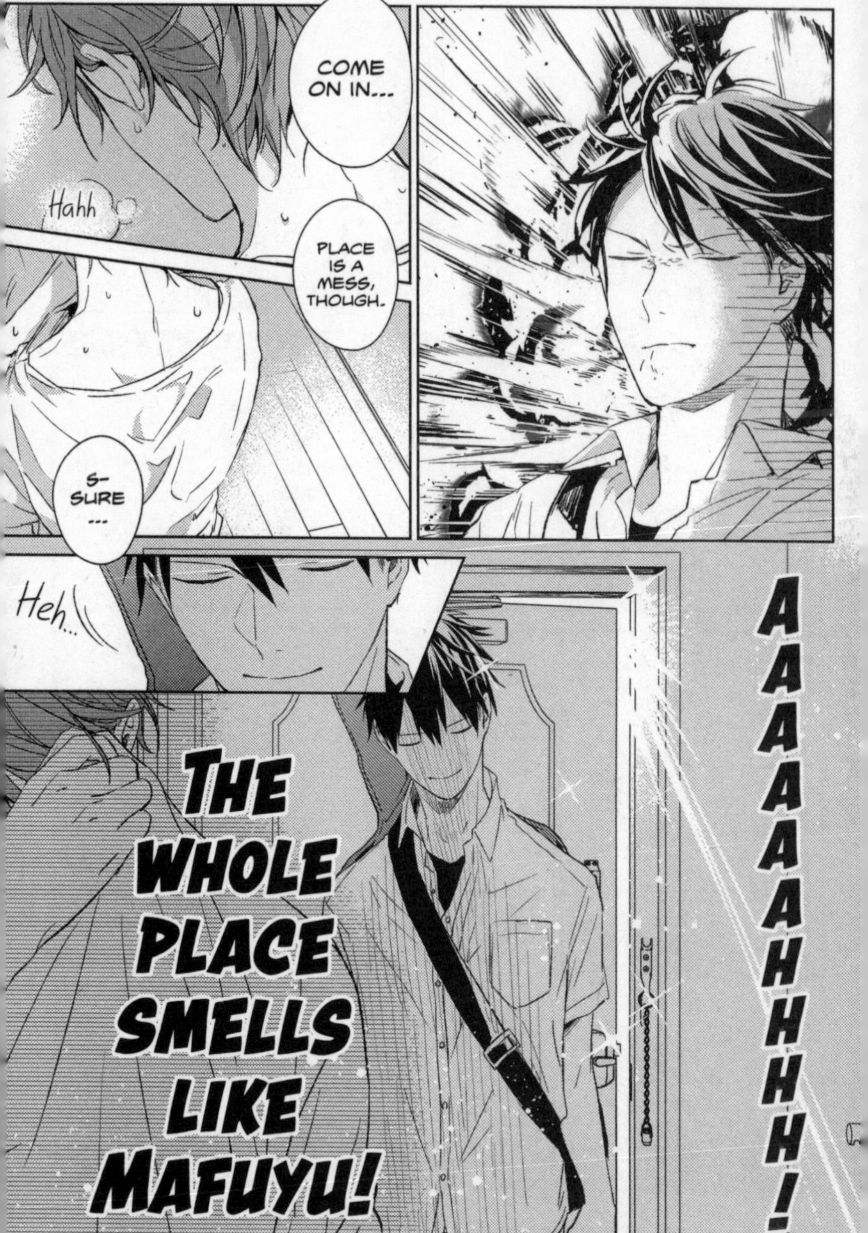
COME ON IN...
Hahh
PLACE IS A MESS, THOUGH.
S-SURE...
Heh...
AAAAAAHHHH!
THE WHOLE PLACE SMELLS LIKE MAFUYU!

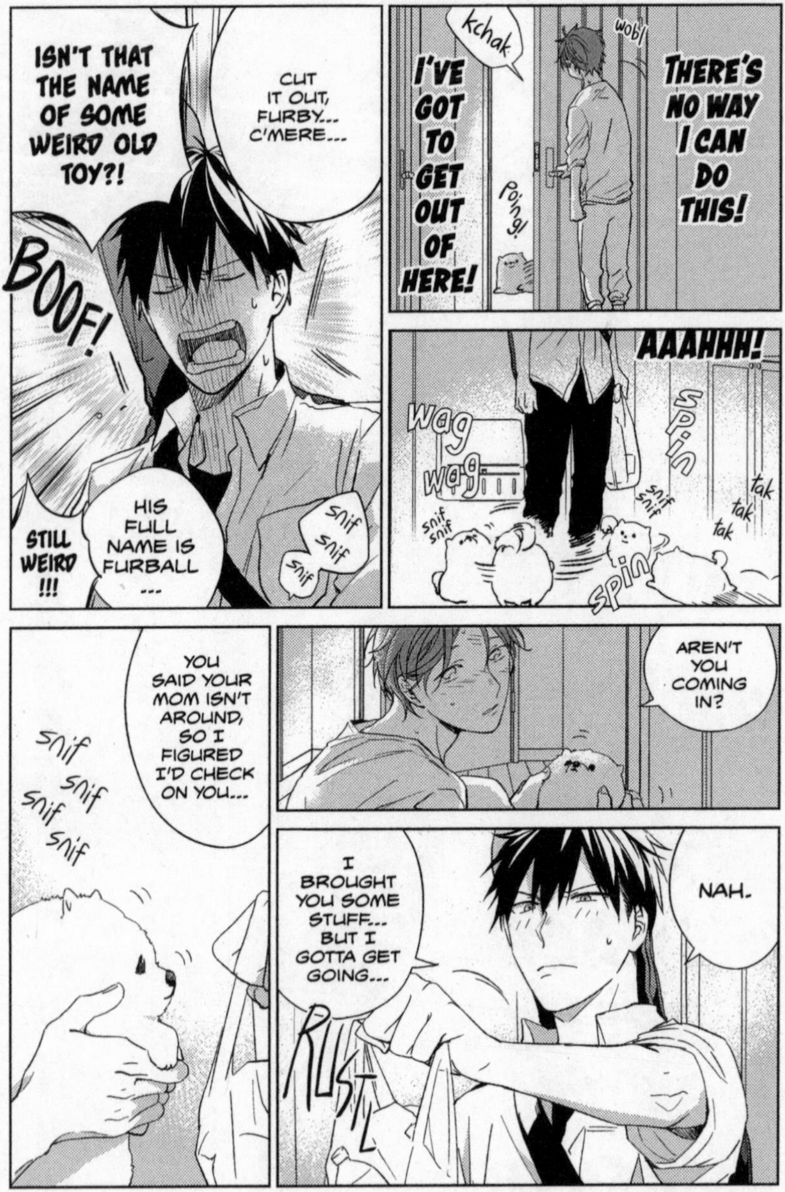
THERE'S NO WAY I CAN DO THIS!
wobl
kchak
I'VE GOT TO GET OUT OF HERE!
Poing!
AAAHHH!
spin
tak tak tak
snif snif
wag wag
snif snif
spin
CUT IT OUT, FURBY... C'MERE...
ISN'T THAT THE NAME OF SOME WEIRD OLD TOY?!
BOOF!
snif snif snif
HIS FULL NAME IS FURBALL ...
STILL WEIRD !!!
AREN'T YOU COMING IN?
NAH.
I BROUGHT YOU SOME STUFF... BUT I GOTTA GET GOING...
RUSTL
YOU SAID YOUR MOM ISN'T AROUND, SO I FIGURED I'D CHECK ON YOU...
snif snif snif snif

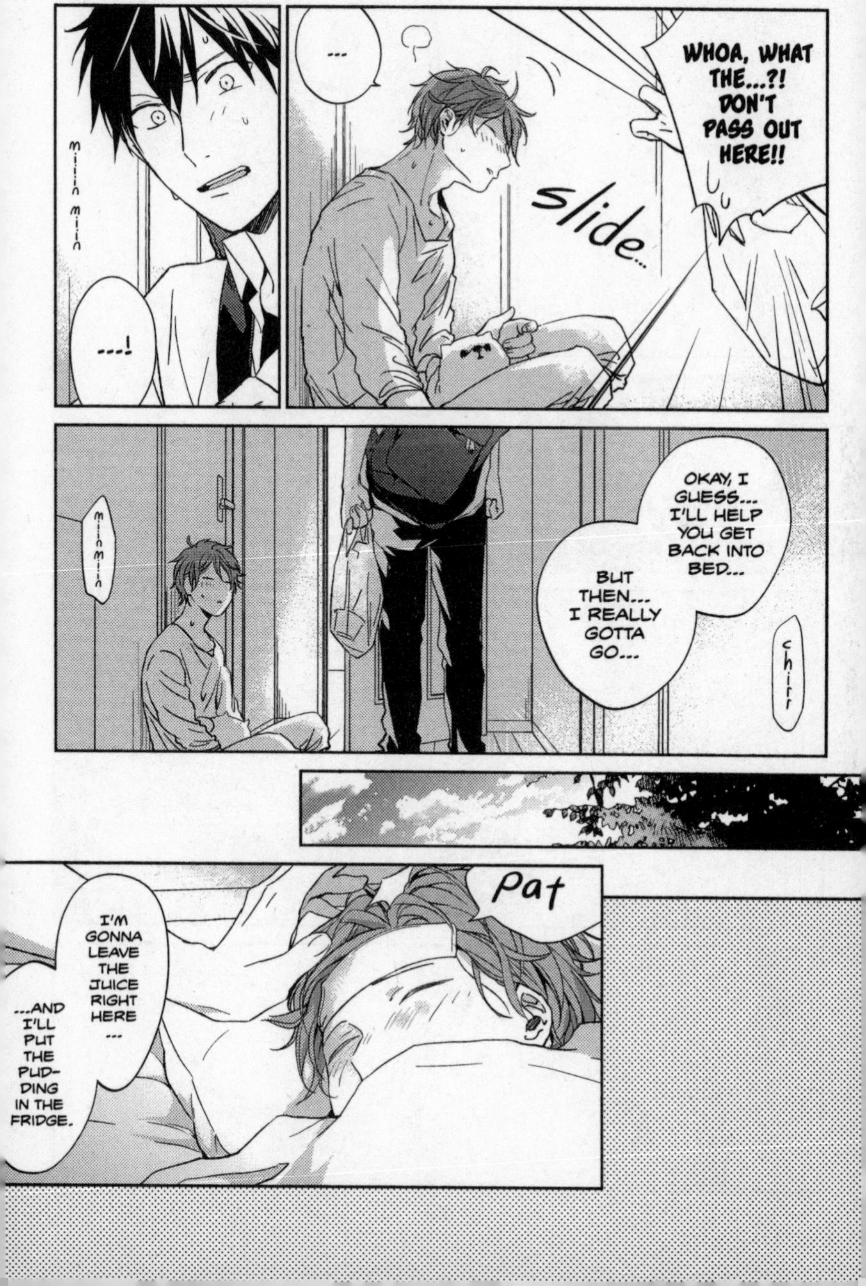
WHOA, WHAT THE...?! DON'T PASS OUT HERE!!
slide...
...
miin miin
...!
OKAY, I GUESS... I'LL HELP YOU GET BACK INTO BED...
BUT THEN... I REALLY GOTTA GO...
chirr
miin miin
Pat
I'M GONNA LEAVE THE JUICE RIGHT HERE...
...AND I'LL PUT THE PUD-DING IN THE FRIDGE.

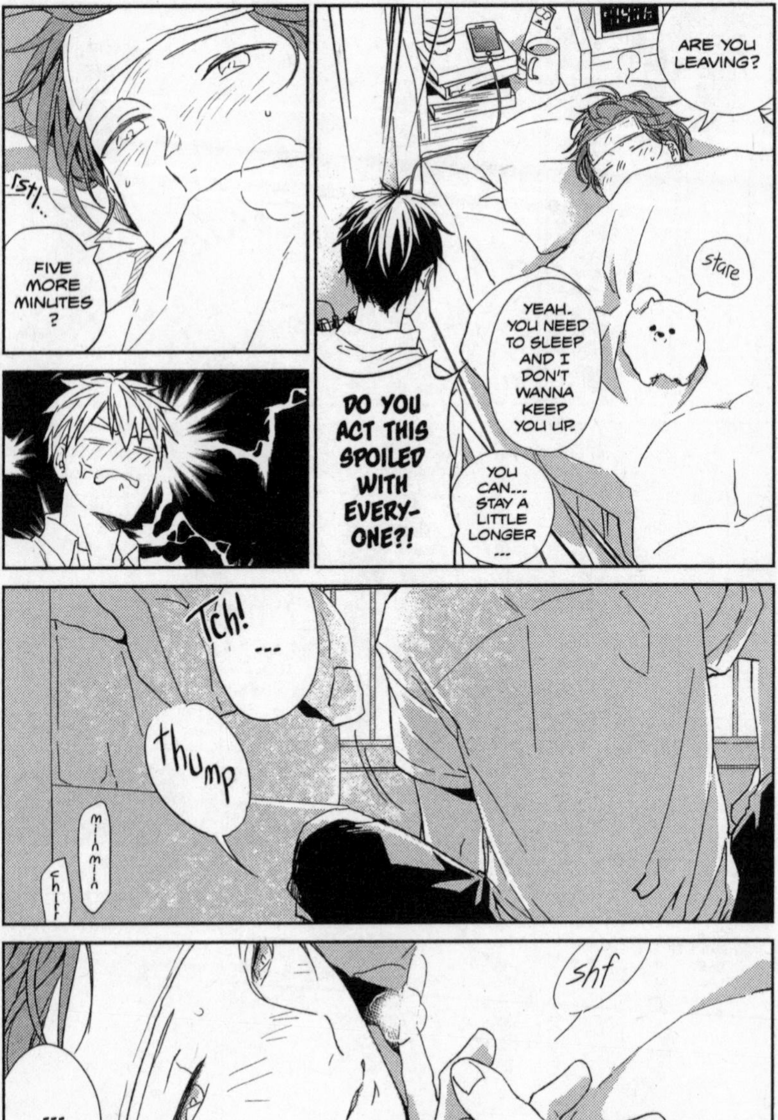
ARE YOU LEAVING?
stare
YEAH. YOU NEED TO SLEEP AND I DON'T WANNA KEEP YOU UP.
YOU CAN... STAY A LITTLE LONGER ...
DO YOU ACT THIS SPOILED WITH EVERY-ONE?!
rstl...
FIVE MORE MINUTES ?
Tch!
...
thump
minmin
chirr
shf
...

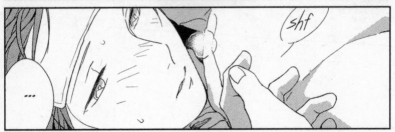

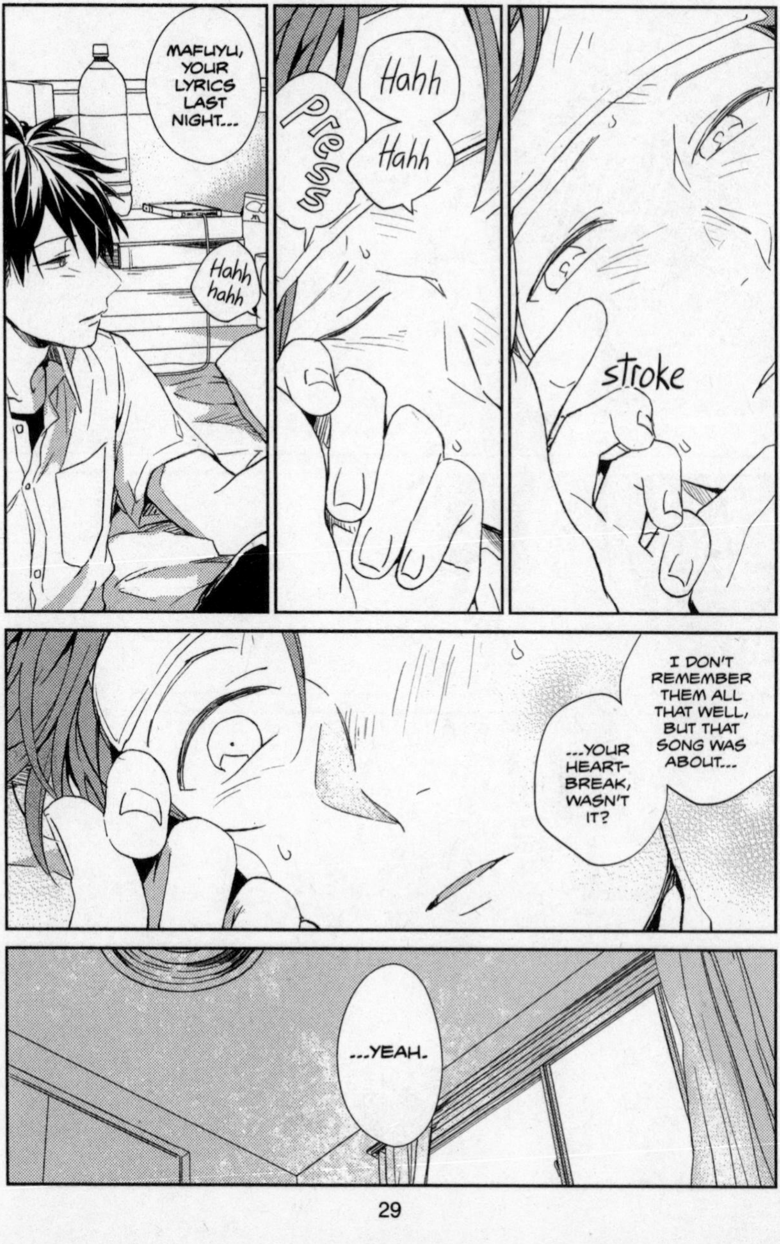
stroke
Hahh
Press
Hahh
MAFUYU, YOUR LYRICS LAST NIGHT...
Hahh hahh
I DON'T REMEMBER THEM ALL THAT WELL, BUT THAT SONG WAS ABOUT...
...YOUR HEART-BREAK, WASN'T IT?
...YEAH.

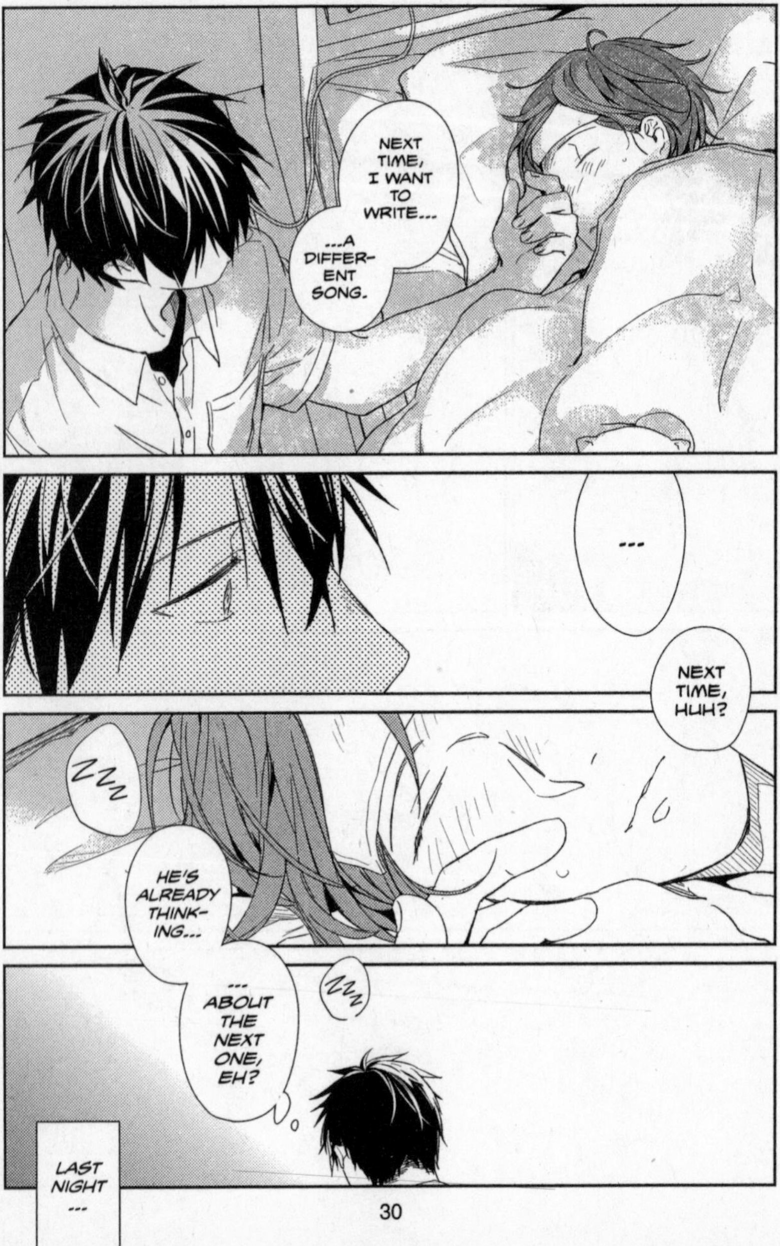
NEXT TIME, I WANT TO WRITE...
...A DIFFERENT SONG.
...
NEXT TIME, HUH?
ZZZ
HE'S ALREADY THINKING...
...ABOUT THE NEXT ONE, EH?
ZZZ
LAST NIGHT...

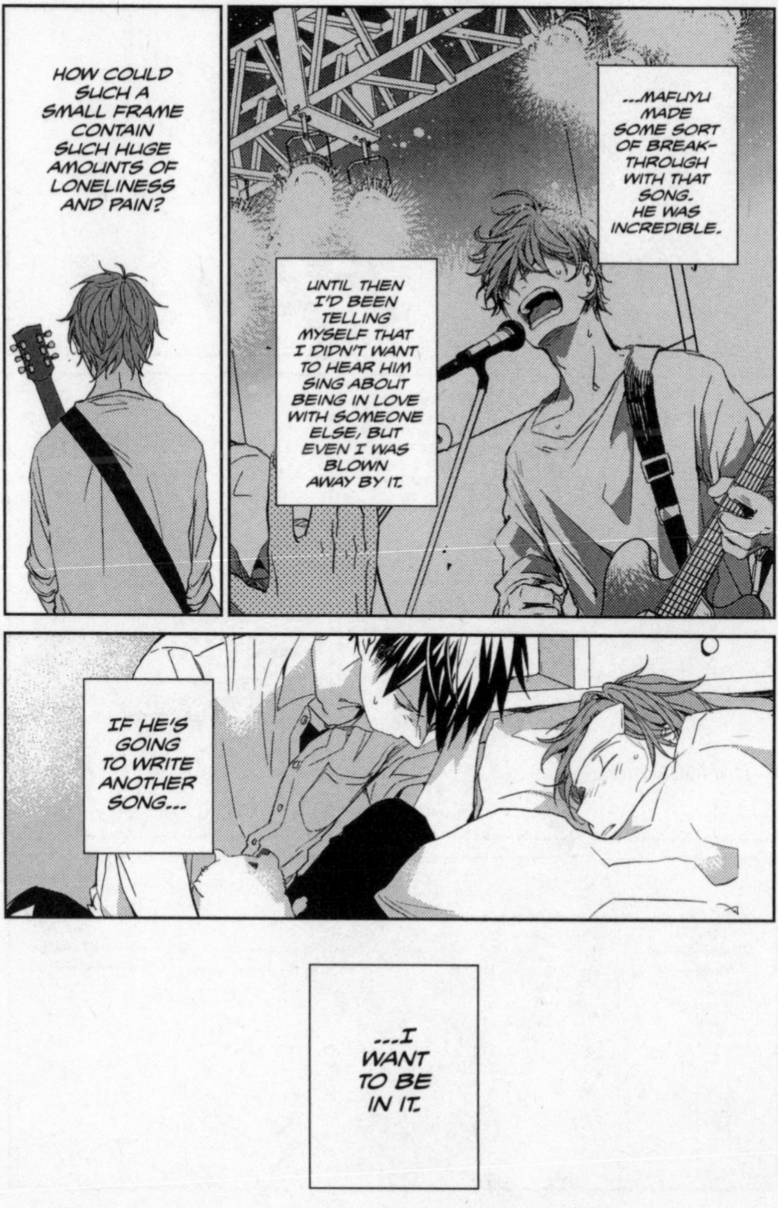
...MAFUYU MADE SOME SORT OF BREAK-THROUGH WITH THAT SONG. HE WAS INCREDIBLE.
UNTIL THEN I'D BEEN TELLING MYSELF THAT I DIDN'T WANT TO HEAR HIM SING ABOUT BEING IN LOVE WITH SOMEONE ELSE, BUT EVEN I WAS BLOWN AWAY BY IT.
HOW COULD SUCH A SMALL FRAME CONTAIN SUCH HUGE AMOUNTS OF LONELINESS AND PAIN?
IF HE'S GOING TO WRITE ANOTHER SONG...
...I WANT TO BE IN IT.

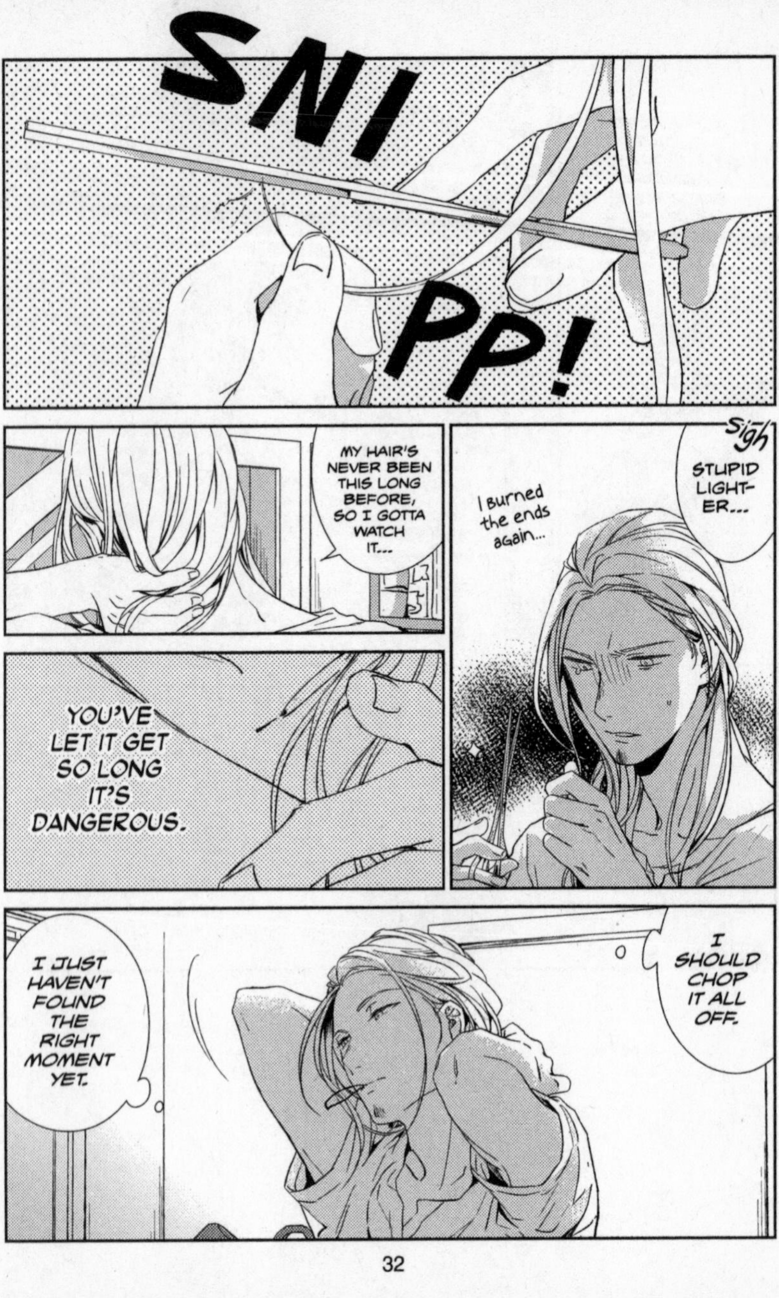
SNIPP!
Sigh
STUPID LIGHTER...
I burned the ends again...
MY HAIR'S NEVER BEEN THIS LONG BEFORE, SO I GOTTA WATCH IT...
YOU'VE LET IT GET SO LONG IT'S DANGEROUS.
I SHOULD CHOP IT ALL OFF.
I JUST HAVEN'T FOUND THE RIGHT MOMENT YET.

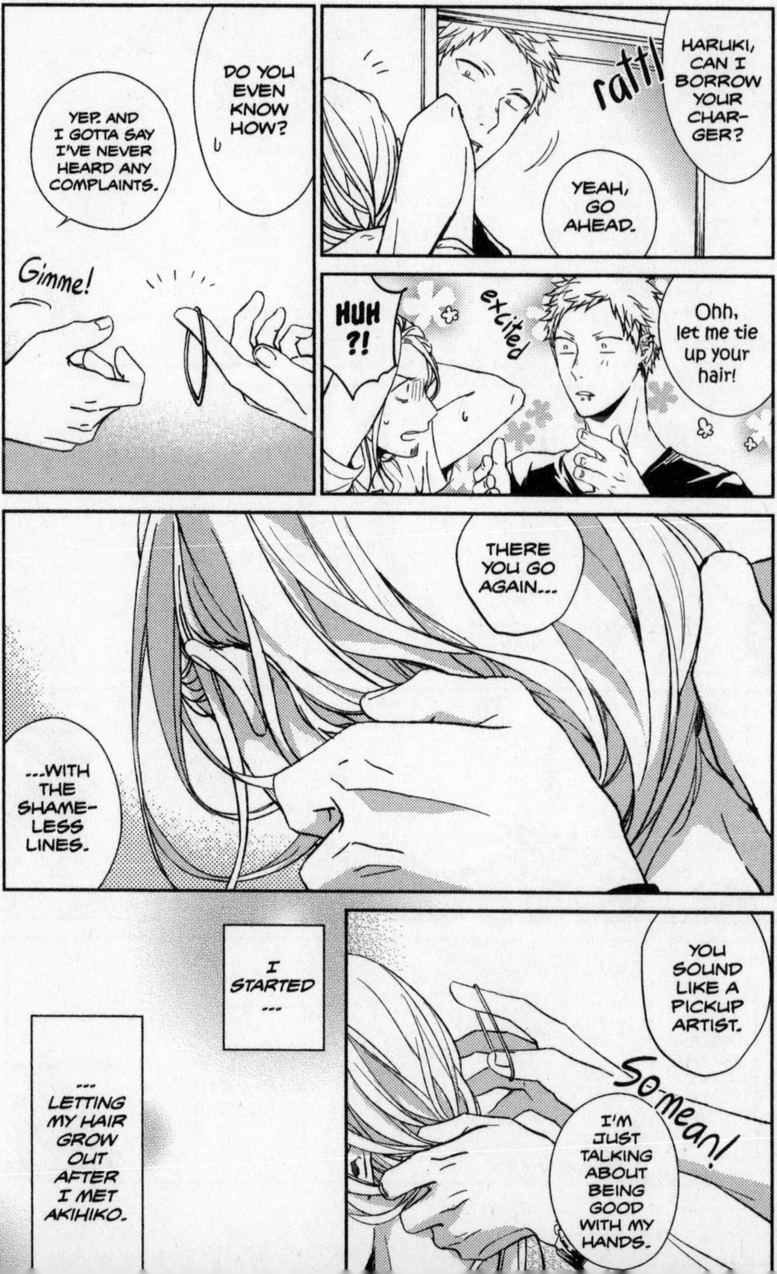
HARUKI, CAN I BORROW YOUR CHARGER?
rattl
YEAH, GO AHEAD.
Ohh, let me tie up your hair!
excited
HUH?!
DO YOU EVEN KNOW HOW?
YEP. AND I GOTTA SAY I'VE NEVER HEARD ANY COMPLAINTS.
Gimme!
THERE YOU GO AGAIN...
...WITH THE SHAMELESS LINES.
YOU SOUND LIKE A PICKUP ARTIST.
So mean!
I'M JUST TALKING ABOUT BEING GOOD WITH MY HANDS.
I STARTED...
...LETTING MY HAIR GROW OUT AFTER I MET AKIHIKO.

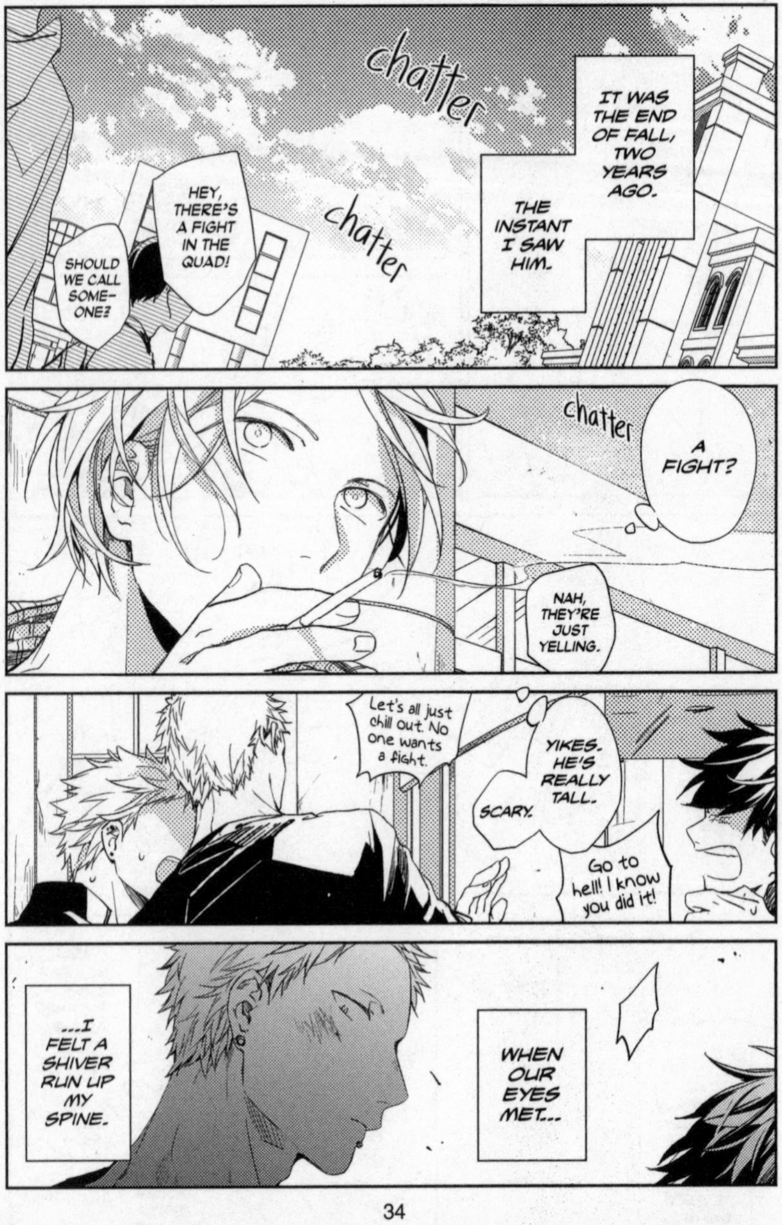
chatter
IT WAS THE END OF FALL, TWO YEARS AGO.
THE INSTANT I SAW HIM.
chatter
HEY, THERE'S A FIGHT IN THE QUAD!
SHOULD WE CALL SOME-ONE?
chatter
A FIGHT?
NAH, THEY'RE JUST YELLING.
YIKES. HE'S REALLY TALL.
SCARY.
Go to hell! I know you did it!
Let's all just chill out. No one wants a fight.
WHEN OUR EYES MET...
...I FELT A SHIVER RUN UP MY SPINE.

I'VE BEEN
LETTING MY HAIR
GROW LONG
SINCE THEN,
LIKE AN OFFERING
OR A PRAYER.

EVER SINCE
THE DAY I
FELL IN LOVE
WITH AKIHIKO.

given

by Natsuki Kizu

Given Drama CD Voice Cast Interview

Cast interviews reveal the inside story!

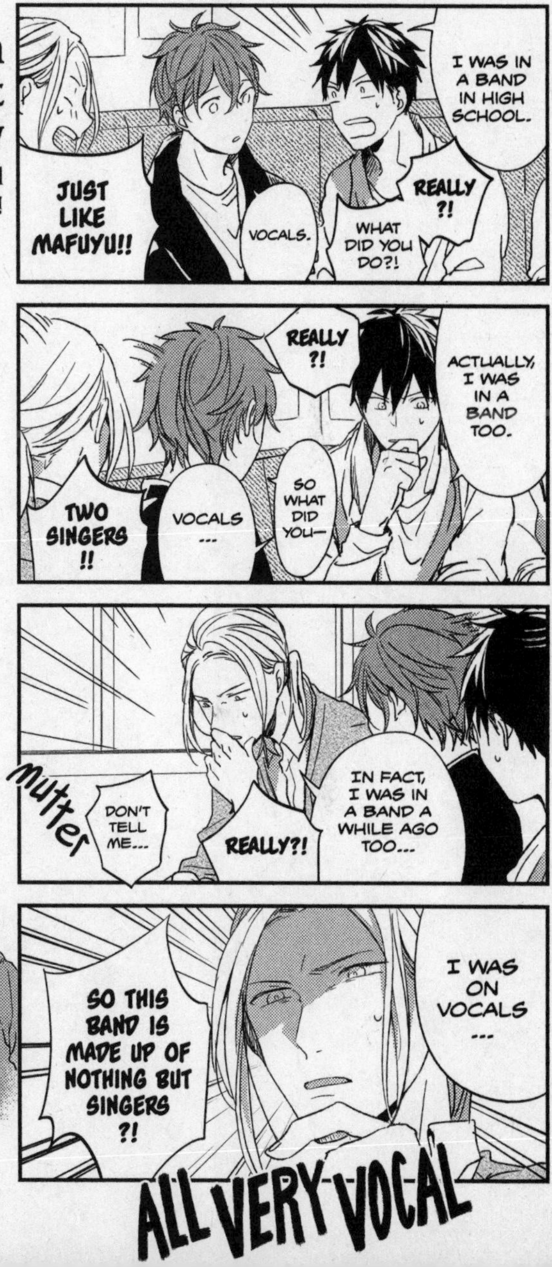
I WAS IN A BAND IN HIGH SCHOOL.
REALLY?!
WHAT DID YOU DO?!
VOCALS.
JUST LIKE MAFUYU!!
ACTUALLY, I WAS IN A BAND TOO.
REALLY?!
SO WHAT DID YOU—
VOCALS...
TWO SINGERS!!
IN FACT, I WAS IN A BAND A WHILE AGO TOO...
REALLY?!
DON'T TELL ME...
mutter
I WAS ON VOCALS...
SO THIS BAND IS MADE UP OF NOTHING BUT SINGERS?!
ALL VERY VOCAL

Mr. Hino's interview was held separately.

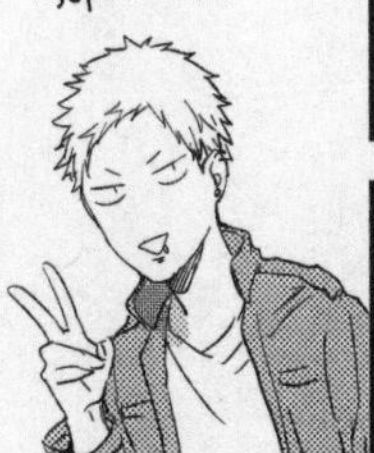

He wasn't in a band too, was he?!

*In a later interview, we found out he wasn't.

given

by Natsuki Kizu

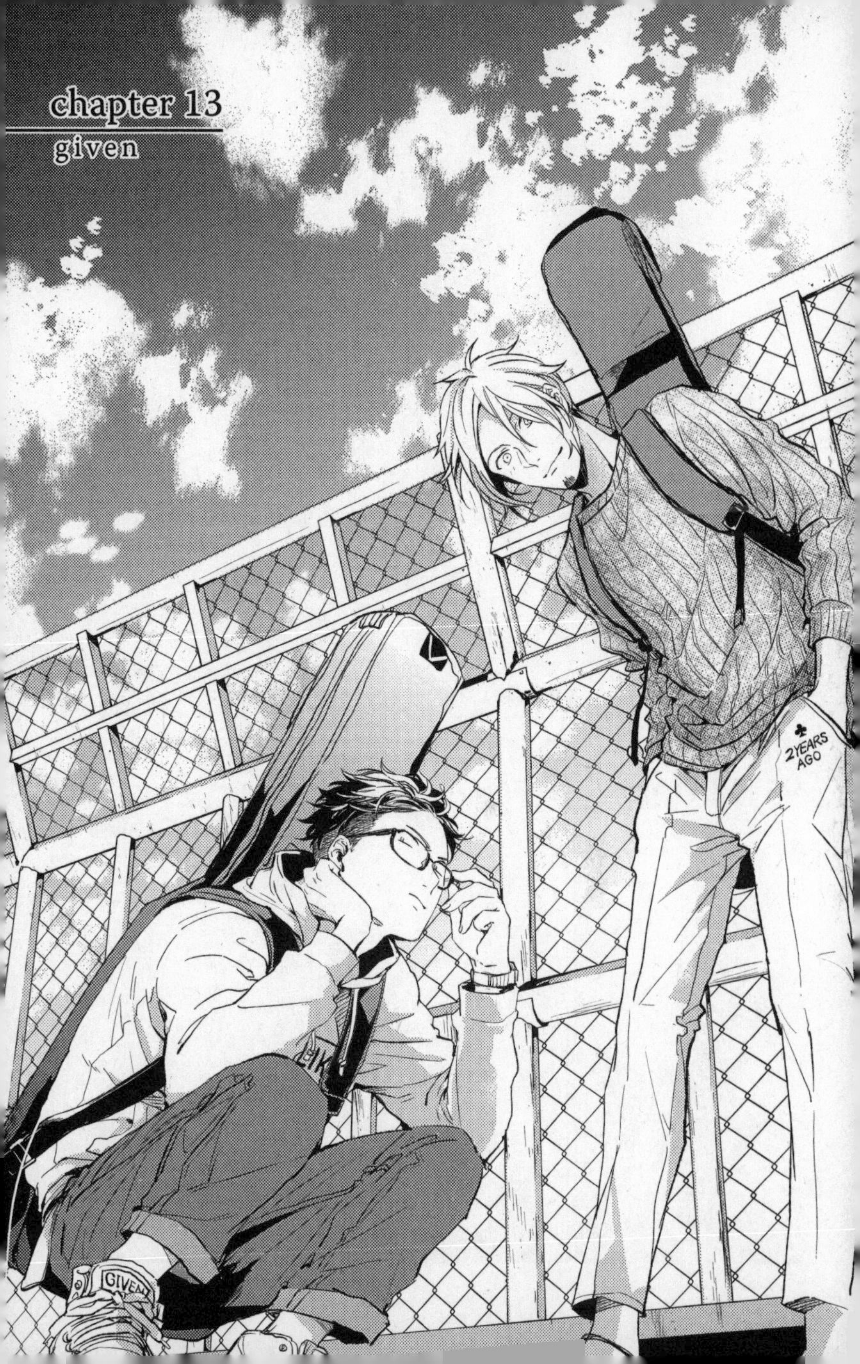
chapter 13
given
2 YEARS AGO
GIVEN

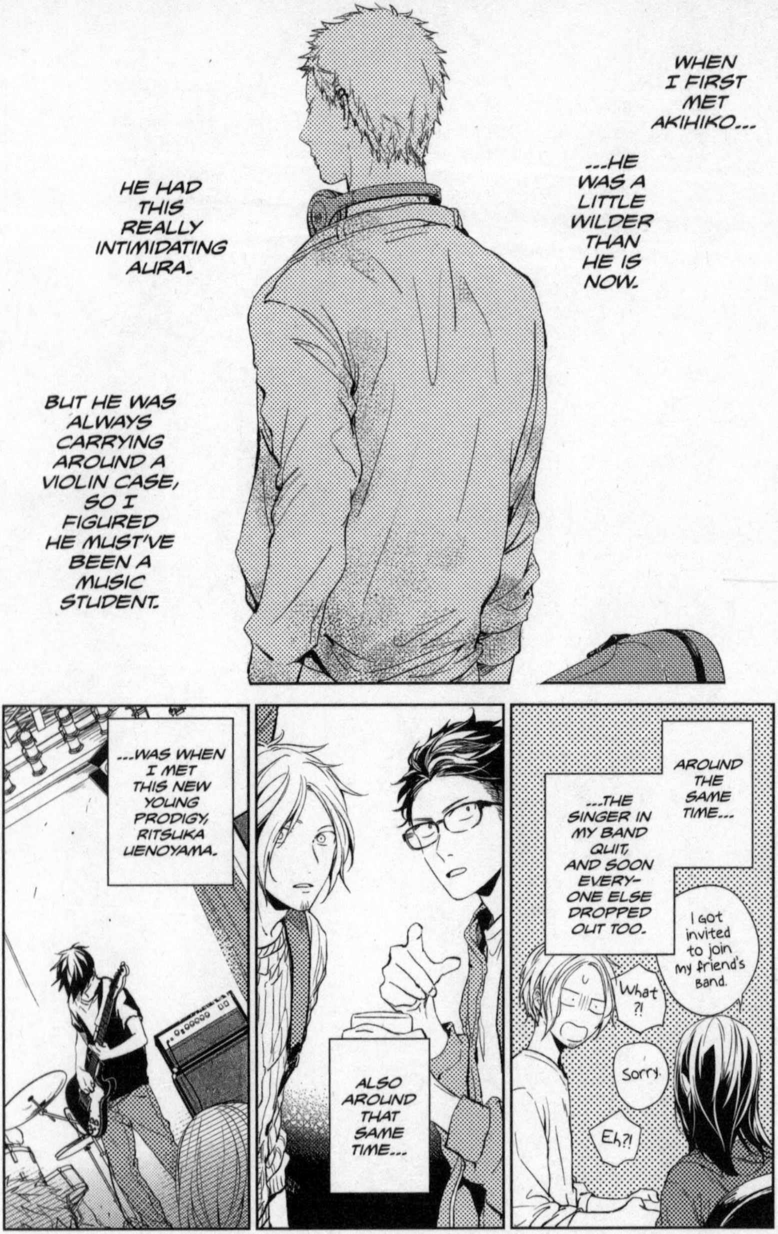
WHEN I FIRST MET AKIHIKO...
...HE WAS A LITTLE WILDER THAN HE IS NOW.
HE HAD THIS REALLY INTIMIDATING AURA.
BUT HE WAS ALWAYS CARRYING AROUND A VIOLIN CASE, SO I FIGURED HE MUST'VE BEEN A MUSIC STUDENT.
AROUND THE SAME TIME...
...THE SINGER IN MY BAND QUIT, AND SOON EVERY-ONE ELSE DROPPED OUT TOO.
I got invited to join my friend's band.
What?!
Sorry.
Eh?!
ALSO AROUND THAT SAME TIME...
...WAS WHEN I MET THIS NEW YOUNG PRODIGY, RITSUKA UENOYAMA.

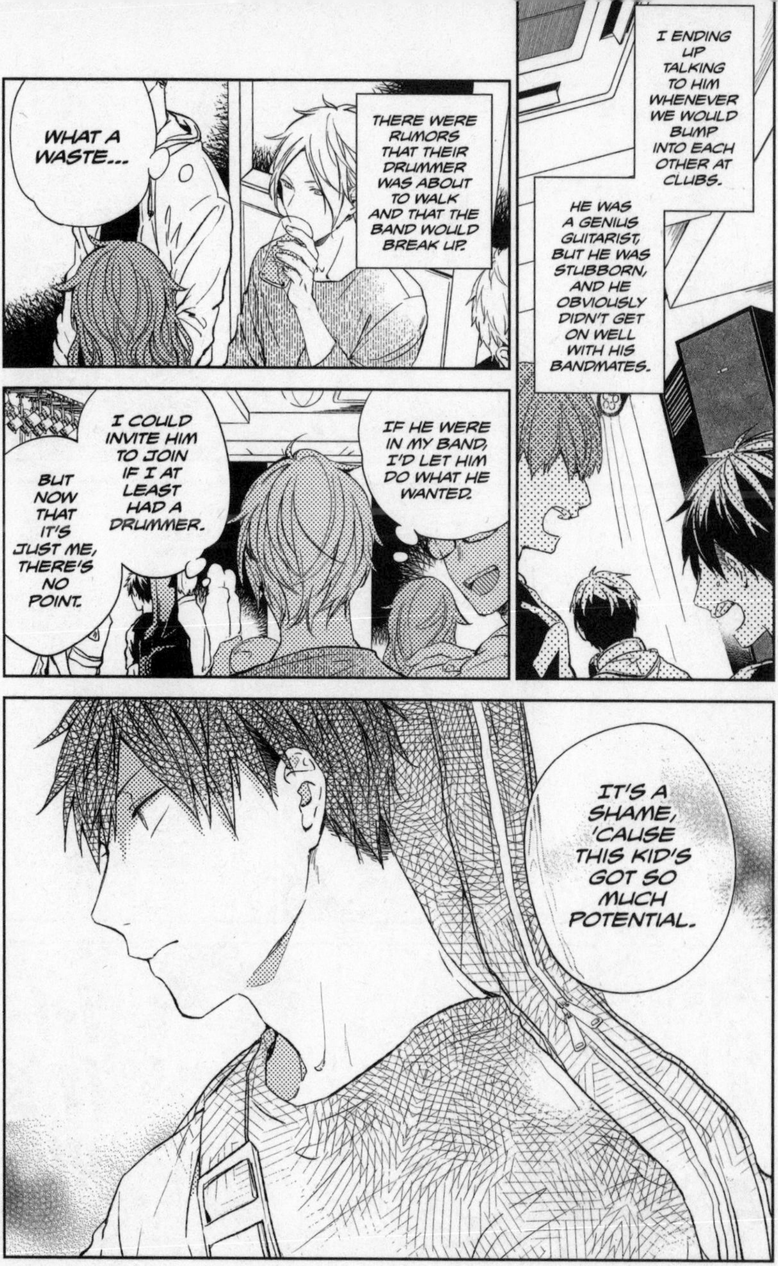
I ENDING UP TALKING TO HIM WHENEVER WE WOULD BUMP INTO EACH OTHER AT CLUBS.
HE WAS A GENIUS GUITARIST, BUT HE WAS STUBBORN, AND HE OBVIOUSLY DIDN'T GET ON WELL WITH HIS BANDMATES.
THERE WERE RUMORS THAT THEIR DRUMMER WAS ABOUT TO WALK AND THAT THE BAND WOULD BREAK UP.
WHAT A WASTE...
IF HE WERE IN MY BAND, I'D LET HIM DO WHAT HE WANTED.
I COULD INVITE HIM TO JOIN IF I AT LEAST HAD A DRUMMER.
BUT NOW THAT IT'S JUST ME, THERE'S NO POINT.
IT'S A SHAME, 'CAUSE THIS KID'S GOT SO MUCH POTENTIAL.

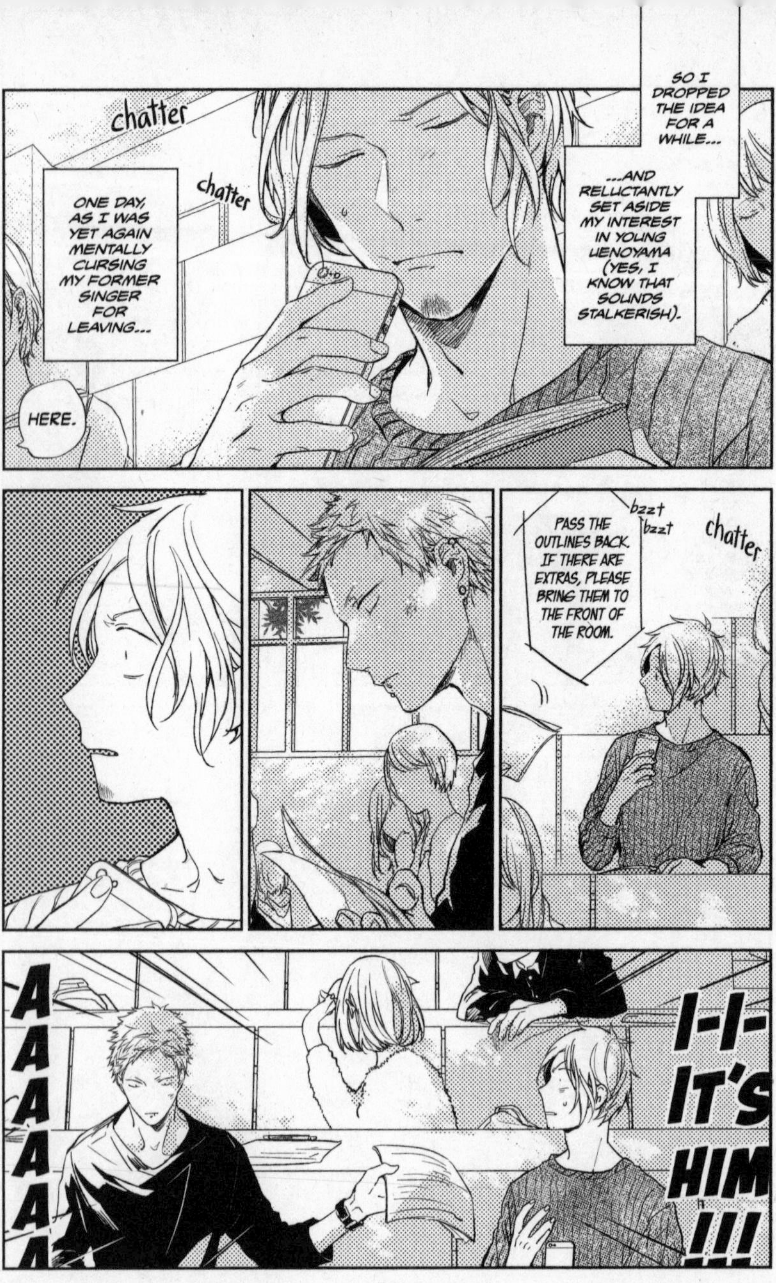
SO I DROPPED THE IDEA FOR A WHILE...
...AND RELUCTANTLY SET ASIDE MY INTEREST IN YOUNG UENOYAMA (YES, I KNOW THAT SOUNDS STALKERISH).
chatter
chatter
ONE DAY, AS I WAS YET AGAIN MENTALLY CURSING MY FORMER SINGER FOR LEAVING...
HERE.
bzzt
bzzt
chatter
PASS THE OUTLINES BACK. IF THERE ARE EXTRAS, PLEASE BRING THEM TO THE FRONT OF THE ROOM.
I-I-IT'S HIM!!!
AAAAAA

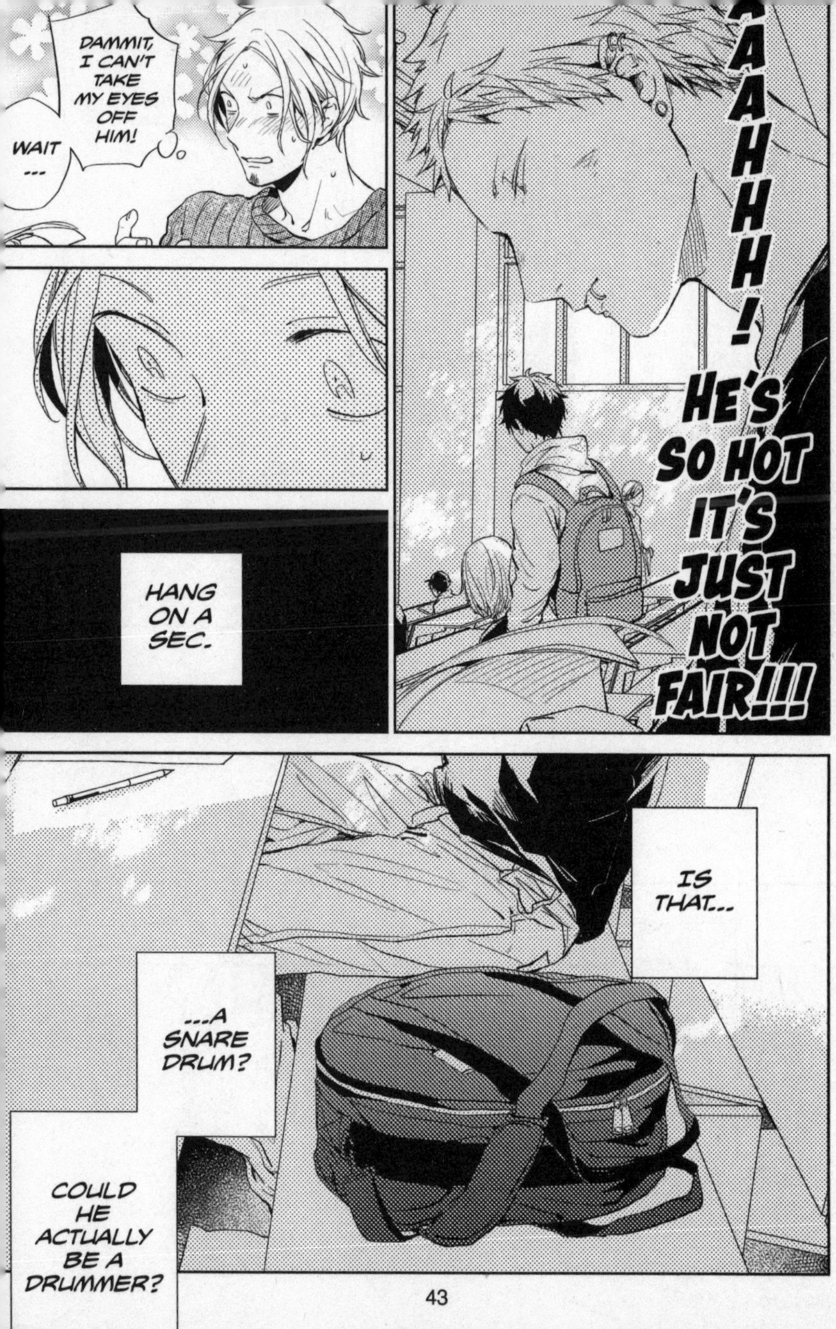
AAAHHHH! HE'S SO HOT IT'S JUST NOT FAIR!!!
DAMMIT, I CAN'T TAKE MY EYES OFF HIM!
WAIT ---
HANG ON A SEC.
IS THAT...
...A SNARE DRUM?
COULD HE ACTUALLY BE A DRUMMER?

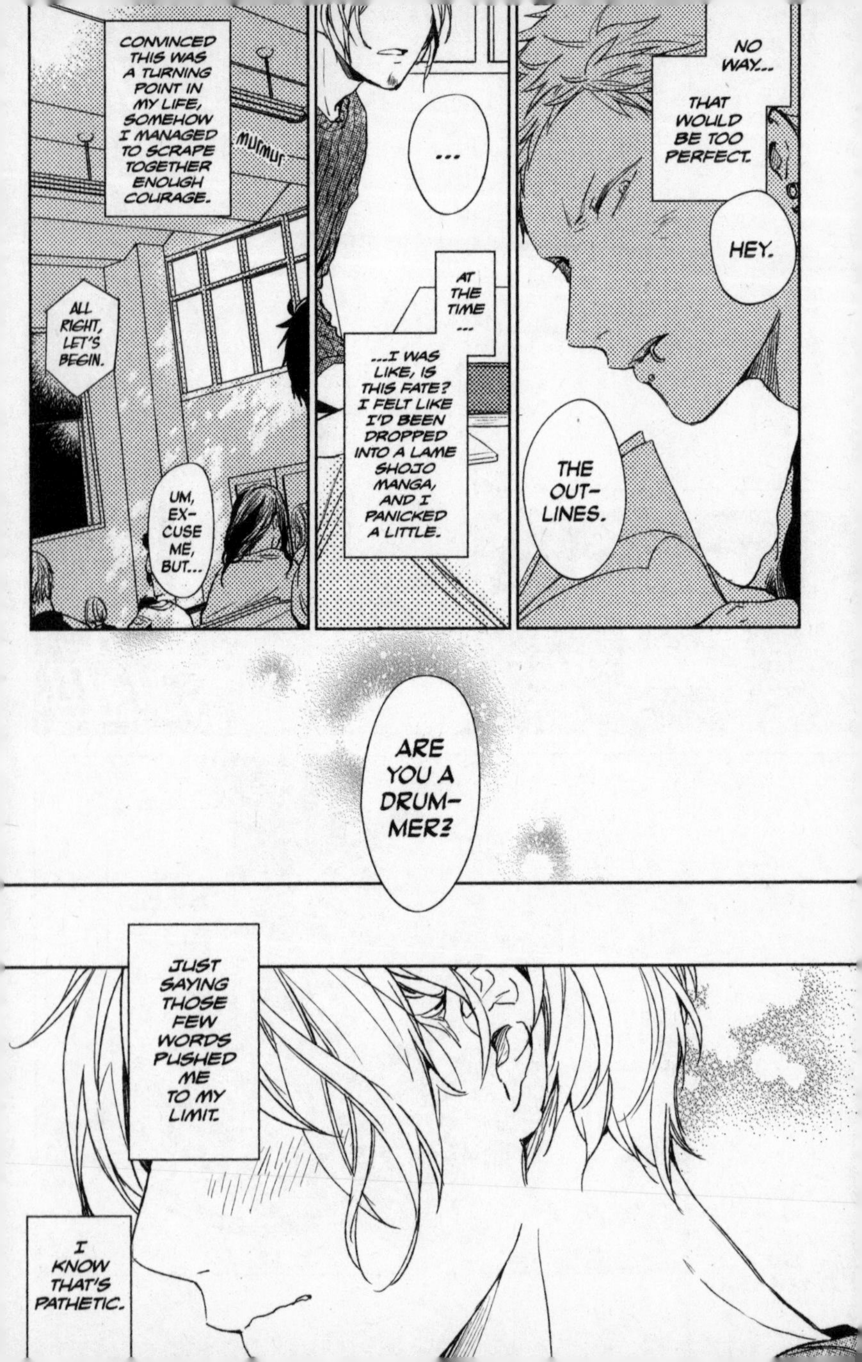
NO WAY...
THAT WOULD BE TOO PERFECT.
HEY.
THE OUT-LINES.
...
AT THE TIME...
...I WAS LIKE, IS THIS FATE? I FELT LIKE I'D BEEN DROPPED INTO A LAME SHOJO MANGA, AND I PANICKED A LITTLE.
CONVINCED THIS WAS A TURNING POINT IN MY LIFE, SOMEHOW I MANAGED TO SCRAPE TOGETHER ENOUGH COURAGE.
murmur
ALL RIGHT, LET'S BEGIN.
UM, EX-CUSE ME, BUT...
ARE YOU A DRUM-MER?
JUST SAYING THOSE FEW WORDS PUSHED ME TO MY LIMIT.
I KNOW THAT'S PATHETIC.

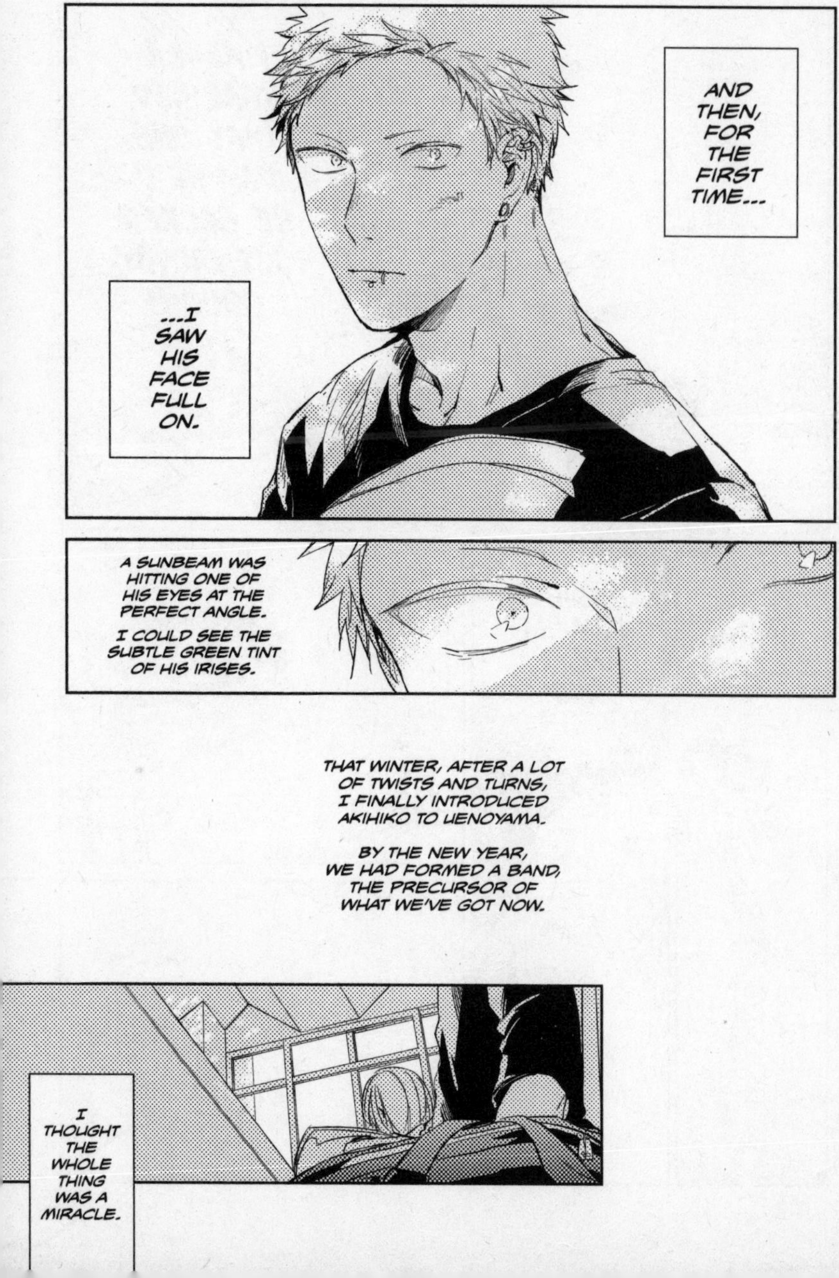
AND THEN, FOR THE FIRST TIME...
...I SAW HIS FACE FULL ON.
A SUNBEAM WAS HITTING ONE OF HIS EYES AT THE PERFECT ANGLE.
I COULD SEE THE SUBTLE GREEN TINT OF HIS IRISES.
THAT WINTER, AFTER A LOT OF TWISTS AND TURNS, I FINALLY INTRODUCED AKIHIKO TO UENOYAMA.
BY THE NEW YEAR, WE HAD FORMED A BAND, THE PRECURSOR OF WHAT WE'VE GOT NOW.
I THOUGHT THE WHOLE THING WAS A MIRACLE.

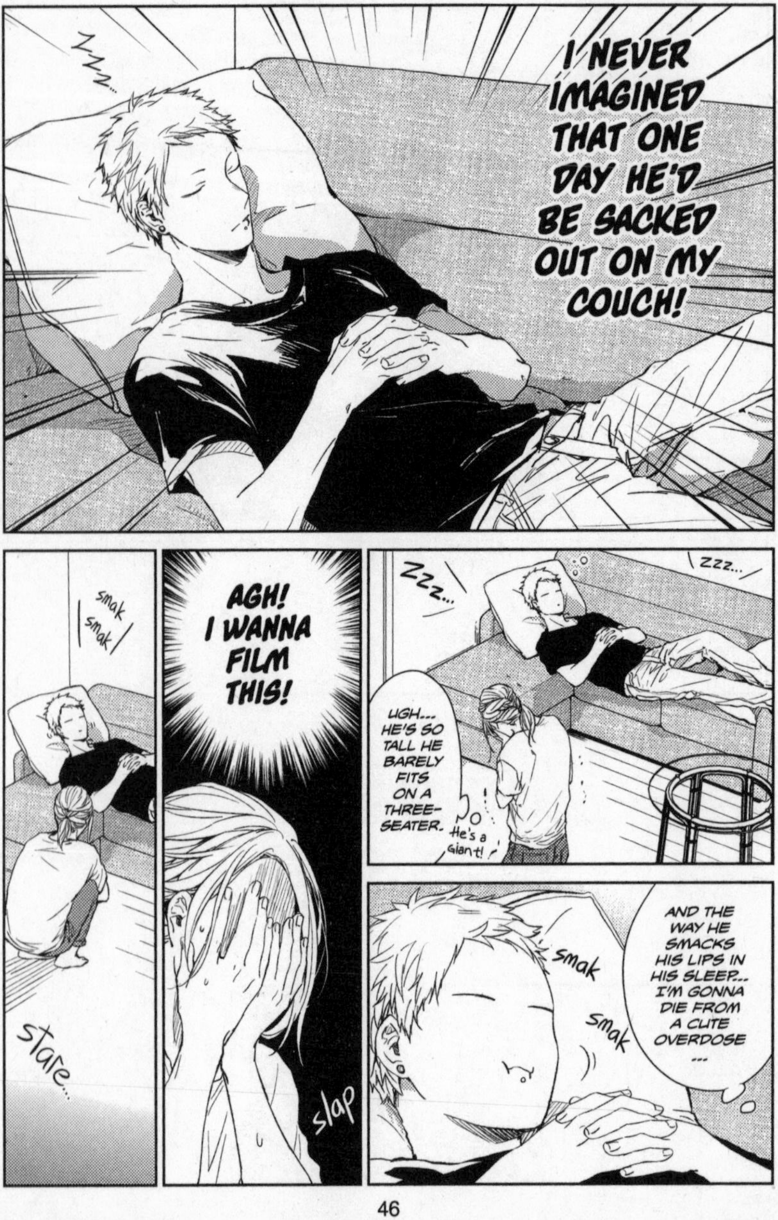
I NEVER IMAGINED THAT ONE DAY HE'D BE SACKED OUT ON MY COUCH!
Zzz...
Zzz...
Zzz...
UGH... HE'S SO TALL HE BARELY FITS ON A THREE-SEATER.
He's a Giant!
AND THE WAY HE SMACKS HIS LIPS IN HIS SLEEP... I'M GONNA DIE FROM A CUTE OVERDOSE...
smak
smak
AGH! I WANNA FILM THIS!
slap
smak smak
stare...

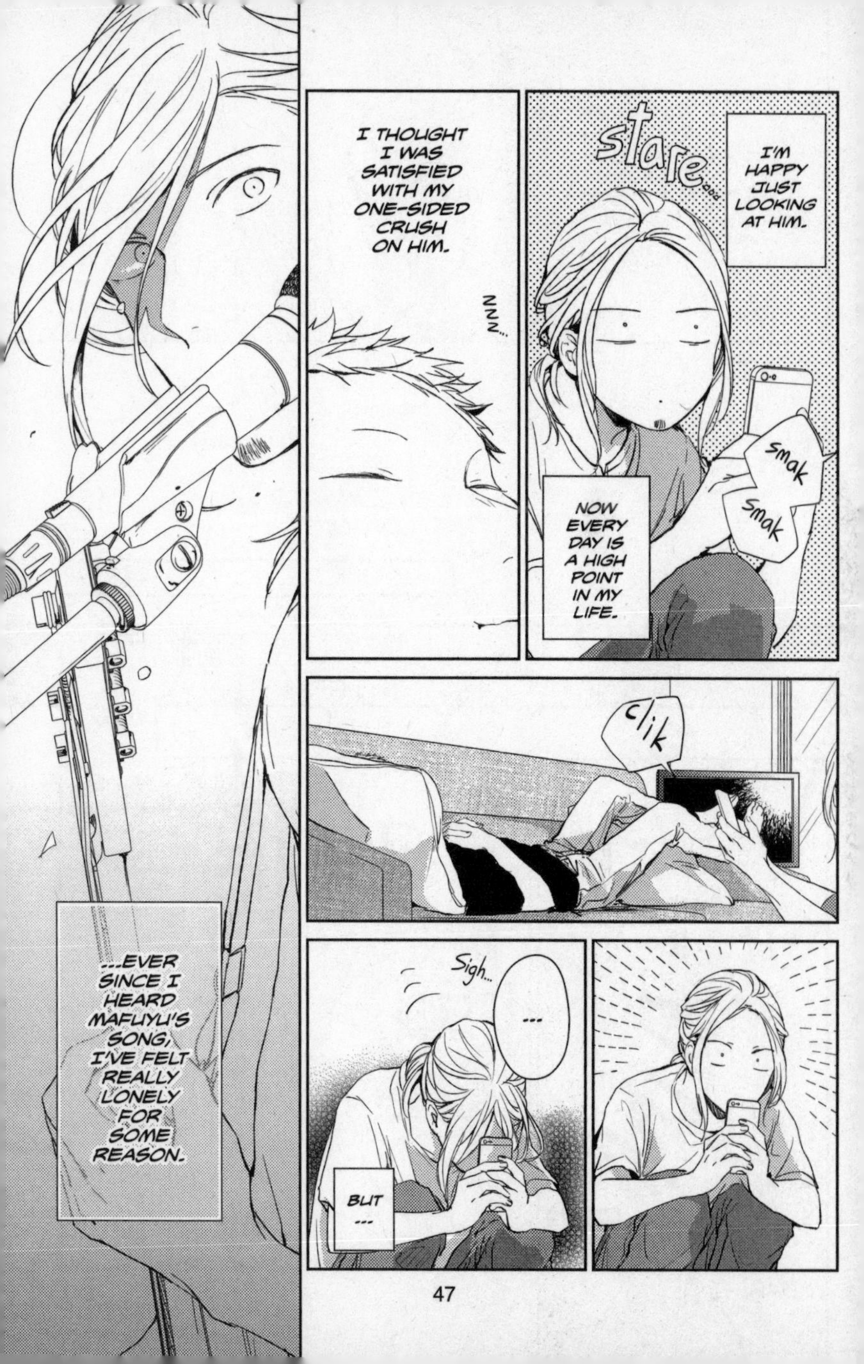
stare...
I'M HAPPY JUST LOOKING AT HIM.
smak
smak
NOW EVERY DAY IS A HIGH POINT IN MY LIFE.
I THOUGHT I WAS SATISFIED WITH MY ONE-SIDED CRUSH ON HIM.
ZZZ...
clik
Sigh...
...
BUT...
...EVER SINCE I HEARD MAFUYU'S SONG, I'VE FELT REALLY LONELY FOR SOME REASON.

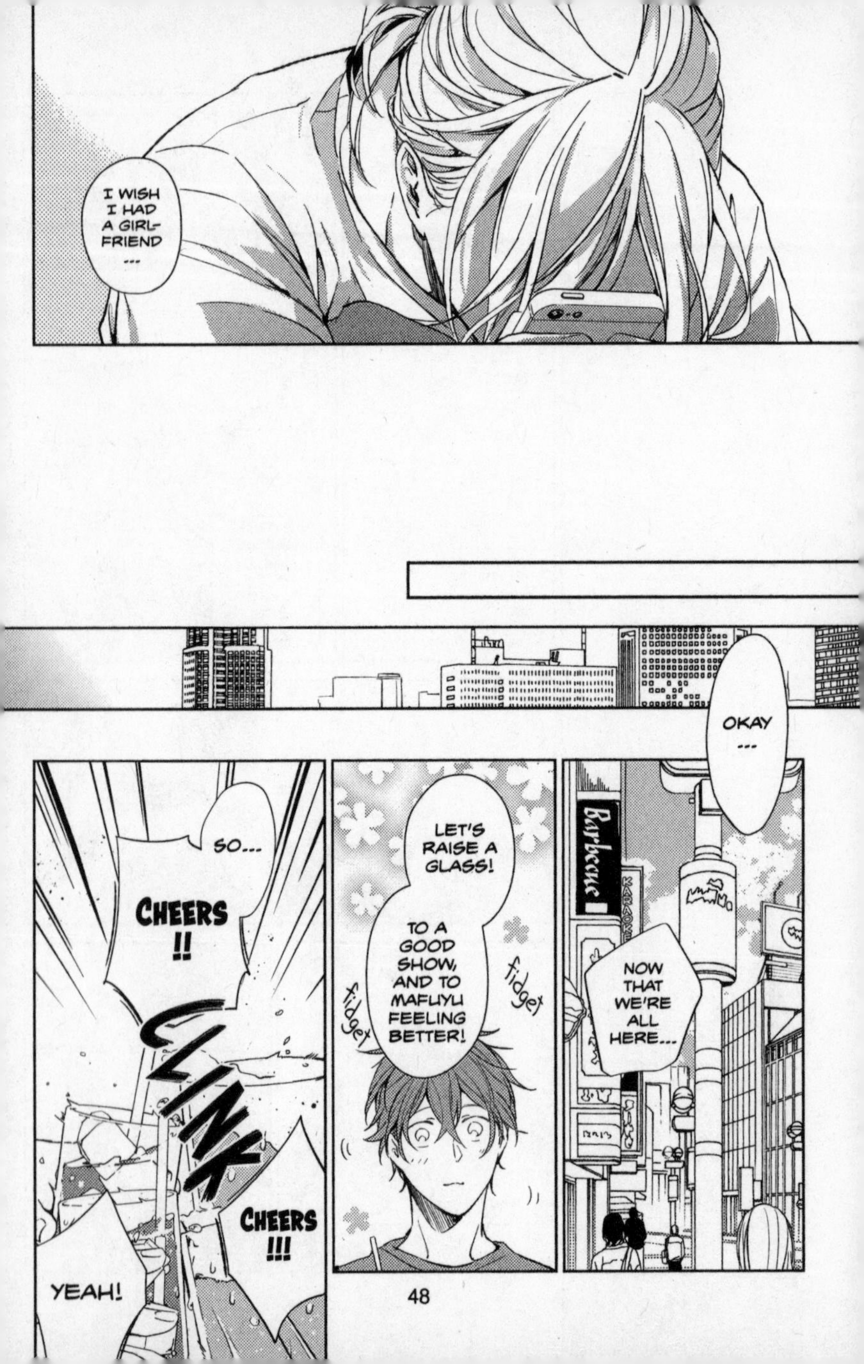
I WISH I HAD A GIRLFRIEND ...
OKAY ...
NOW THAT WE'RE ALL HERE...
LET'S RAISE A GLASS!
TO A GOOD SHOW, AND TO MAFUYU FEELING BETTER!
fidget
fidget
SO...
CHEERS!!
CLINK
CHEERS!!!
YEAH!

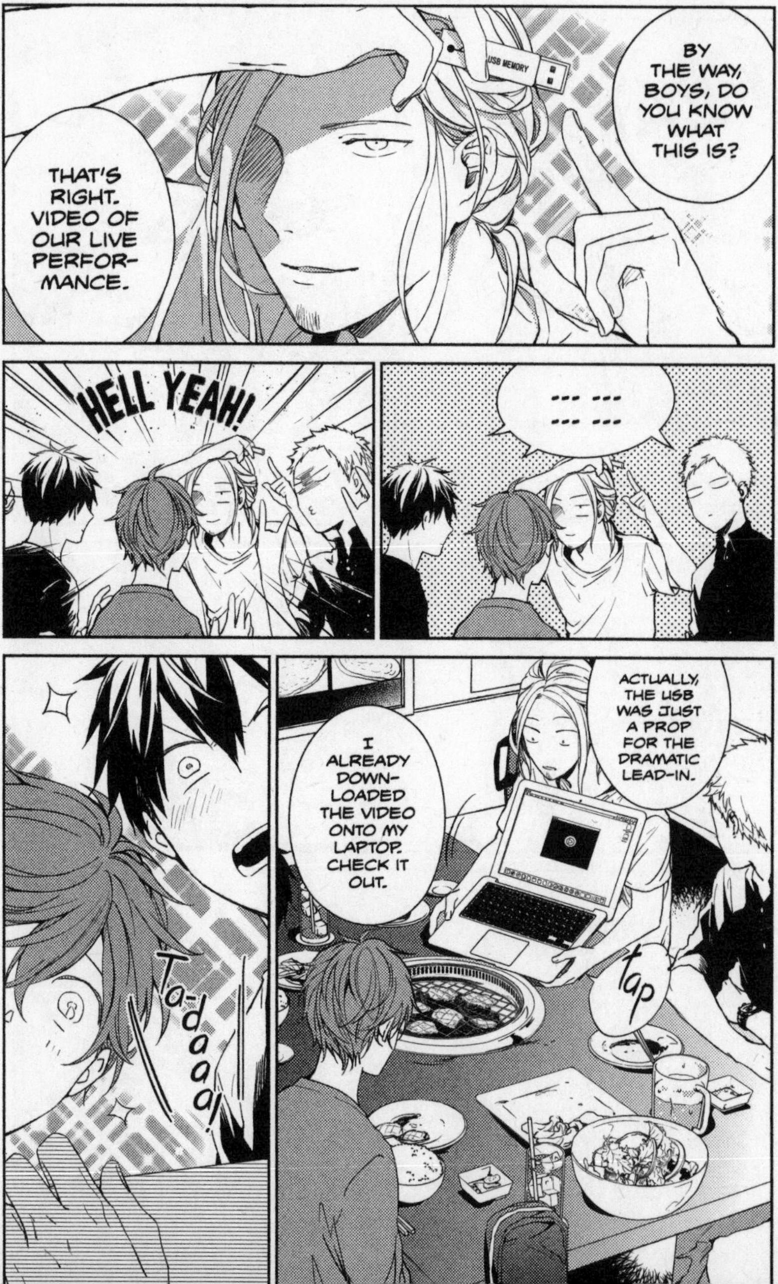
BY THE WAY, BOYS, DO YOU KNOW WHAT THIS IS?
USB MEMORY
THAT'S RIGHT. VIDEO OF OUR LIVE PERFORMANCE.
--- --- --- ---
HELL YEAH!
ACTUALLY, THE USB WAS JUST A PROP FOR THE DRAMATIC LEAD-IN.
I ALREADY DOWNLOADED THE VIDEO ONTO MY LAPTOP. CHECK IT OUT.
tap
Ta-daaa!

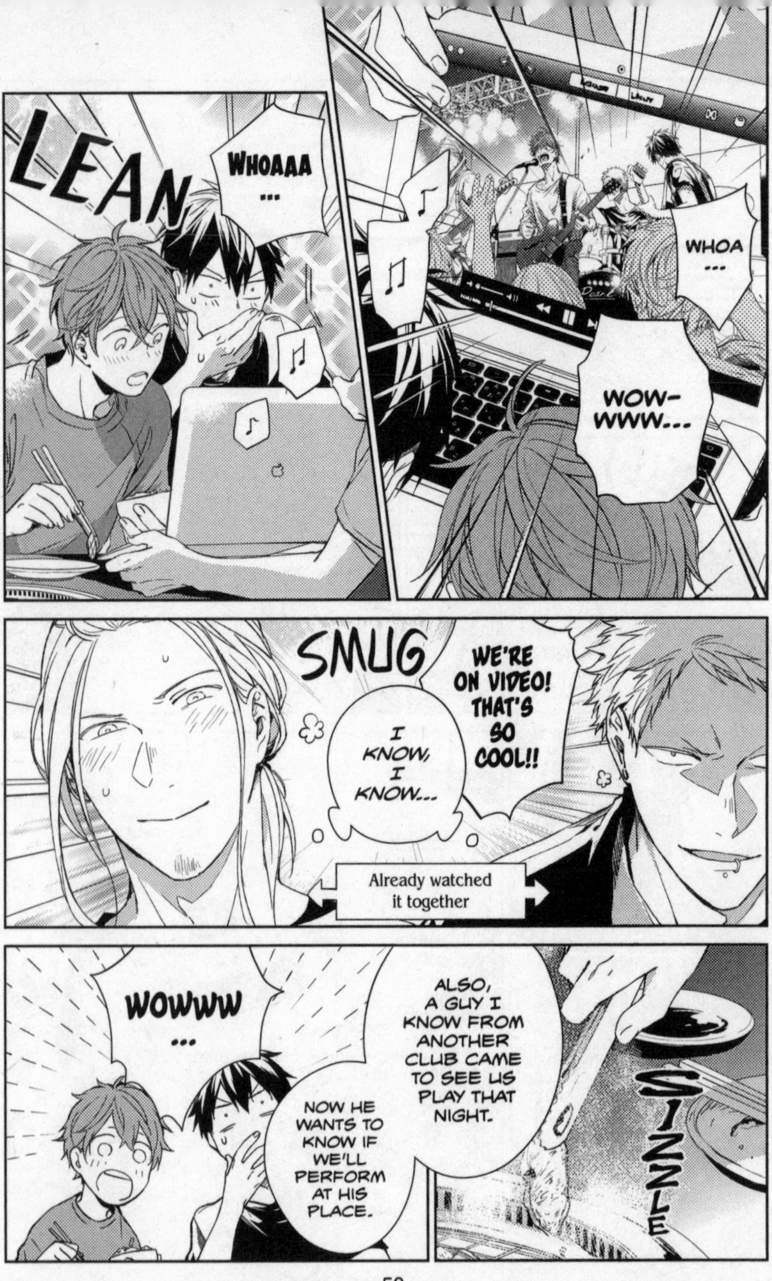
WHOA ...
WOW-WWW...
WHOAAA ...
LEAN
WE'RE ON VIDEO! THAT'S SO COOL!!
SMUG
I KNOW, I KNOW...
Already watched it together
SIZZLE
ALSO, A GUY I KNOW FROM ANOTHER CLUB CAME TO SEE US PLAY THAT NIGHT.
NOW HE WANTS TO KNOW IF WE'LL PERFORM AT HIS PLACE.
WOWWW ...

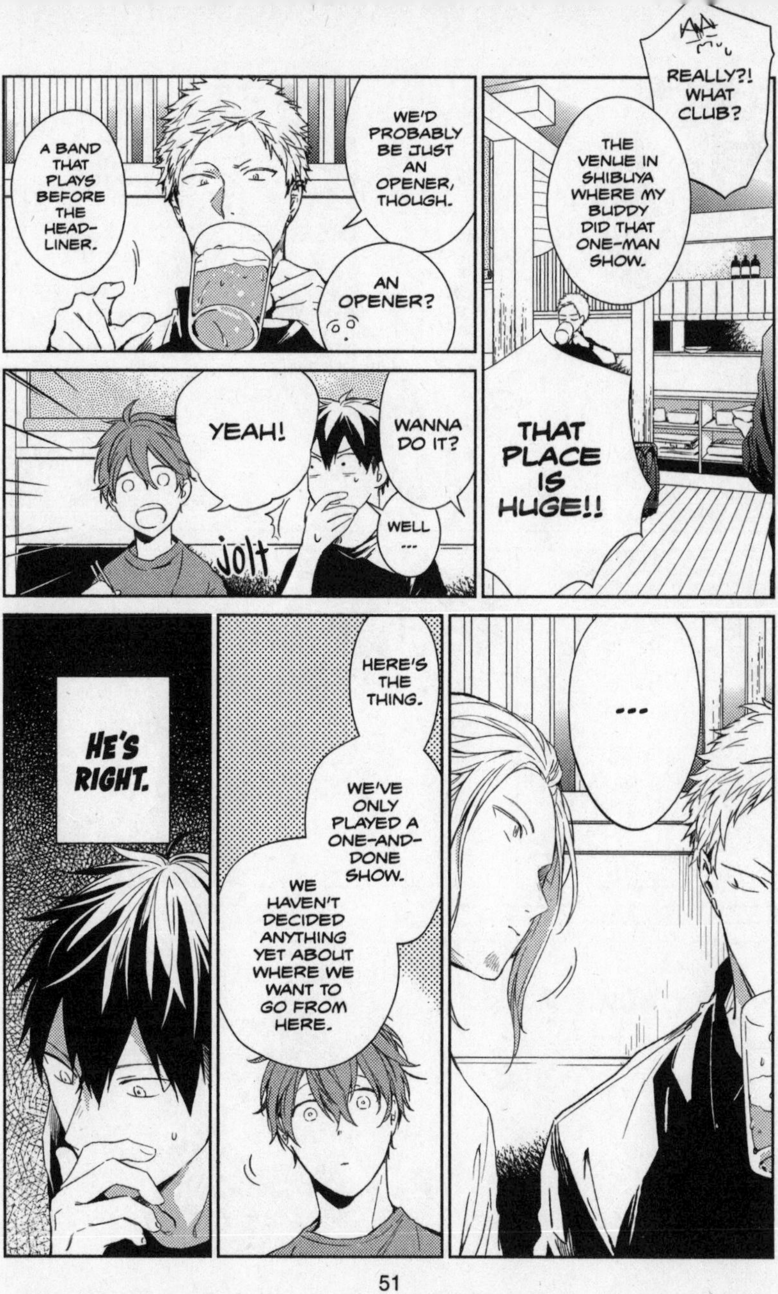
REALLY?! WHAT CLUB?
THE VENUE IN SHIBUYA WHERE MY BUDDY DID THAT ONE-MAN SHOW.
THAT PLACE IS HUGE!!
WE'D PROBABLY BE JUST AN OPENER, THOUGH.
AN OPENER?
A BAND THAT PLAYS BEFORE THE HEAD-LINER.
WANNA DO IT?
YEAH!
WELL...
JOLT
...
HERE'S THE THING.
WE'VE ONLY PLAYED A ONE-AND-DONE SHOW.
WE HAVEN'T DECIDED ANYTHING YET ABOUT WHERE WE WANT TO GO FROM HERE.
HE'S RIGHT.

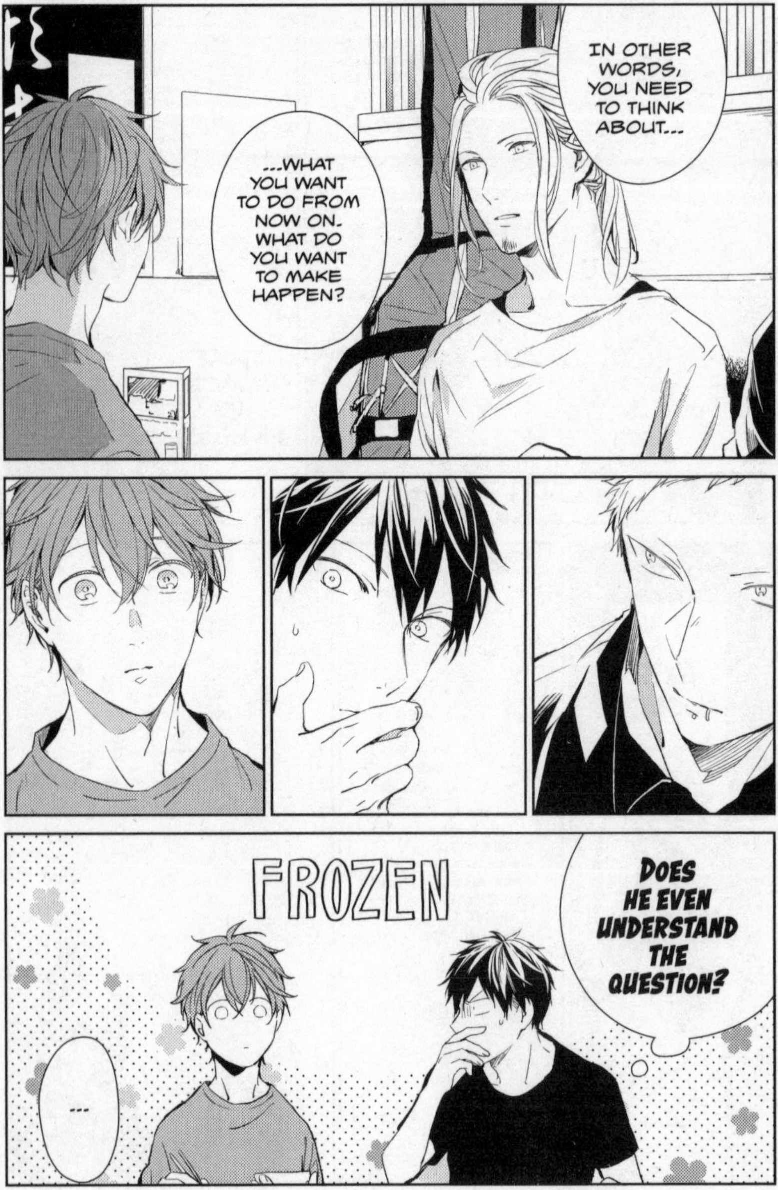
IN OTHER WORDS, YOU NEED TO THINK ABOUT...
...WHAT YOU WANT TO DO FROM NOW ON. WHAT DO YOU WANT TO MAKE HAPPEN?
DOES HE EVEN UNDERSTAND THE QUESTION?
FROZEN
...

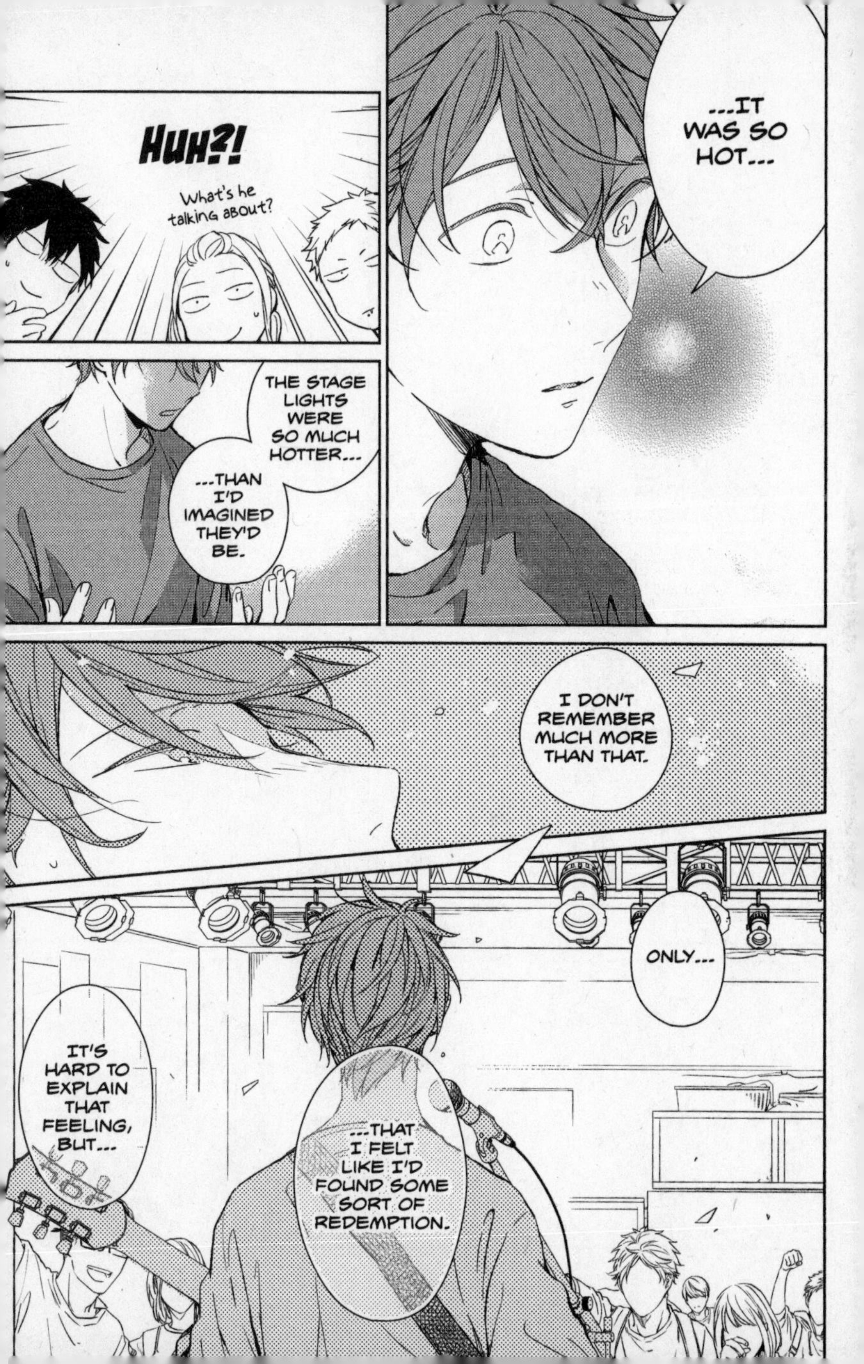
...IT WAS SO HOT...
HUH?!
What's he talking about?
THE STAGE LIGHTS WERE SO MUCH HOTTER...
...THAN I'D IMAGINED THEY'D BE.
I DON'T REMEMBER MUCH MORE THAN THAT.
ONLY...
...THAT I FELT LIKE I'D FOUND SOME SORT OF REDEMPTION.
IT'S HARD TO EXPLAIN THAT FEELING, BUT...

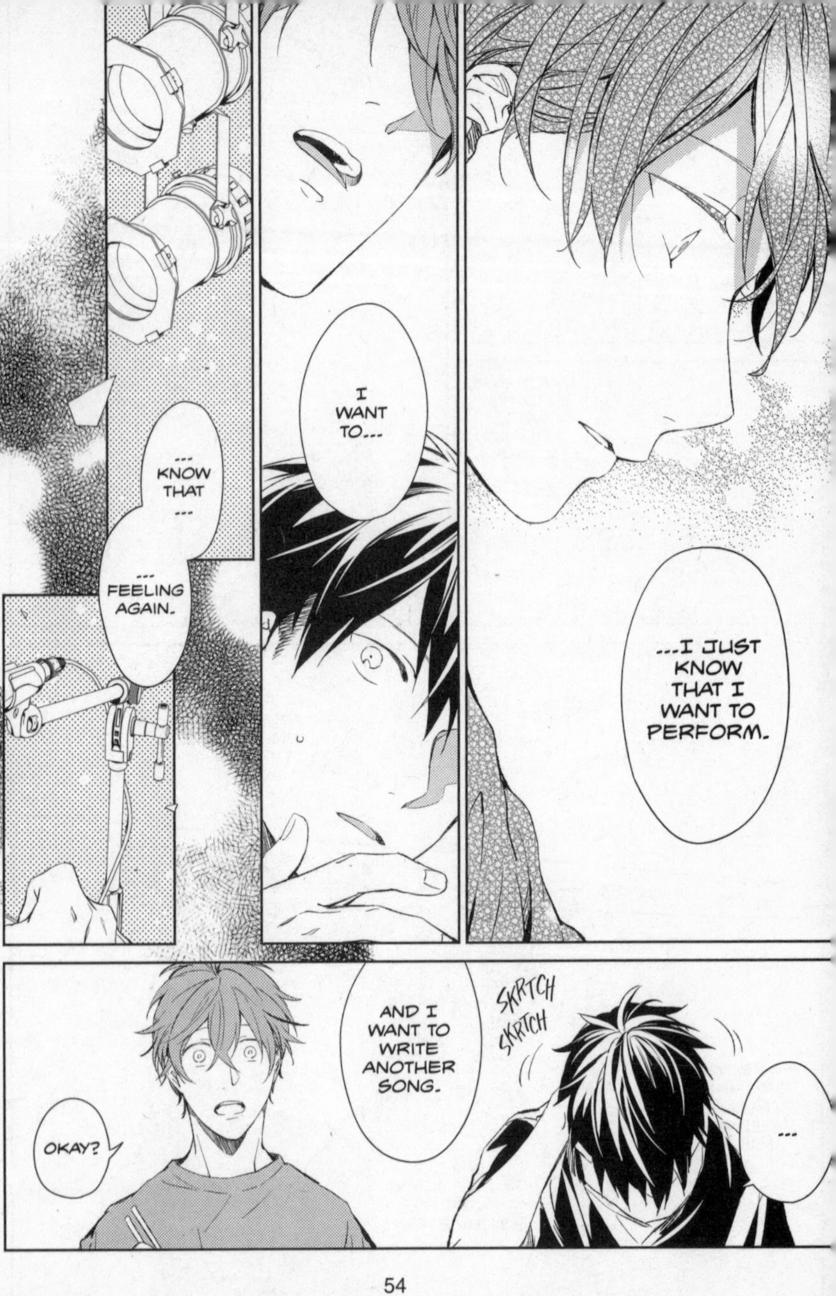

...I JUST KNOW THAT I WANT TO PERFORM.
I WANT TO...
...KNOW THAT ...
...FEELING AGAIN.
...
SKRTCH SKRTCH
AND I WANT TO WRITE ANOTHER SONG.
OKAY?

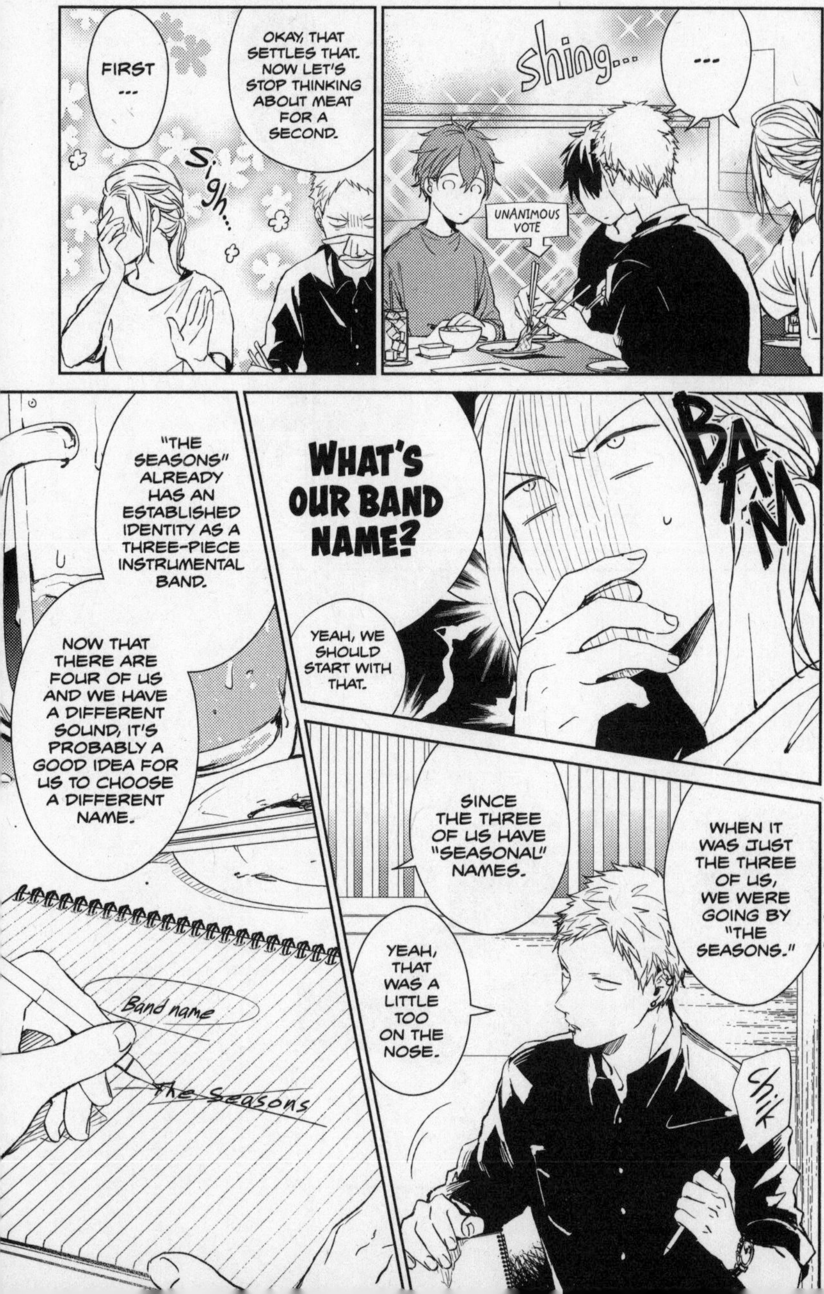
shing...
...
UNANIMOUS VOTE
OKAY, THAT SETTLES THAT. NOW LET'S STOP THINKING ABOUT MEAT FOR A SECOND.
FIRST ...
Sigh...
WHAT'S OUR BAND NAME?
BAM
YEAH, WE SHOULD START WITH THAT.
WHEN IT WAS JUST THE THREE OF US, WE WERE GOING BY "THE SEASONS."
SINCE THE THREE OF US HAVE "SEASONAL" NAMES.
YEAH, THAT WAS A LITTLE TOO ON THE NOSE.
chik
"THE SEASONS" ALREADY HAS AN ESTABLISHED IDENTITY AS A THREE-PIECE INSTRUMENTAL BAND.
NOW THAT THERE ARE FOUR OF US AND WE HAVE A DIFFERENT SOUND, IT'S PROBABLY A GOOD IDEA FOR US TO CHOOSE A DIFFERENT NAME.
Band name
The Seasons

Note: "Haru" = spring, "Ka" = summer, "Aki" = fall.

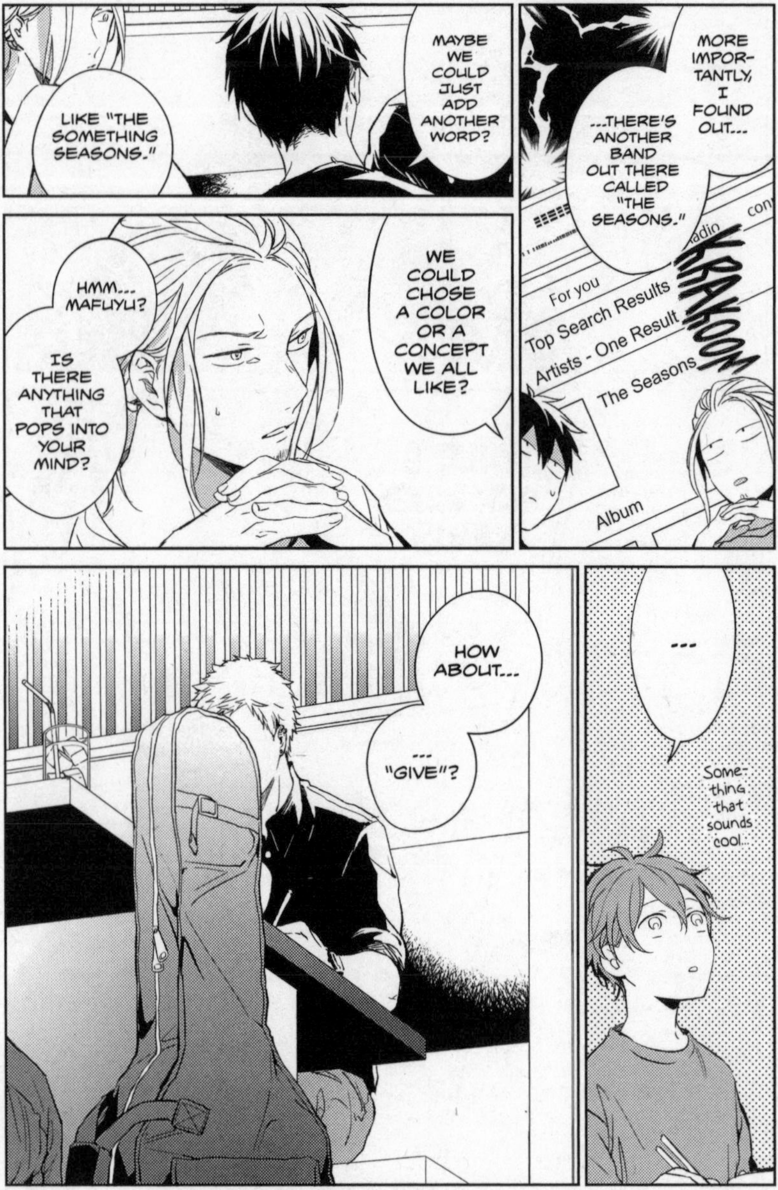
MORE IMPORTANTLY, I FOUND OUT...
...THERE'S ANOTHER BAND OUT THERE CALLED "THE SEASONS."
For you
Top Search Results
Artists - One Result
The Seasons
Album
KRAKOOM
MAYBE WE COULD JUST ADD ANOTHER WORD?
LIKE "THE SOMETHING SEASONS."
WE COULD CHOSE A COLOR OR A CONCEPT WE ALL LIKE?
HMM... MAFUYU?
IS THERE ANYTHING THAT POPS INTO YOUR MIND?
...
Something that sounds cool...
HOW ABOUT...
..."GIVE"?

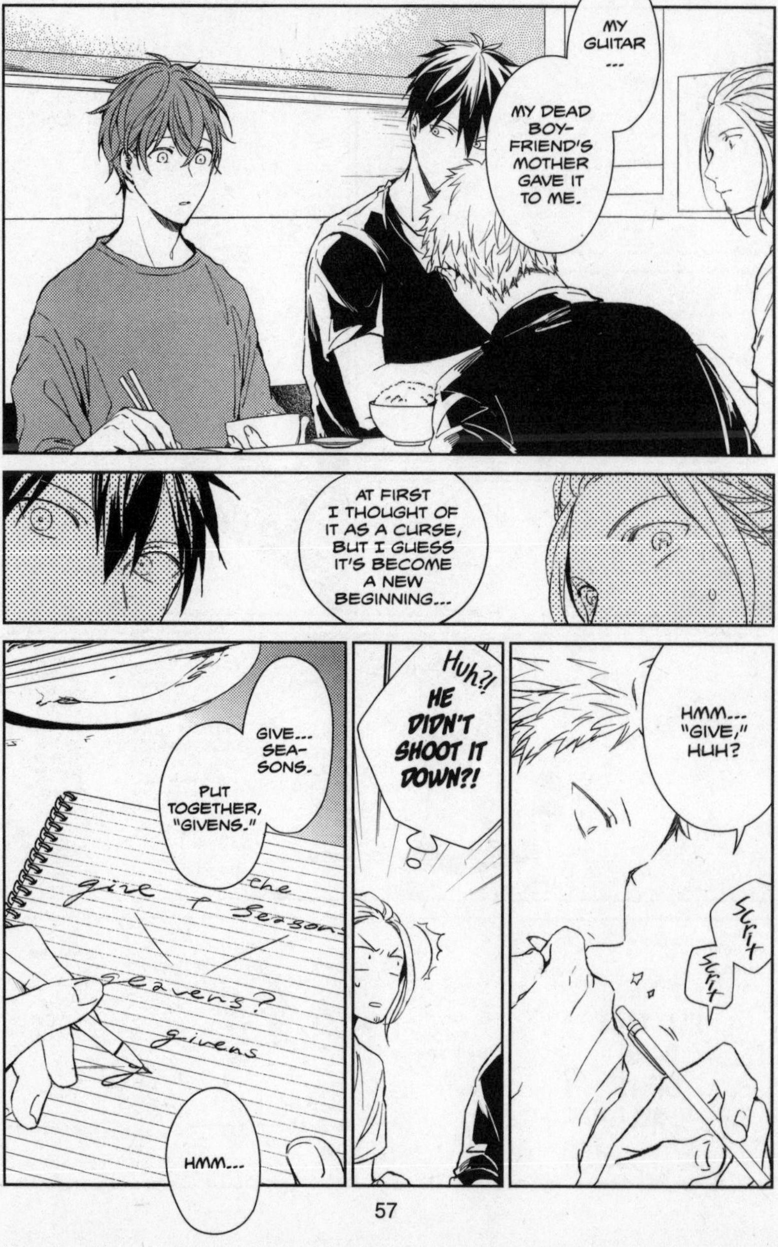
MY GUITAR ...
MY DEAD BOY-FRIEND'S MOTHER GAVE IT TO ME.
AT FIRST I THOUGHT OF IT AS A CURSE, BUT I GUESS IT'S BECOME A NEW BEGINNING...
HMM... "GIVE," HUH?
SCRIT
SCRIT
Huh?!
HE DIDN'T SHOOT IT DOWN?!
GIVE... SEA-SONS.
PUT TOGETHER, "GIVENS."
give
the
+ seasons
seavens?
givens
HMM...

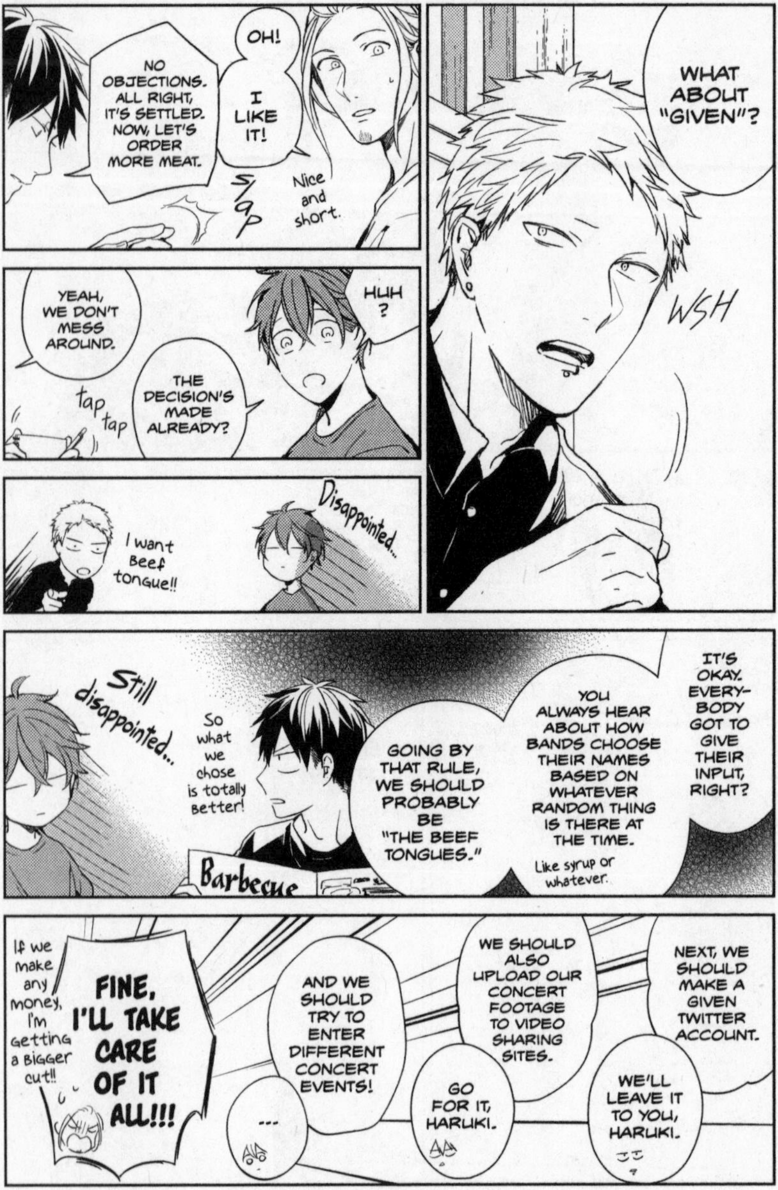
WHAT ABOUT "GIVEN"?
WSH
OH!
I LIKE IT!
Nice and short.
NO OBJECTIONS. ALL RIGHT, IT'S SETTLED. NOW, LET'S ORDER MORE MEAT.
Slap
HUH?
THE DECISION'S MADE ALREADY?
YEAH, WE DON'T MESS AROUND.
tap tap
Disappointed...
I want Beef tongue!!
IT'S OKAY. EVERYBODY GOT TO GIVE THEIR INPUT, RIGHT?
YOU ALWAYS HEAR ABOUT HOW BANDS CHOOSE THEIR NAMES BASED ON WHATEVER RANDOM THING IS THERE AT THE TIME.
Like syrup or whatever.
GOING BY THAT RULE, WE SHOULD PROBABLY BE "THE BEEF TONGUES."
So what we chose is totally better!
Still disappointed...
Barbecue
NEXT, WE SHOULD MAKE A GIVEN TWITTER ACCOUNT.
WE'LL LEAVE IT TO YOU, HARUKI.
WE SHOULD ALSO UPLOAD OUR CONCERT FOOTAGE TO VIDEO SHARING SITES.
GO FOR IT, HARUKI.
AND WE SHOULD TRY TO ENTER DIFFERENT CONCERT EVENTS!
...
FINE, I'LL TAKE CARE OF IT ALL!!!
If we make any money, I'm getting a bigger cut!!

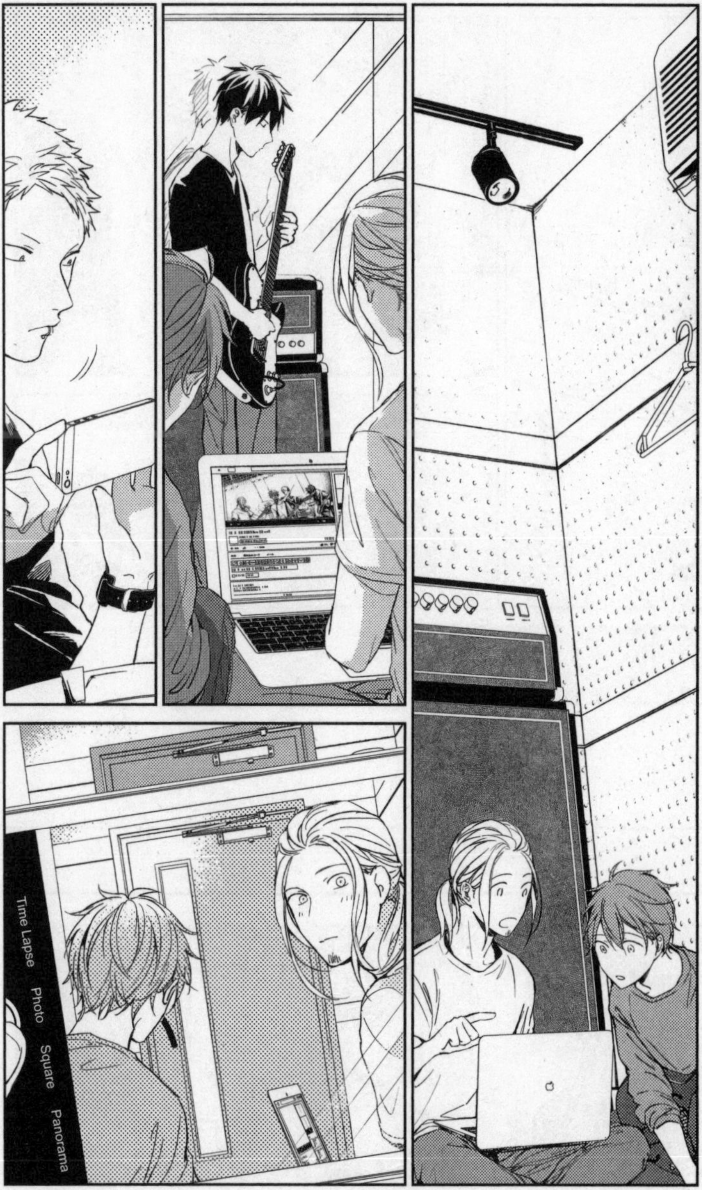
Time Lapse
Photo
Square
Panorama

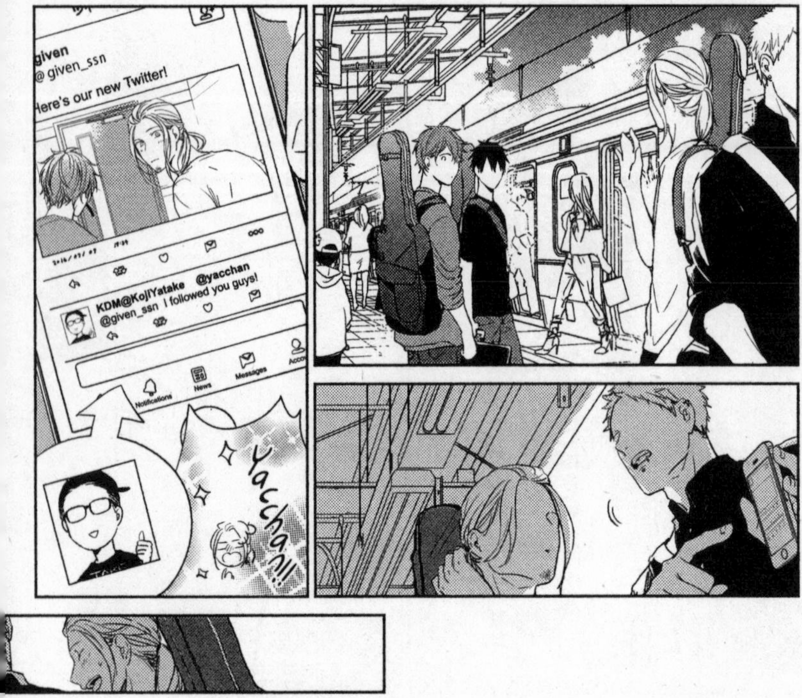
given
@ given_ssn
Here's our new Twitter!
KDM@KojiYatake @yacchan
@given_ssn I followed you guys!
Notifications
News
Messages
Yacchan!!!

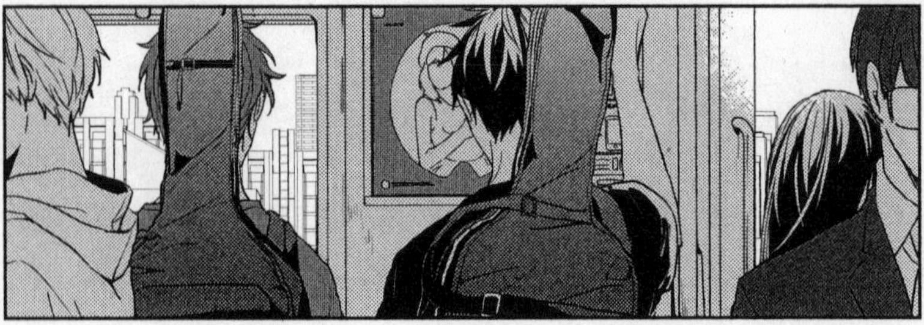

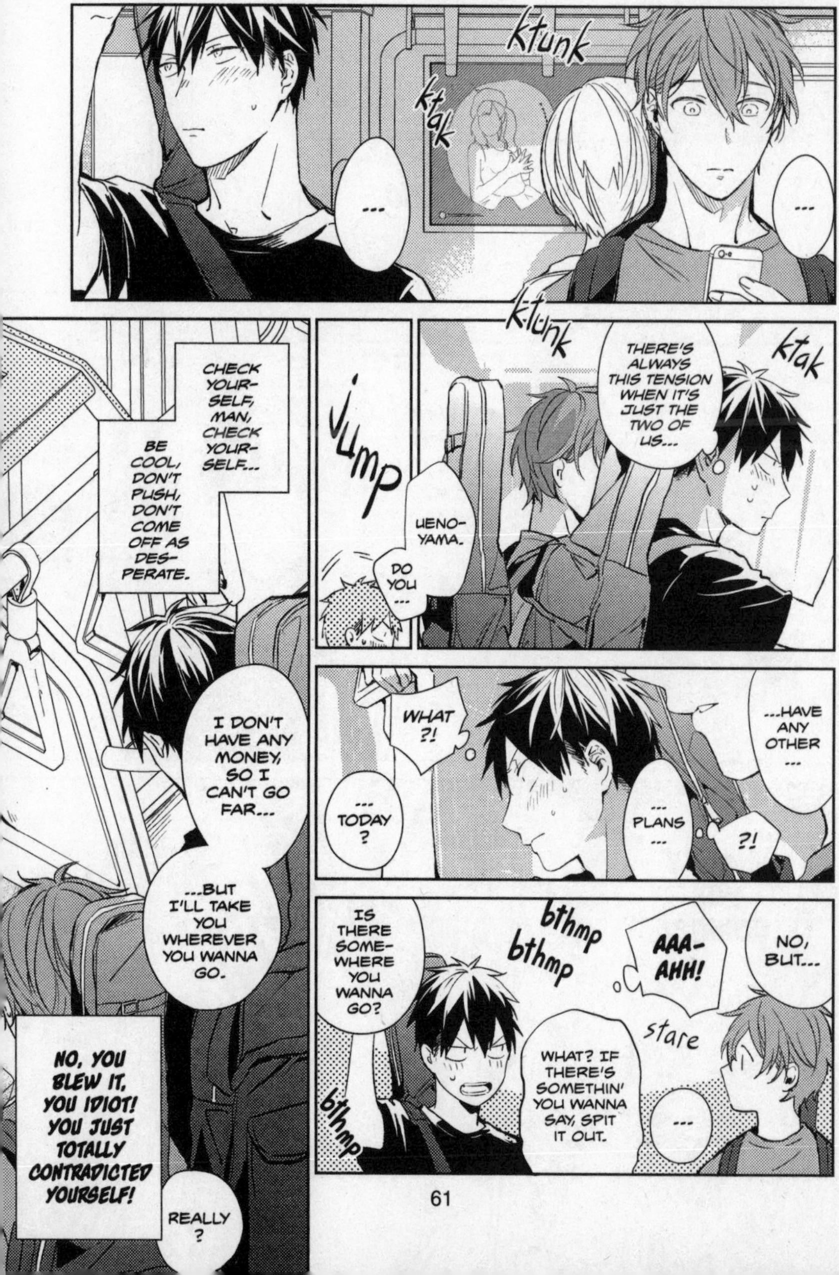
...
kTunk
kTak
...
kTunk
kTak
THERE'S ALWAYS THIS TENSION WHEN IT'S JUST THE TWO OF US...
jump
UENO-YAMA.
DO YOU...
...HAVE ANY OTHER...
?!
...PLANS...
WHAT?!
...TODAY?
NO, BUT...
AAA-AHH!
bthmp bthmp
IS THERE SOME-WHERE YOU WANNA GO?
stare
...
WHAT? IF THERE'S SOMETHIN' YOU WANNA SAY, SPIT IT OUT.
bthmp
CHECK YOUR-SELF, MAN, CHECK YOUR-SELF...
BE COOL, DON'T PUSH, DON'T COME OFF AS DES-PERATE.
I DON'T HAVE ANY MONEY, SO I CAN'T GO FAR...
...BUT I'LL TAKE YOU WHEREVER YOU WANNA GO.
NO, YOU BLEW IT, YOU IDIOT! YOU JUST TOTALLY CONTRADICTED YOURSELF!
REALLY?

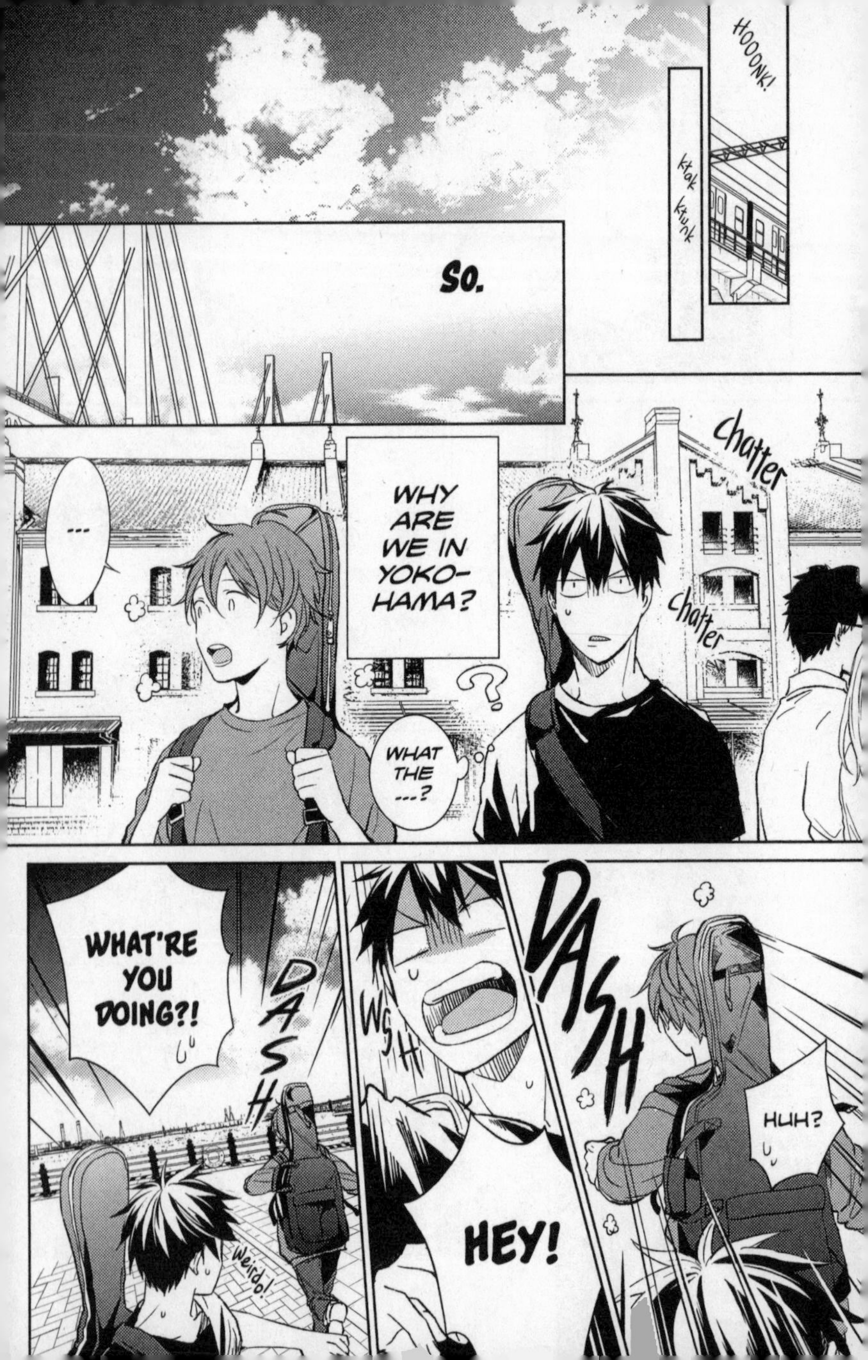
HOOONK!
ktok ktunk
SO.
chatter
chatter
WHY ARE WE IN YOKO-HAMA?
WHAT THE ...?
...
DASH
HUH?
HEY!
WSH
WHAT'RE YOU DOING?!
DASH
weirdo!

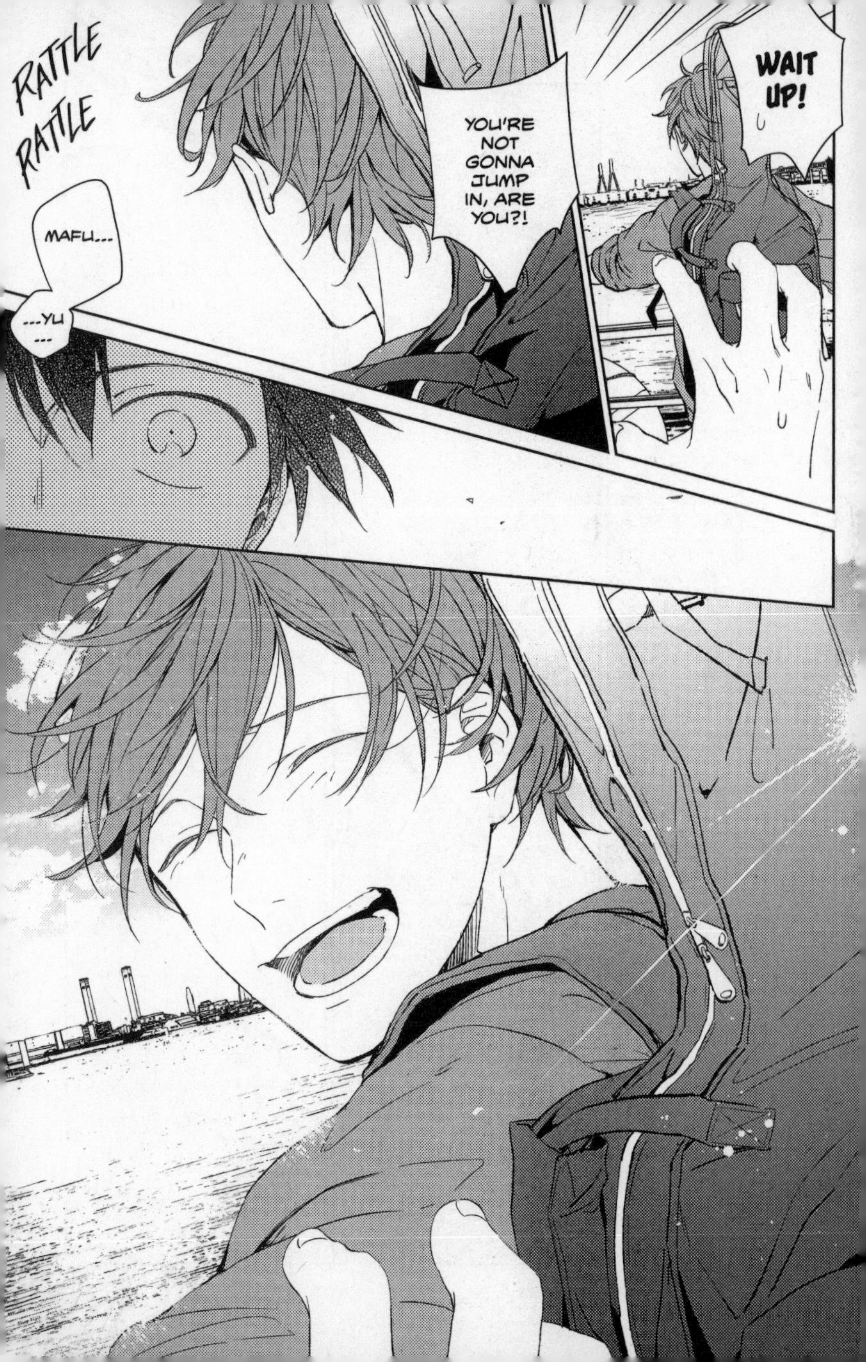
WAIT UP!
YOU'RE NOT GONNA JUMP IN, ARE YOU?!
RATTLE RATTLE
MAFU...
...YU ...

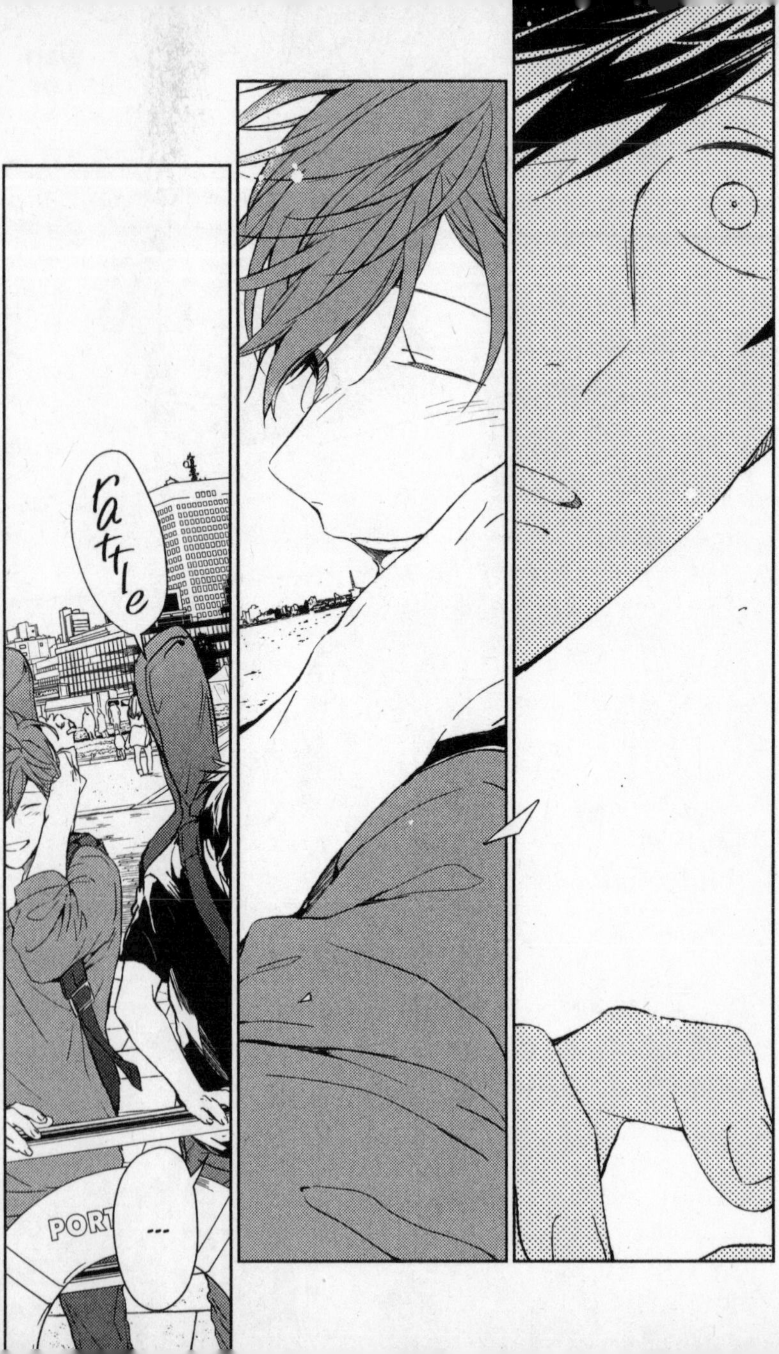
...
rattle
PORT

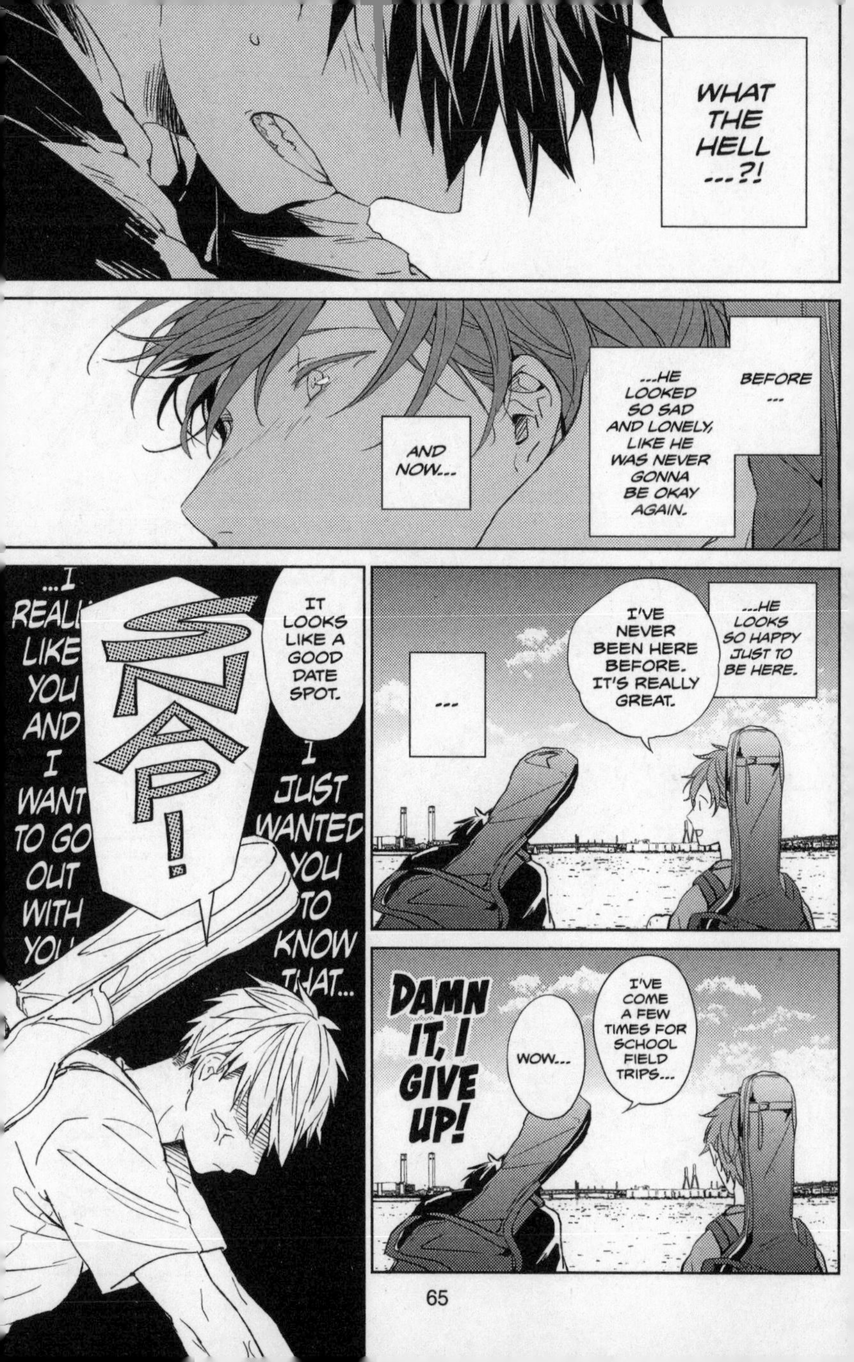
WHAT THE HELL ...?!
BEFORE ...
...HE LOOKED SO SAD AND LONELY, LIKE HE WAS NEVER GONNA BE OKAY AGAIN.
AND NOW...
...HE LOOKS SO HAPPY JUST TO BE HERE.
I'VE NEVER BEEN HERE BEFORE. IT'S REALLY GREAT.
...
I'VE COME A FEW TIMES FOR SCHOOL FIELD TRIPS...
WOW...
DAMN IT, I GIVE UP!
IT LOOKS LIKE A GOOD DATE SPOT.
SNAP!
I JUST WANTED YOU TO KNOW THAT...
...I REALL LIKE YOU AND I WANT TO GO OUT WITH YO

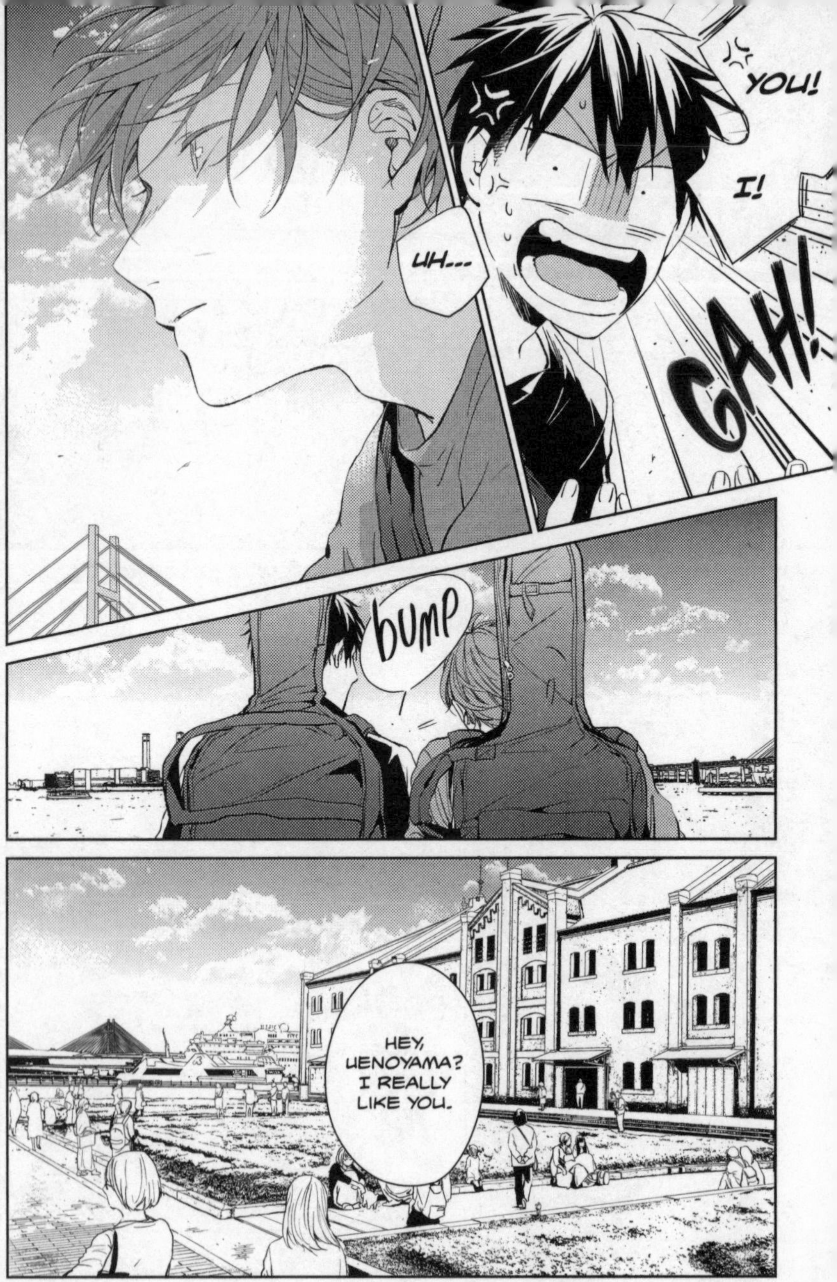
YOU!
I!
UH...
GAH!
bump
HEY, UENOYAMA? I REALLY LIKE YOU.

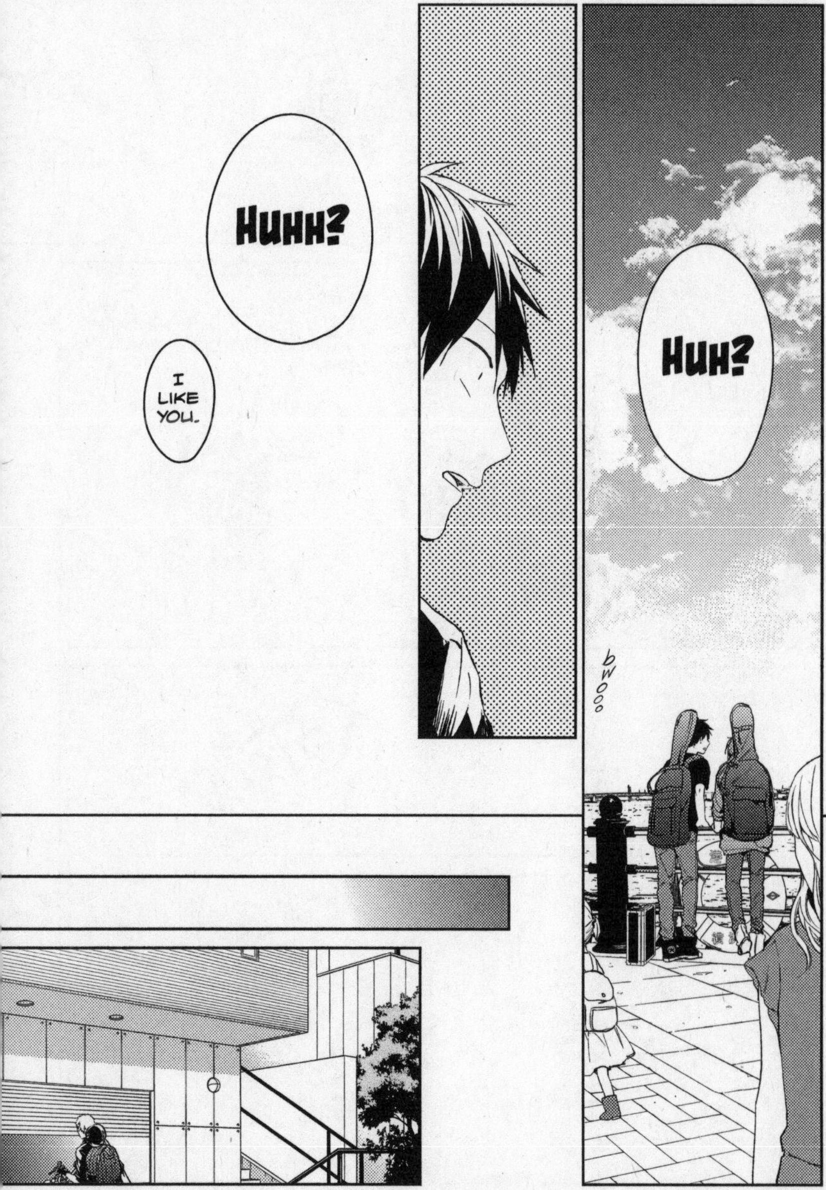

HUH?
bwooo
HUHH?
I LIKE YOU.

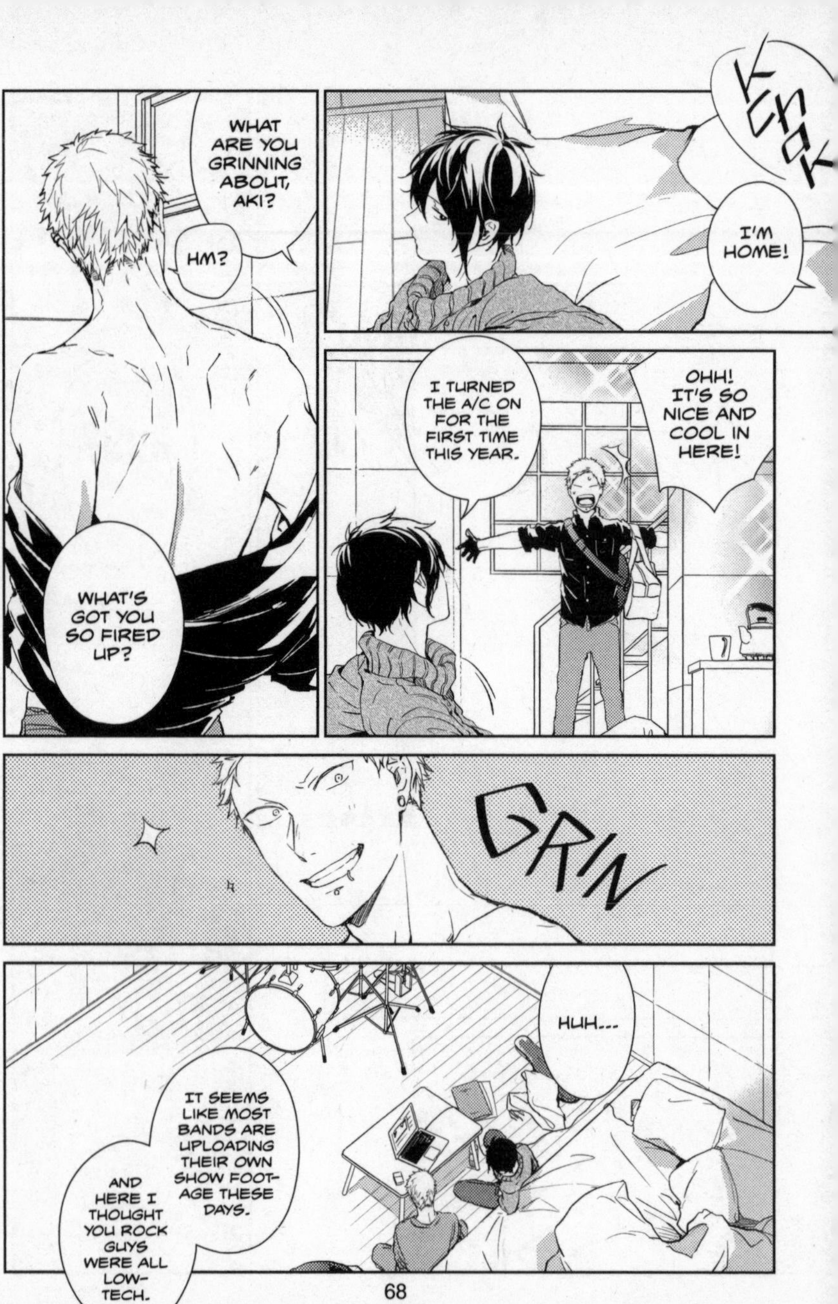
KCHAK
I'M HOME!
WHAT ARE YOU GRINNING ABOUT, AKI?
HM?
OHH! IT'S SO NICE AND COOL IN HERE!
I TURNED THE A/C ON FOR THE FIRST TIME THIS YEAR.
WHAT'S GOT YOU SO FIRED UP?
GRIN
HUH...
IT SEEMS LIKE MOST BANDS ARE UPLOADING THEIR OWN SHOW FOOT-AGE THESE DAYS.
AND HERE I THOUGHT YOU ROCK GUYS WERE ALL LOW-TECH.

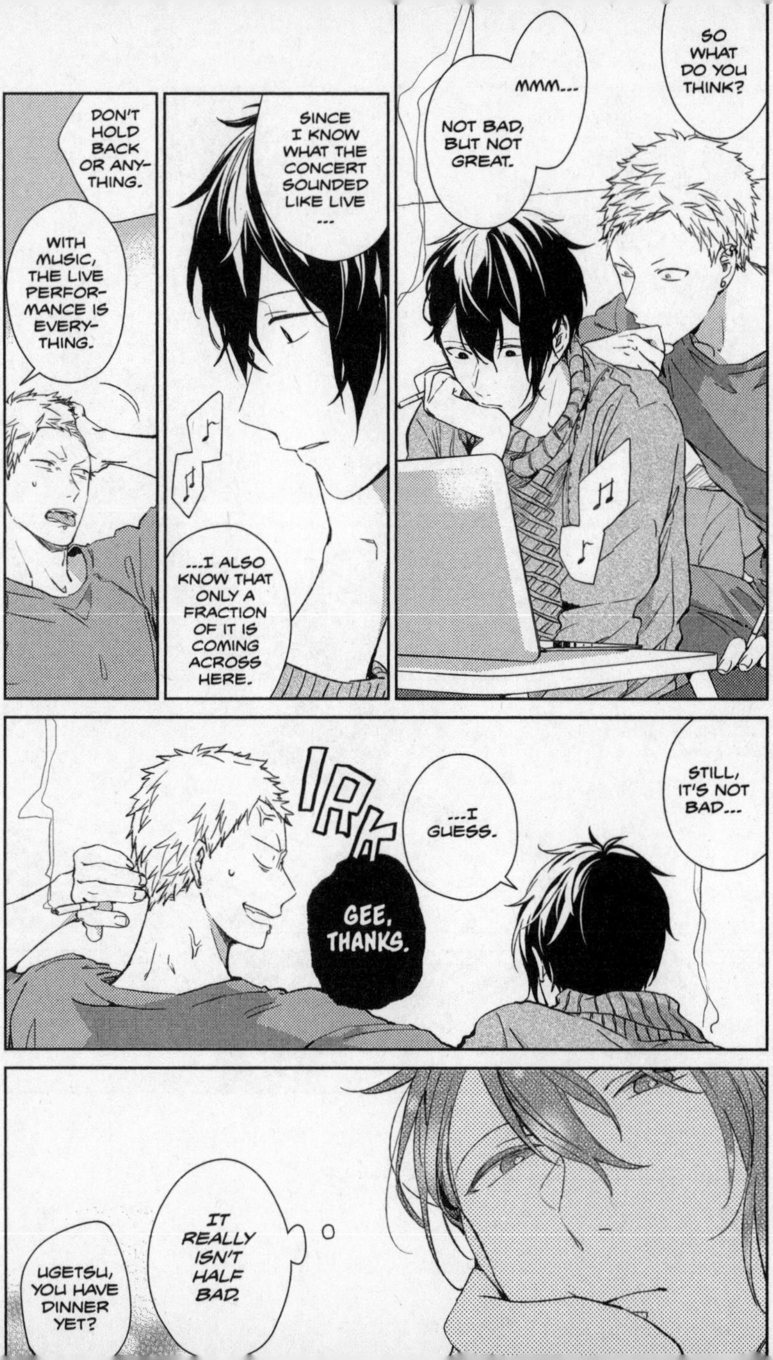
SO WHAT DO YOU THINK?
MMM... NOT BAD, BUT NOT GREAT.
SINCE I KNOW WHAT THE CONCERT SOUNDED LIKE LIVE ...
...I ALSO KNOW THAT ONLY A FRACTION OF IT IS COMING ACROSS HERE.
DON'T HOLD BACK OR ANYTHING.
WITH MUSIC, THE LIVE PERFORMANCE IS EVERYTHING.
STILL, IT'S NOT BAD...
...I GUESS.
IRK
GEE, THANKS.
IT REALLY ISN'T HALF BAD.
UGETSU, YOU HAVE DINNER YET?

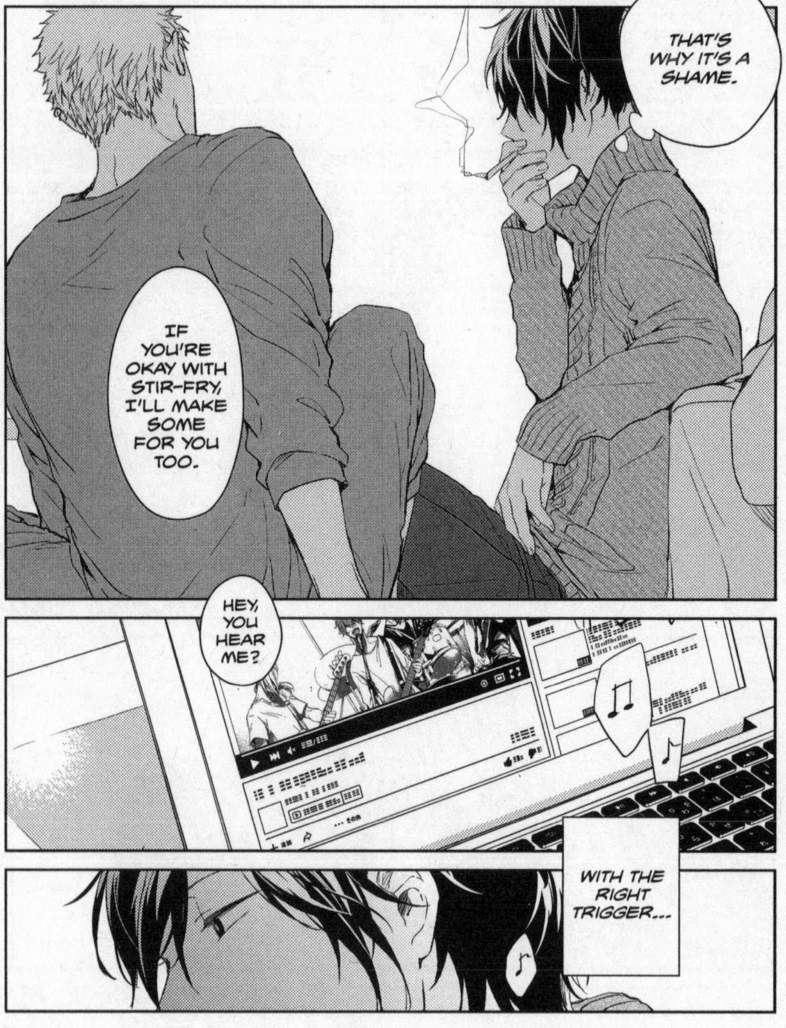
THAT'S WHY IT'S A SHAME.
IF YOU'RE OKAY WITH STIR-FRY, I'LL MAKE SOME FOR YOU TOO.
HEY, YOU HEAR ME?
WITH THE RIGHT TRIGGER...

...HE WOULD EVOLVE, TOO.

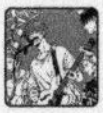

given
@given_ssn

Official band formation barbecue (beef tongue)

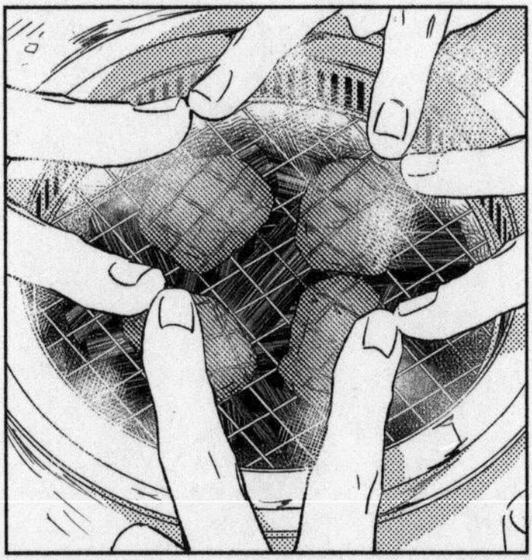

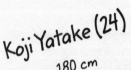

Koji Yatake (24)

180 cm

(Entered university the same time as Haruki after spending a year studying for the entrance exam.)

(Graduated, has a bachelor's degree.)

Birthday: 5/10 Sign: Taurus

Blood Type: A

Video editor at a small production company.

Plays bass and sings vocals.

Friends with Haruki ever since they were in the same visual arts course at school.

Creates music videos for bands both as a hobby and a side hustle.

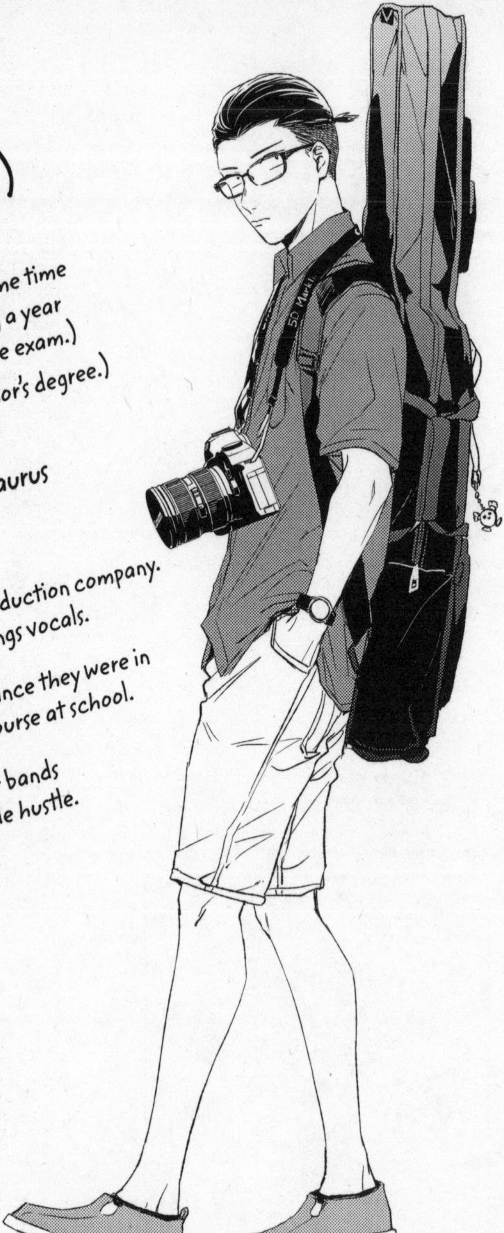

It's Not Like I Hate the Guy, But...

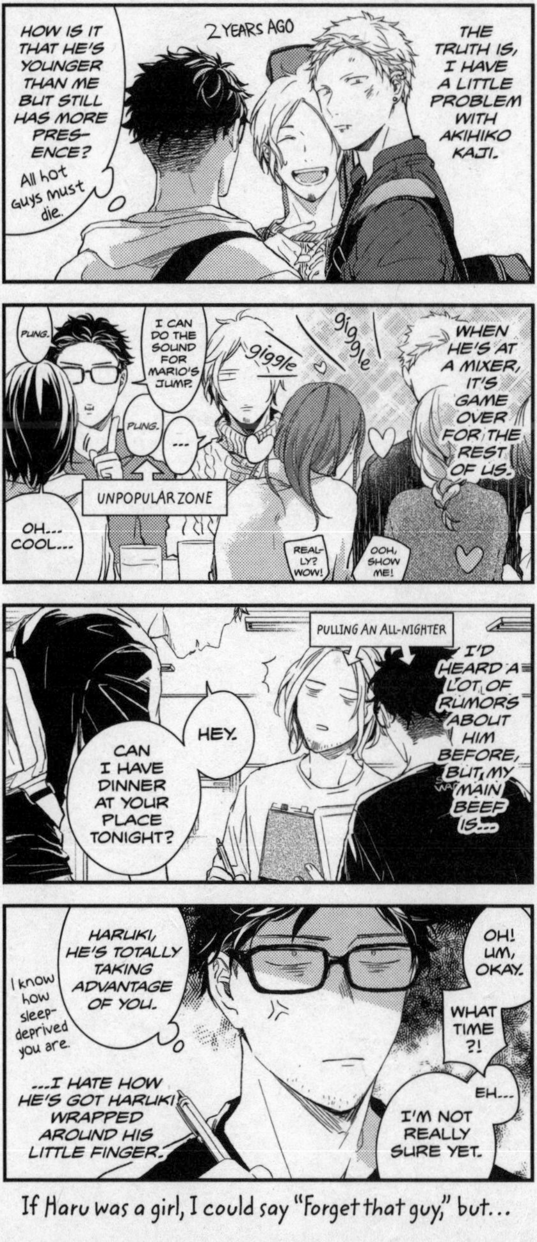
2 YEARS AGO
THE TRUTH IS, I HAVE A LITTLE PROBLEM WITH AKIHIKO KAJI.
HOW IS IT THAT HE'S YOUNGER THAN ME BUT STILL HAS MORE PRES-ENCE?
All hot guys must die.
WHEN HE'S AT A MIXER, IT'S GAME OVER FOR THE REST OF US.
giggle
giggle
I CAN DO THE SOUND FOR MARIO'S JUMP.
PLING.
PLING.
...
UNPOPULAR ZONE
OH... COOL...
OOH, SHOW ME!
REAL-LY? WOW!
PULLING AN ALL-NIGHTER
I'D HEARD A LOT OF RUMORS ABOUT HIM BEFORE, BUT MY MAIN BEEF IS...
HEY.
CAN I HAVE DINNER AT YOUR PLACE TONIGHT?
OH! UM, OKAY.
WHAT TIME?!
EH...
I'M NOT REALLY SURE YET.
HARUKI, HE'S TOTALLY TAKING ADVANTAGE OF YOU.
I know how sleep-deprived you are.
...I HATE HOW HE'S GOT HARUKI WRAPPED AROUND HIS LITTLE FINGER.

If Haru was a girl, I could say "Forget that guy," but...

given

by Natsuki Kizu

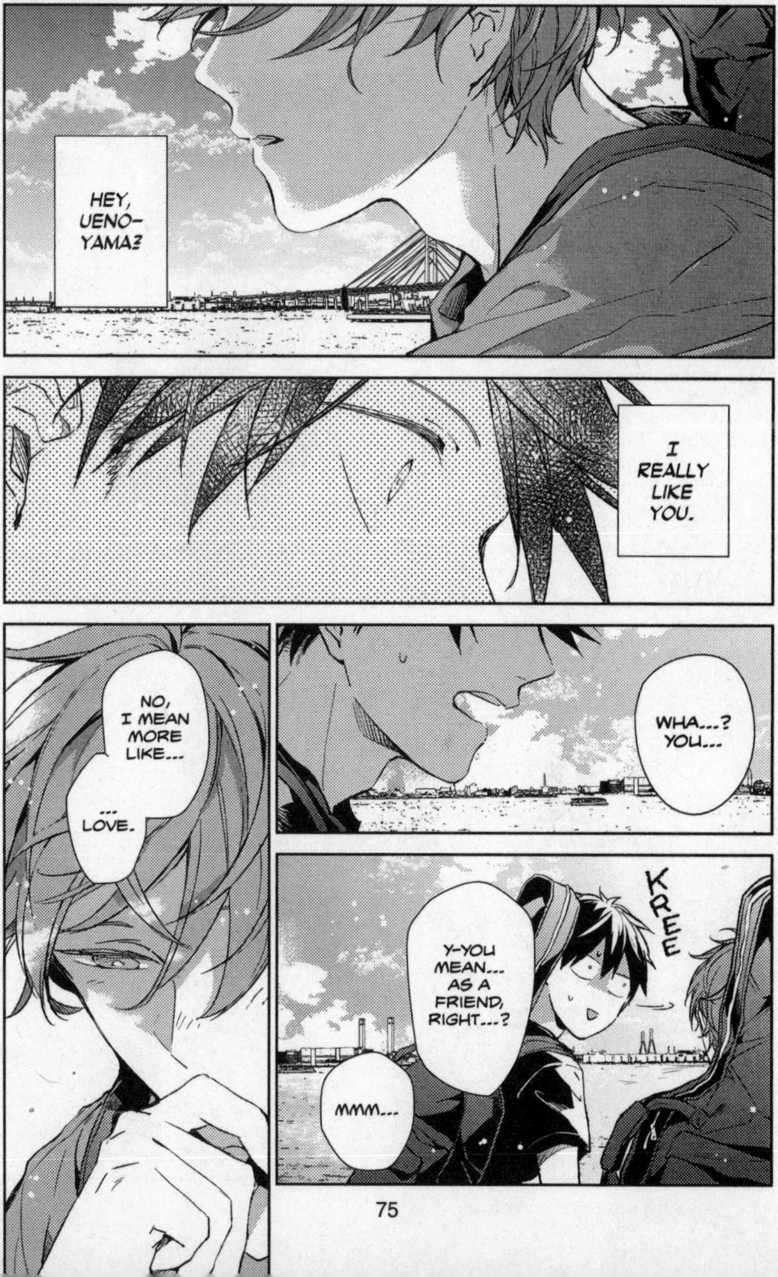
HEY, UENO-YAMA?
I REALLY LIKE YOU.
WHA...? YOU...
Y-YOU MEAN... AS A FRIEND, RIGHT...?
KREE
MMM...
NO, I MEAN MORE LIKE...
... LOVE.

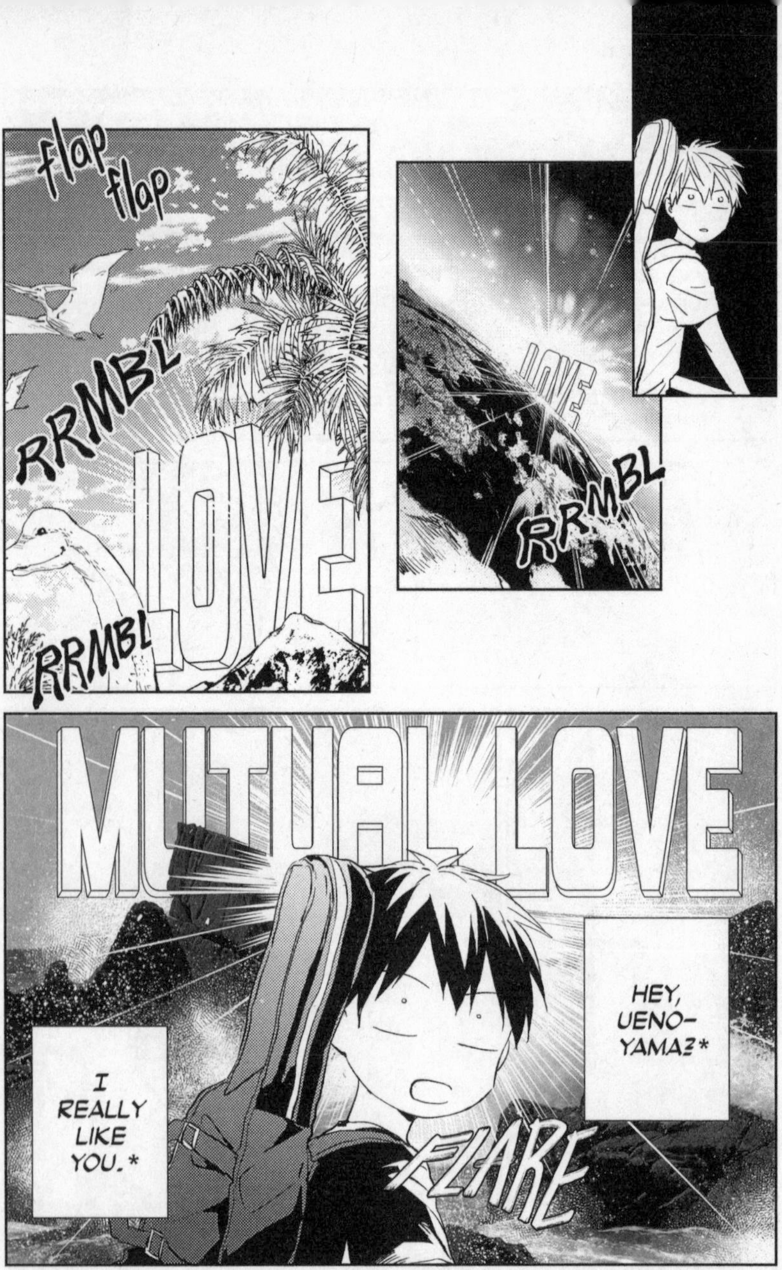
LOVE
RRMBL
flap flap
RRMBL
LOVE
RRMBL
MUTUAL LOVE
HEY, UENO-YAMA?*
I REALLY LIKE YOU.*
FLARE

*The playback is still looping in his head.

chapter 14

given

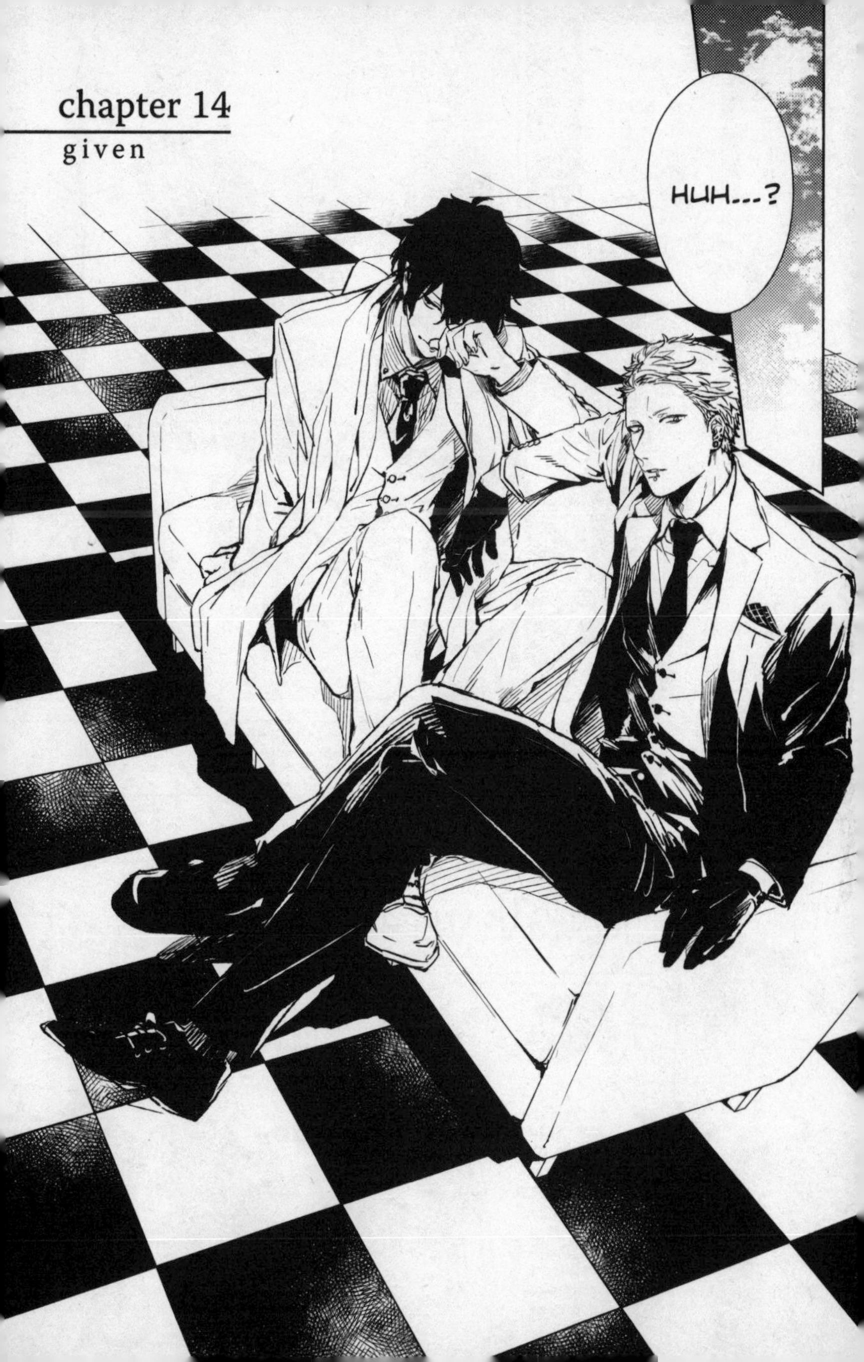
HUH...?

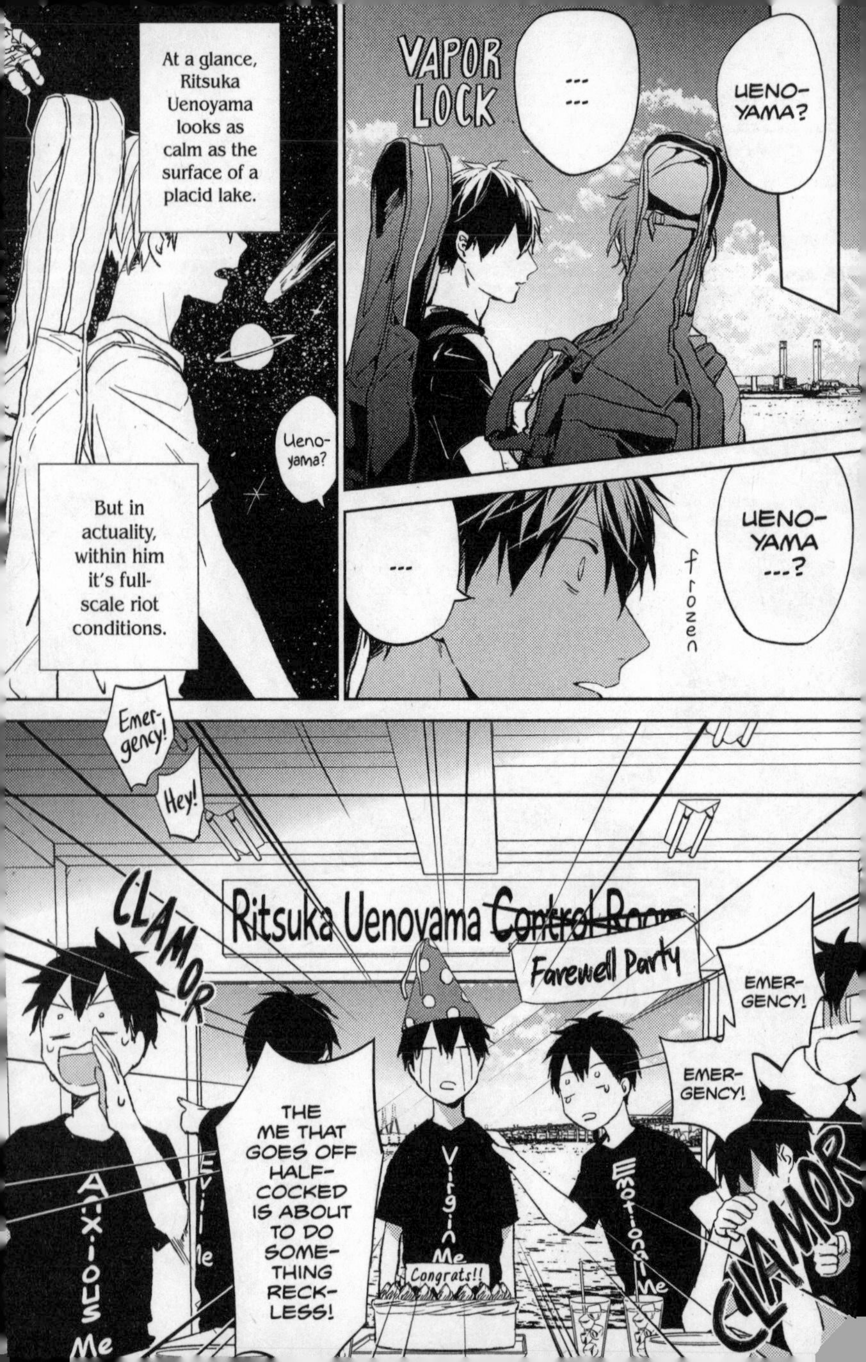
UENO-YAMA?

VAPOR LOCK
UENO-YAMA ---?
frozen

At a glance, Ritsuka Uenoyama looks as calm as the surface of a placid lake.
Ueno-yama?
But in actuality, within him it's full-scale riot conditions.
EMER-GENCY!
EMER-GENCY!
CLAMOR
Farewell Party
Ritsuka Uenoyama Control Room
Emotional Me
Virgin Me
Congrats!!
THE ME THAT GOES OFF HALF-COCKED IS ABOUT TO DO SOMETHING RECK-LESS!
Emer-gency!
Hey!
CLAMOR
Evil Me
Anxious Me

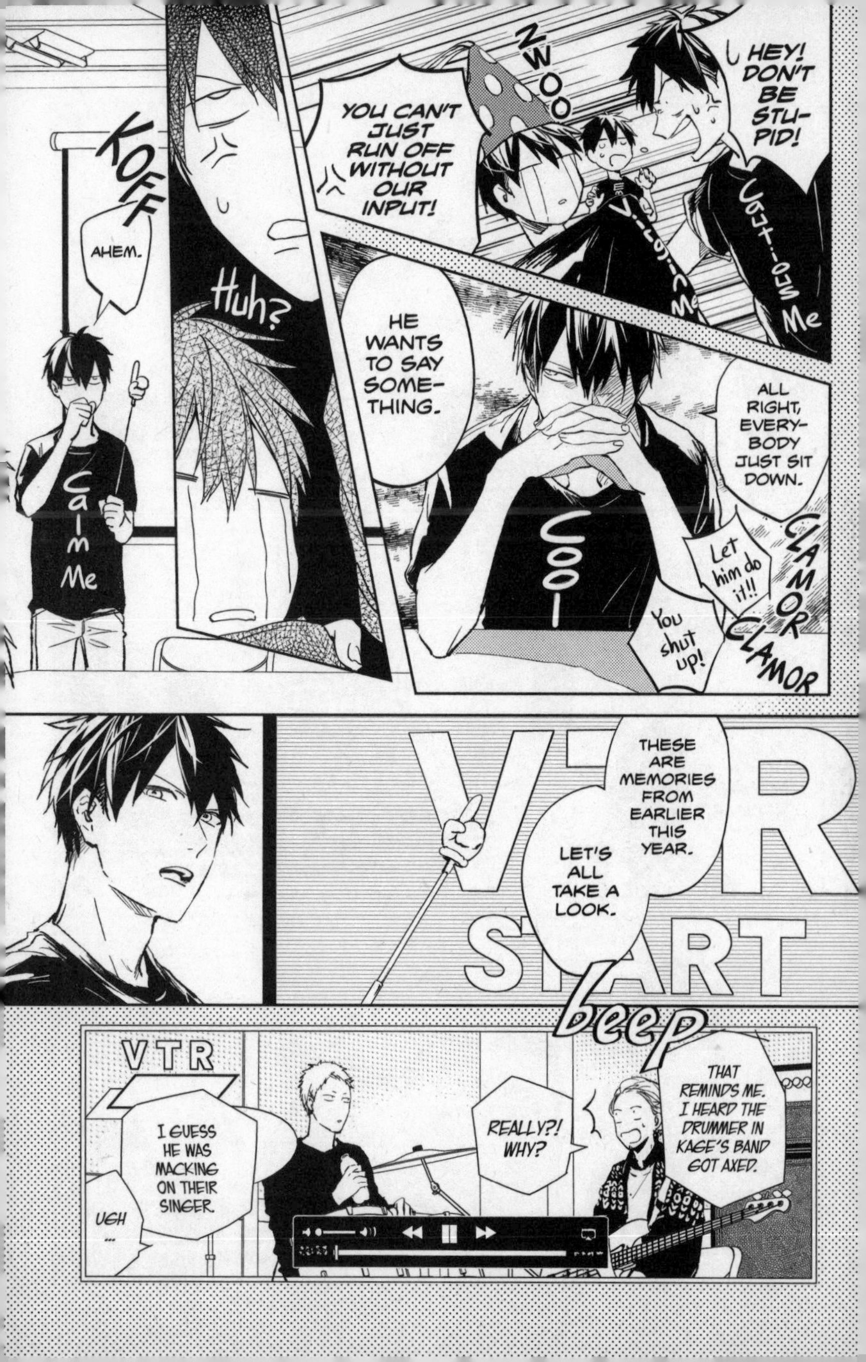
ZWOO
HEY! DON'T BE STU-PID!
Cautious Me
YOU CAN'T JUST RUN OFF WITHOUT OUR INPUT!
ALL RIGHT, EVERYBODY JUST SIT DOWN.
CLAMOR CLAMOR
Let him do it!!
You shut up!
Cool
HE WANTS TO SAY SOMETHING.
Huh?
KOFF
AHEM.
Calm Me
VTR START
THESE ARE MEMORIES FROM EARLIER THIS YEAR.
LET'S ALL TAKE A LOOK.
beep
THAT REMINDS ME. I HEARD THE DRUMMER IN KAGE'S BAND GOT AXED.
REALLY?! WHY?
I GUESS HE WAS MACKING ON THEIR SINGER.
UGH...
VTR

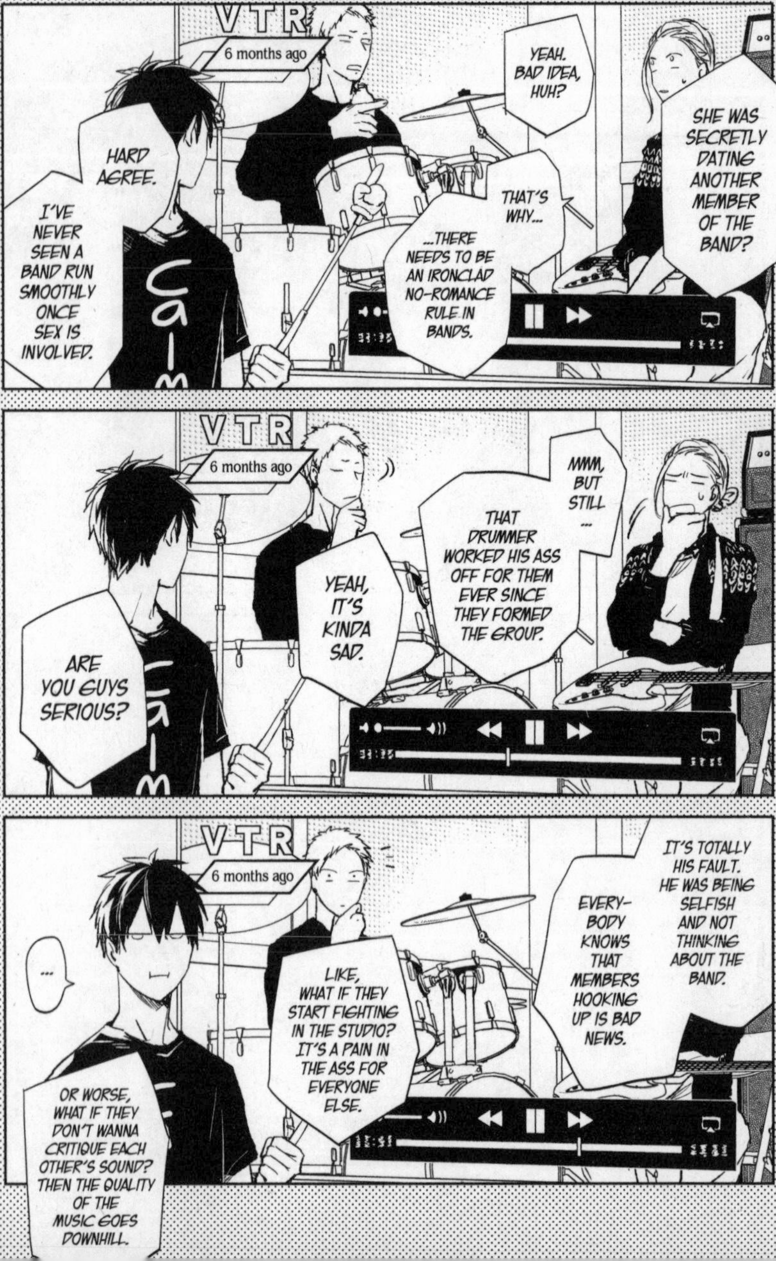
VTR
6 months ago
SHE WAS SECRETLY DATING ANOTHER MEMBER OF THE BAND?
YEAH. BAD IDEA, HUH?
THAT'S WHY...
...THERE NEEDS TO BE AN IRONCLAD NO-ROMANCE RULE IN BANDS.
HARD AGREE.
I'VE NEVER SEEN A BAND RUN SMOOTHLY ONCE SEX IS INVOLVED.
VTR
6 months ago
MMM, BUT STILL ...
THAT DRUMMER WORKED HIS ASS OFF FOR THEM EVER SINCE THEY FORMED THE GROUP.
YEAH, IT'S KINDA SAD.
ARE YOU GUYS SERIOUS?
VTR
6 months ago
IT'S TOTALLY HIS FAULT. HE WAS BEING SELFISH AND NOT THINKING ABOUT THE BAND.
EVERYBODY KNOWS THAT MEMBERS HOOKING UP IS BAD NEWS.
LIKE, WHAT IF THEY START FIGHTING IN THE STUDIO? IT'S A PAIN IN THE ASS FOR EVERYONE ELSE.
...
OR WORSE, WHAT IF THEY DON'T WANNA CRITIQUE EACH OTHER'S SOUND? THEN THE QUALITY OF THE MUSIC GOES DOWNHILL.

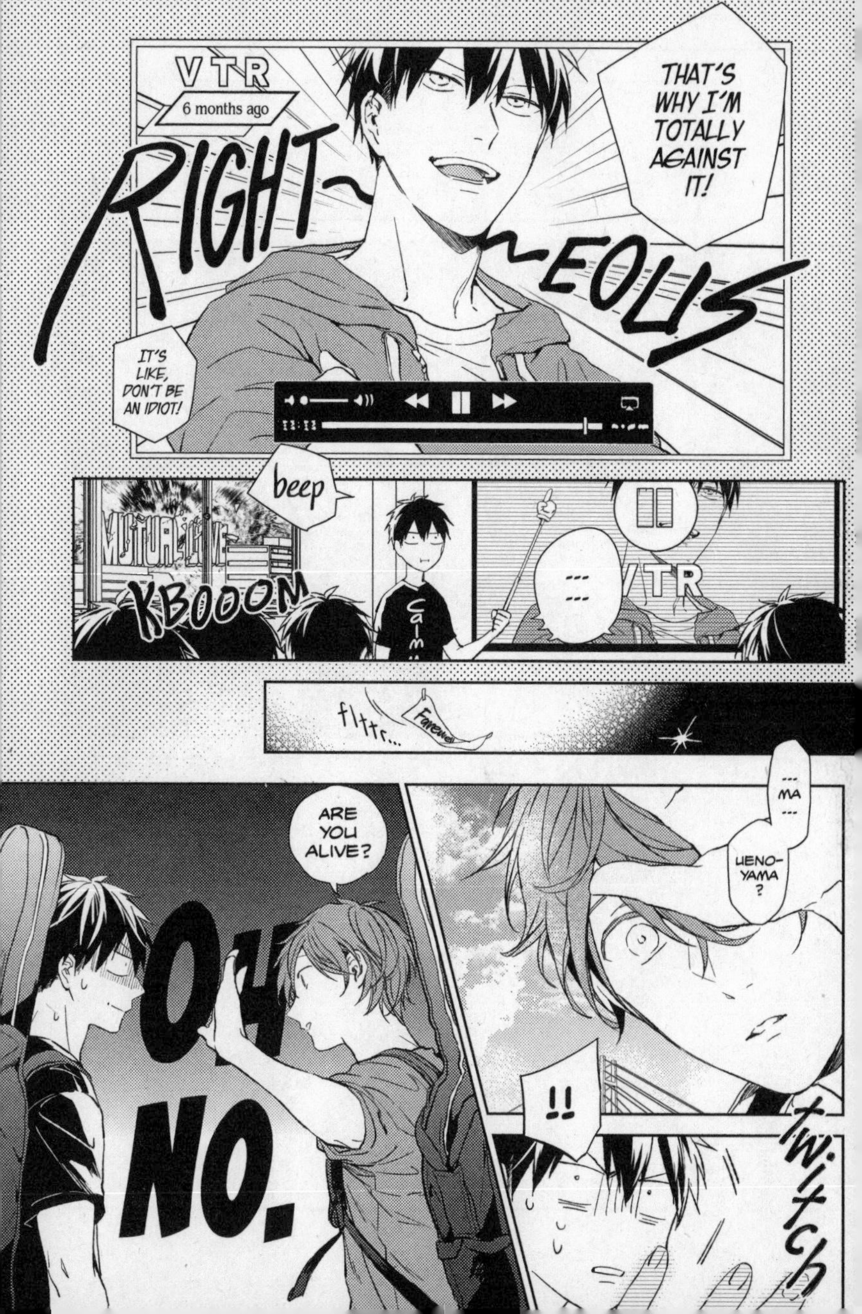
VTR
6 months ago
THAT'S WHY I'M TOTALLY AGAINST IT!
RIGHT~
~EOLIS
IT'S LIKE, DON'T BE AN IDIOT!
II
...
VTR
beep
KBOOOM
flttr...
...MA...
UENO-YAMA?
!!
twitch
ARE YOU ALIVE?
OH
NO.

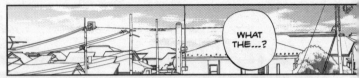

WHAT THE...?

Chirp

Chirp

Miiiiin

Miin

Miin

WHAT'RE YOU TWO DOING HERE?

Miin

Miin

GOOD MORNING!

IT'S EARLY— KEEP YOUR VOICE DOWN.

82

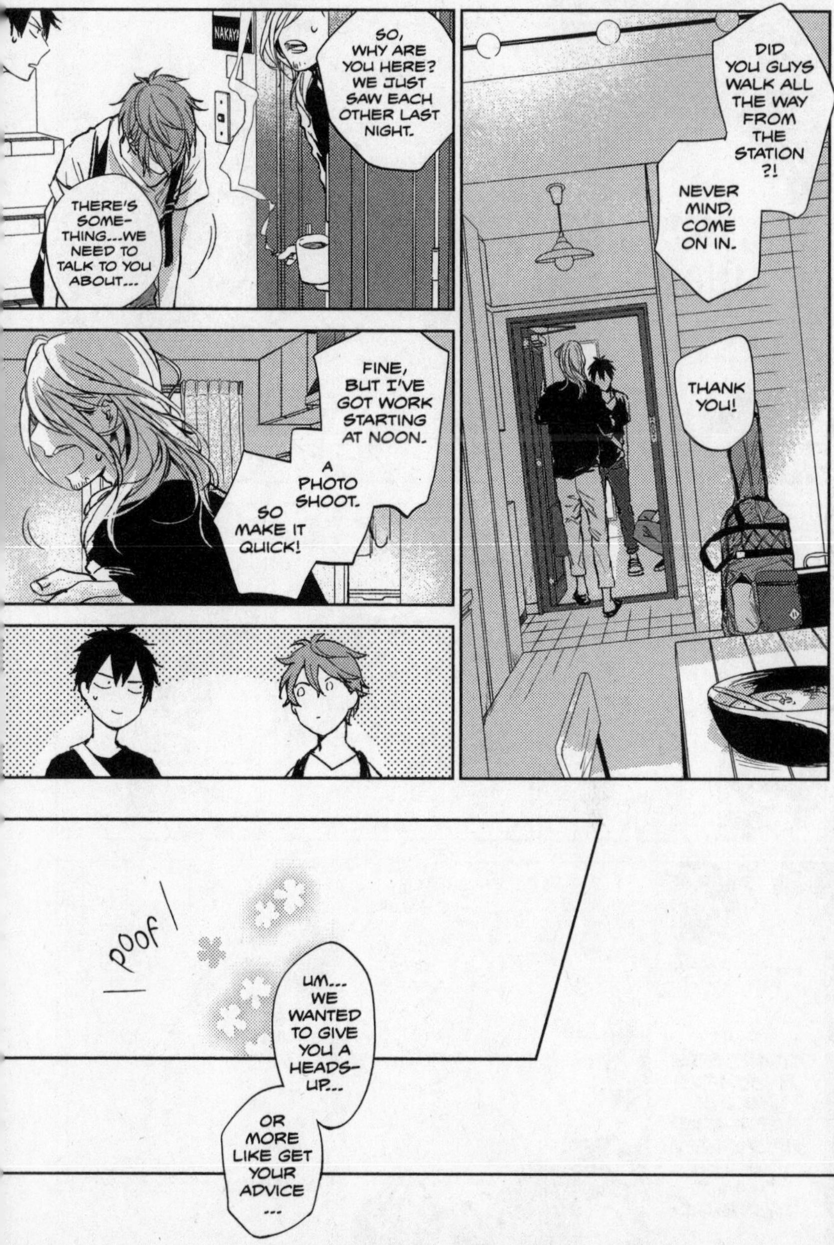
DID YOU GUYS WALK ALL THE WAY FROM THE STATION ?!
NEVER MIND, COME ON IN.
THANK YOU!
SO, WHY ARE YOU HERE? WE JUST SAW EACH OTHER LAST NIGHT.
THERE'S SOME-THING...WE NEED TO TALK TO YOU ABOUT...
FINE, BUT I'VE GOT WORK STARTING AT NOON.
A PHOTO SHOOT.
SO MAKE IT QUICK!
poof
UM... WE WANTED TO GIVE YOU A HEADS-UP...
OR MORE LIKE GET YOUR ADVICE ...

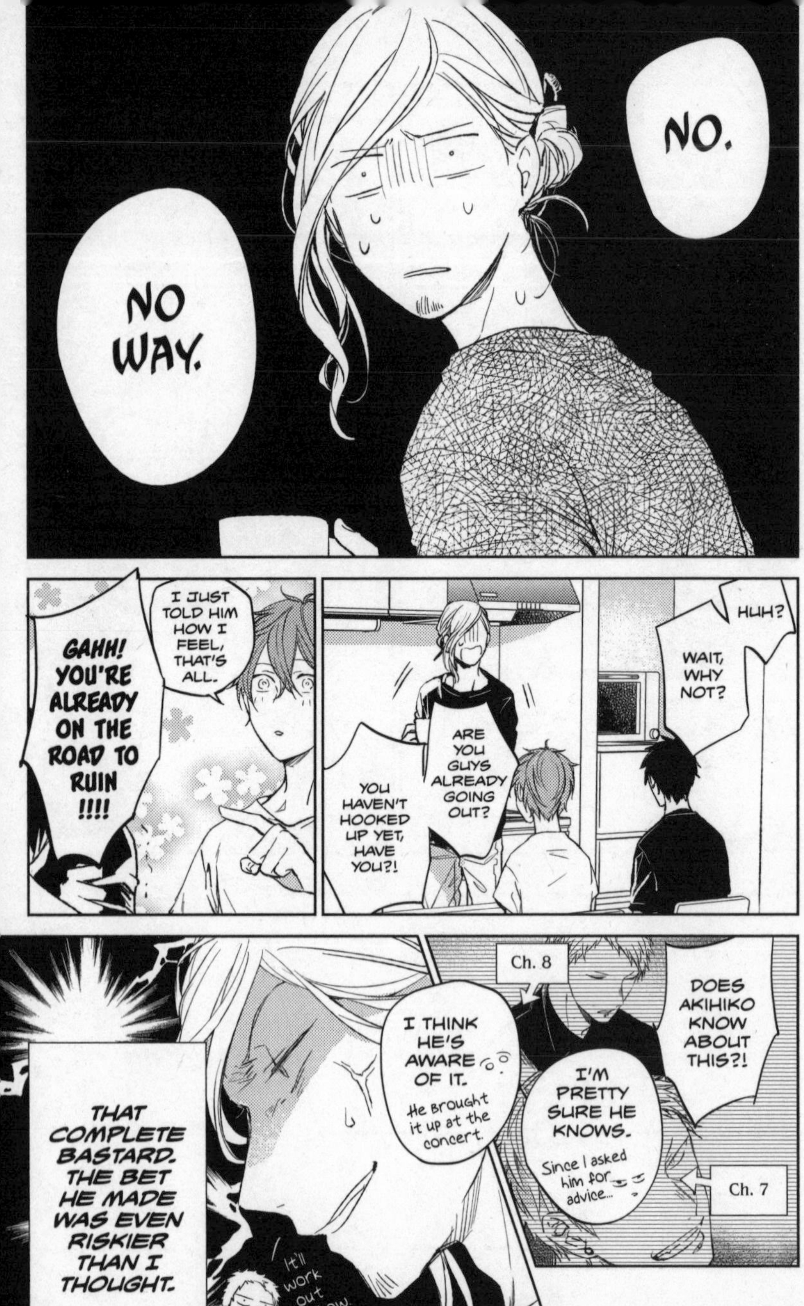
NO.
NO WAY.
HUH?
WAIT, WHY NOT?
ARE YOU GUYS ALREADY GOING OUT?
YOU HAVEN'T HOOKED UP YET, HAVE YOU?!
I JUST TOLD HIM HOW I FEEL, THAT'S ALL.
GAHH! YOU'RE ALREADY ON THE ROAD TO RUIN !!!!
DOES AKIHIKO KNOW ABOUT THIS?!
Ch. 8
I THINK HE'S AWARE OF IT.
He brought it up at the concert.
I'M PRETTY SURE HE KNOWS.
Since I asked him for advice...
Ch. 7
THAT COMPLETE BASTARD. THE BET HE MADE WAS EVEN RISKIER THAN I THOUGHT.
It'll work out somehow.

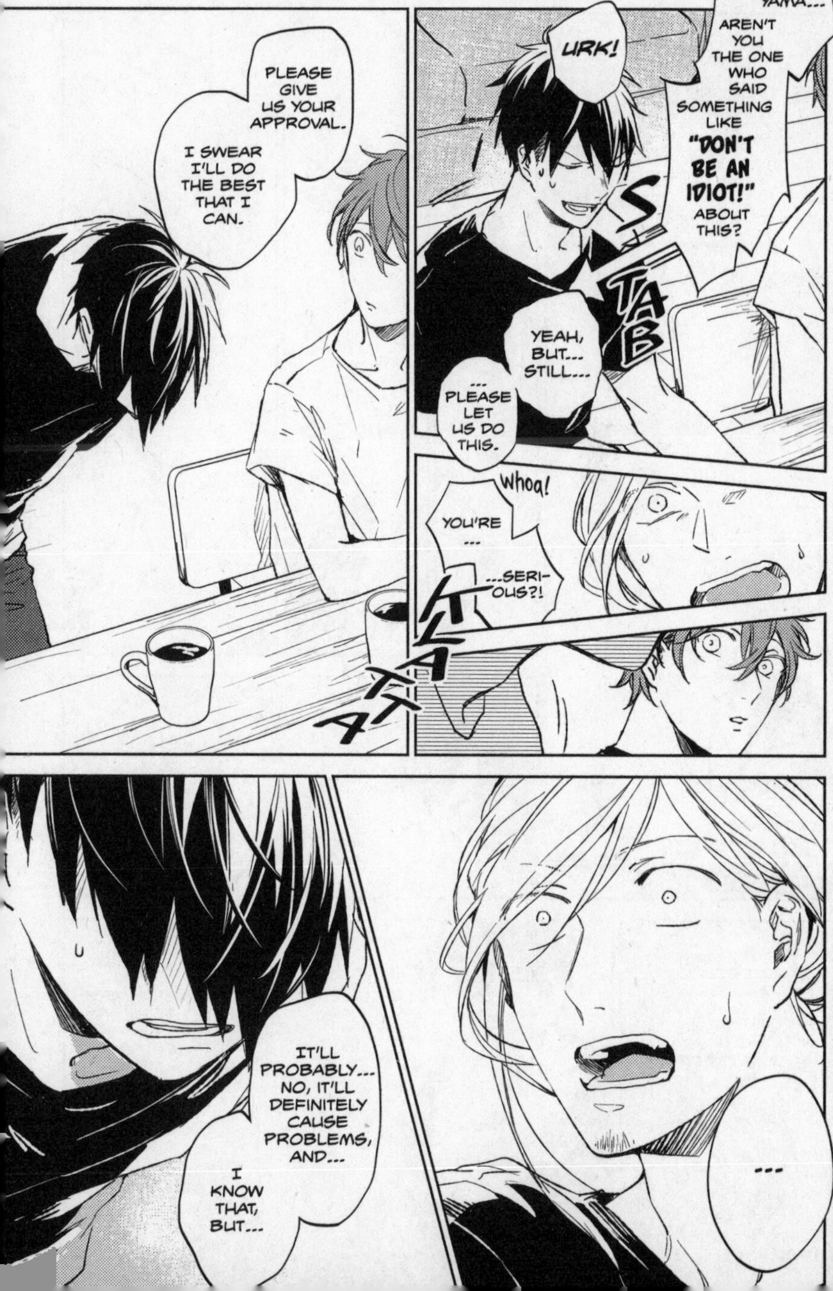
UENO-YAMA...
AREN'T YOU THE ONE WHO SAID SOMETHING LIKE **"DON'T BE AN IDIOT!"** ABOUT THIS?
URK!
STAB
YEAH, BUT... STILL...
...PLEASE LET US DO THIS.
Whoa!
YOU'RE...
...SERI-OUS?!
PLEASE GIVE US YOUR APPROVAL.
I SWEAR I'LL DO THE BEST THAT I CAN.
...
IT'LL PROBABLY... NO, IT'LL DEFINITELY CAUSE PROBLEMS, AND...
I KNOW THAT, BUT...

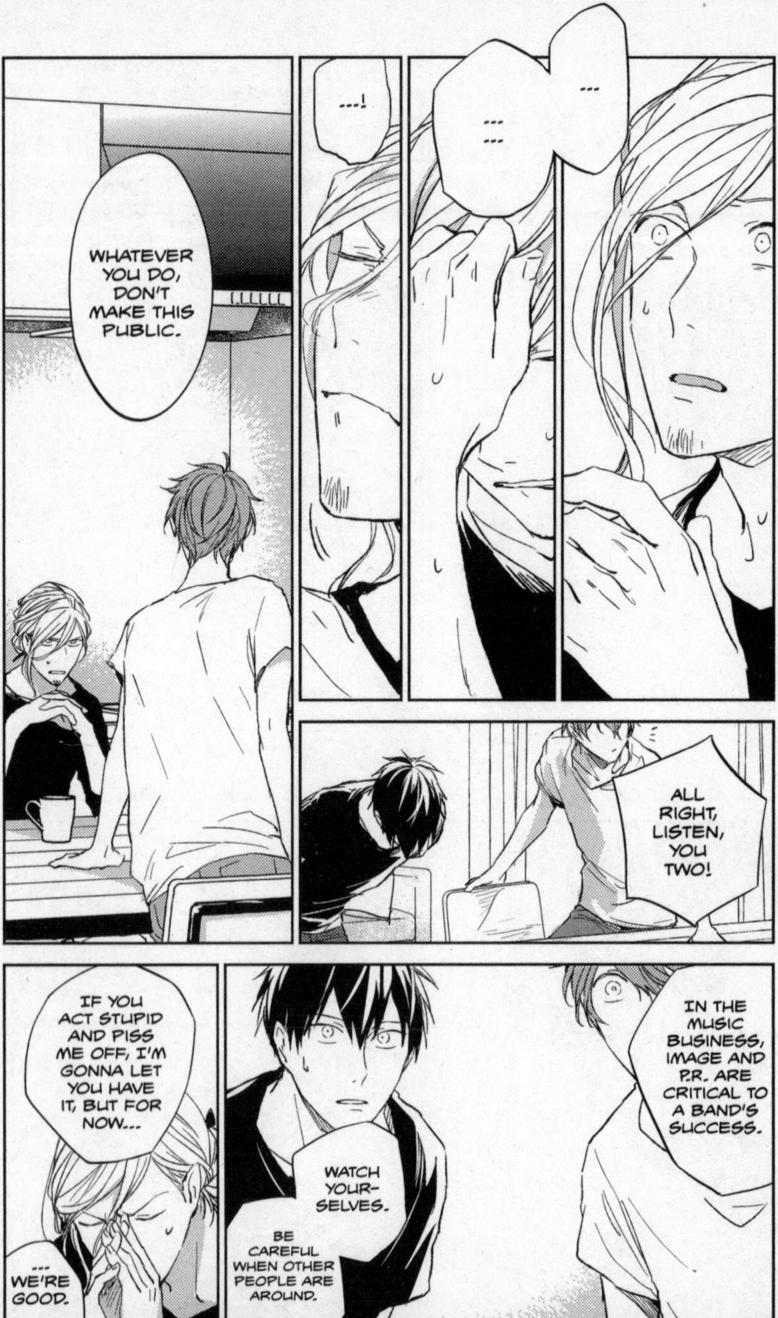
...
... ...
...!
ALL RIGHT, LISTEN, YOU TWO!
WHATEVER YOU DO, DON'T MAKE THIS PUBLIC.
IN THE MUSIC BUSINESS, IMAGE AND P.R. ARE CRITICAL TO A BAND'S SUCCESS.
WATCH YOUR-SELVES.
BE CAREFUL WHEN OTHER PEOPLE ARE AROUND.
IF YOU ACT STUPID AND PISS ME OFF, I'M GONNA LET YOU HAVE IT, BUT FOR NOW...
...WE'RE GOOD.

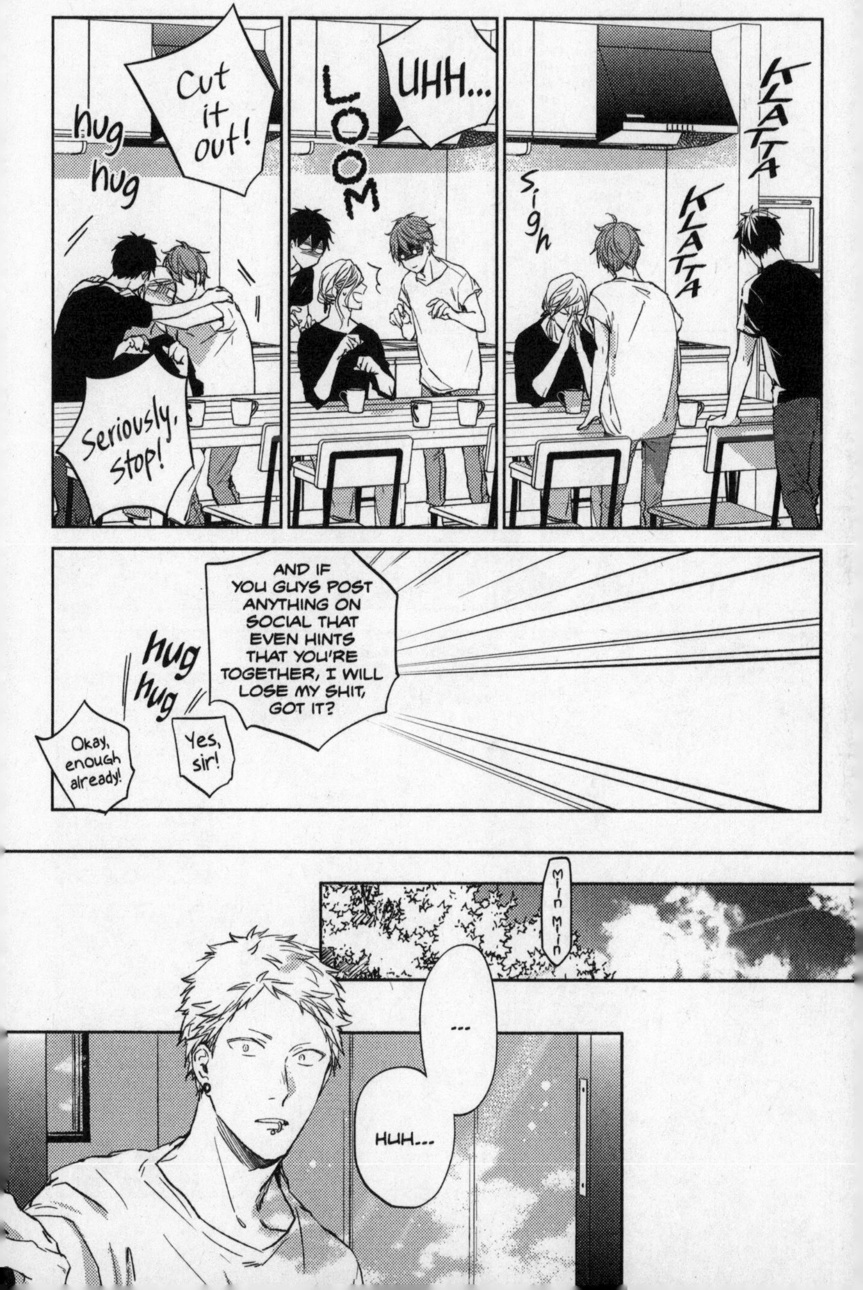
KLATTA
KLATTA
Sigh
UHH...
LOOM
Cut it out!
hug hug
Seriously, stop!
AND IF YOU GUYS POST ANYTHING ON SOCIAL THAT EVEN HINTS THAT YOU'RE TOGETHER, I WILL LOSE MY SHIT, GOT IT?
hug hug
Yes, sir!
Okay, enough already!
Miin miin
...
HUH...

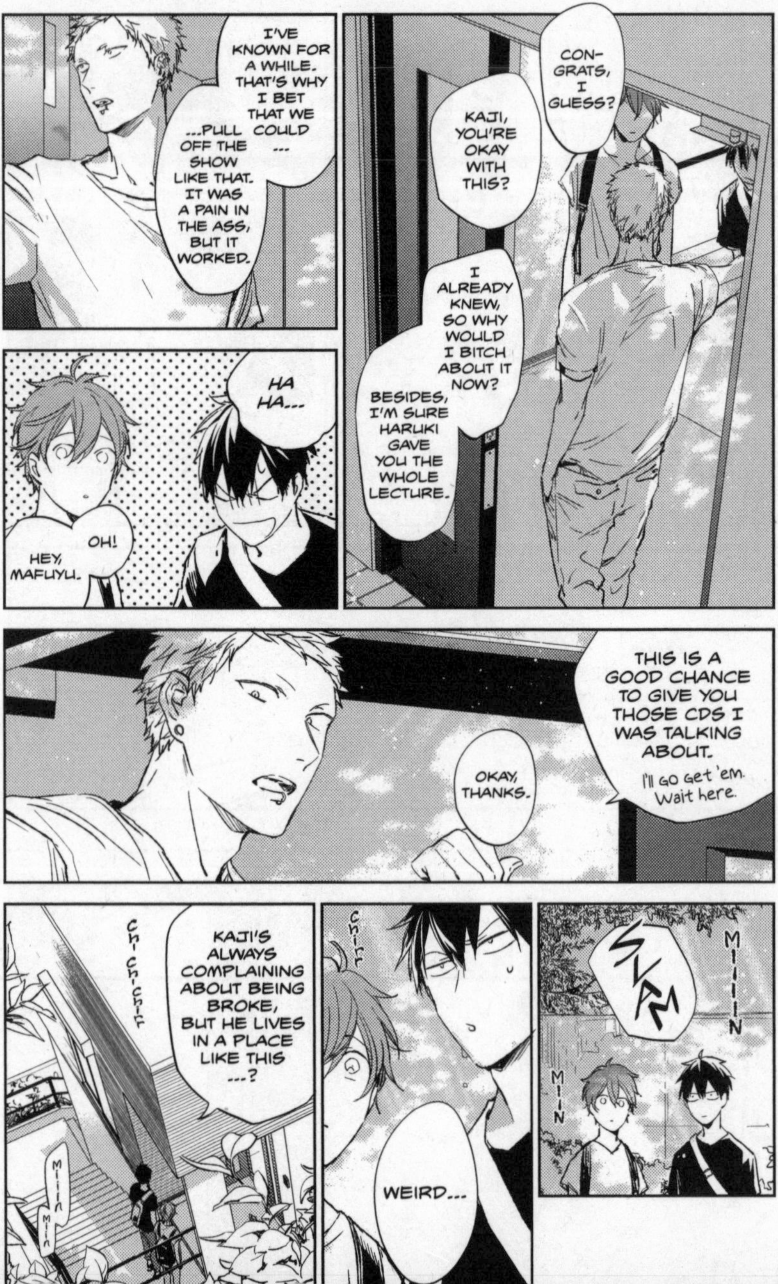
CON-GRATS, I GUESS?
KAJI, YOU'RE OKAY WITH THIS?
I ALREADY KNEW, SO WHY WOULD I BITCH ABOUT IT NOW?
BESIDES, I'M SURE HARUKI GAVE YOU THE WHOLE LECTURE.
I'VE KNOWN FOR A WHILE. THAT'S WHY I BET THAT WE COULD ...
...PULL OFF THE SHOW LIKE THAT. IT WAS A PAIN IN THE ASS, BUT IT WORKED.
HA HA...
OH!
HEY, MAFUYU.
THIS IS A GOOD CHANCE TO GIVE YOU THOSE CDS I WAS TALKING ABOUT.
I'll go get 'em. Wait here.
OKAY, THANKS.
MIIIN
MIIN
Chirr
WEIRD...
Chi-chi-chirr
KAJI'S ALWAYS COMPLAINING ABOUT BEING BROKE, BUT HE LIVES IN A PLACE LIKE THIS ...?
Miiin
Min

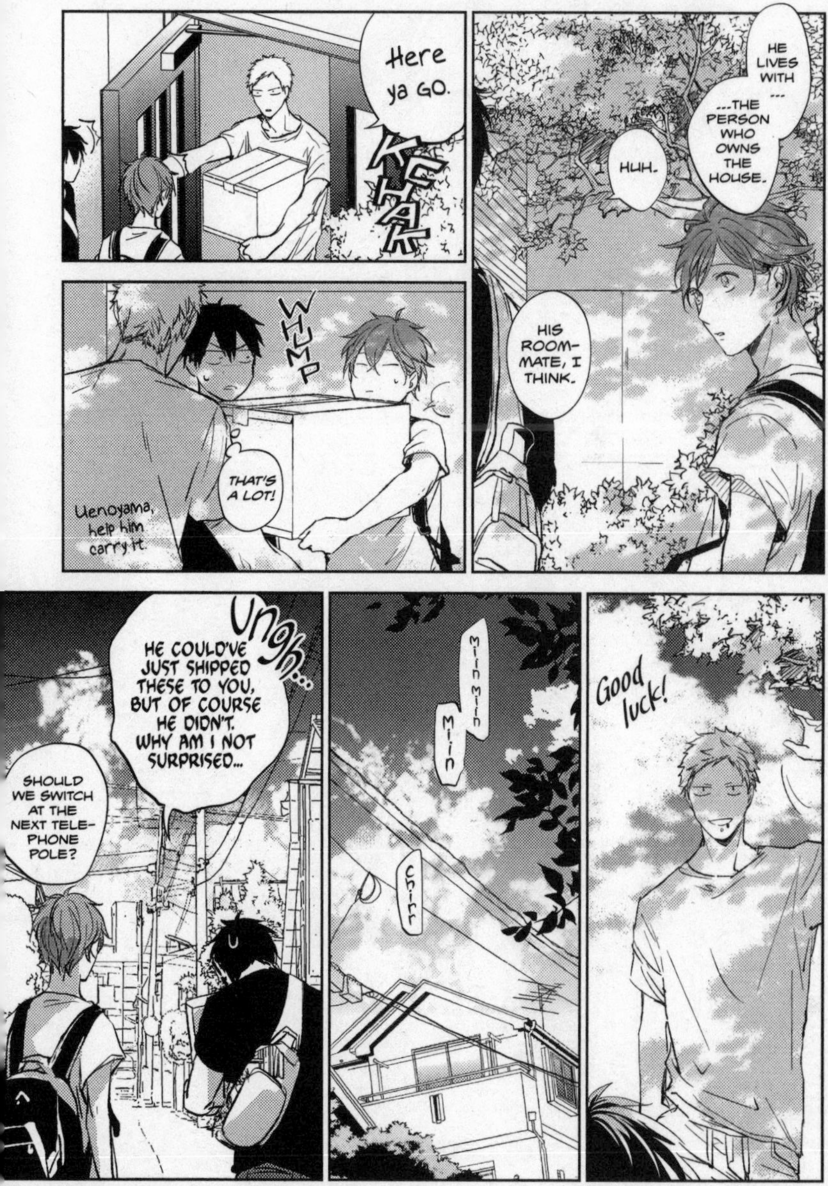
HE LIVES WITH ---
---THE PERSON WHO OWNS THE HOUSE.
HUH.
HIS ROOMMATE, I THINK.
Here ya GO.
KCHAK
WHUMP
THAT'S A LOT!
Uenoyama, help him carry it.
Good luck!
Miin miin
Miin
Chirr
Ungh...
HE COULD'VE JUST SHIPPED THESE TO YOU, BUT OF COURSE HE DIDN'T. WHY AM I NOT SURPRISED...
SHOULD WE SWITCH AT THE NEXT TELEPHONE POLE?

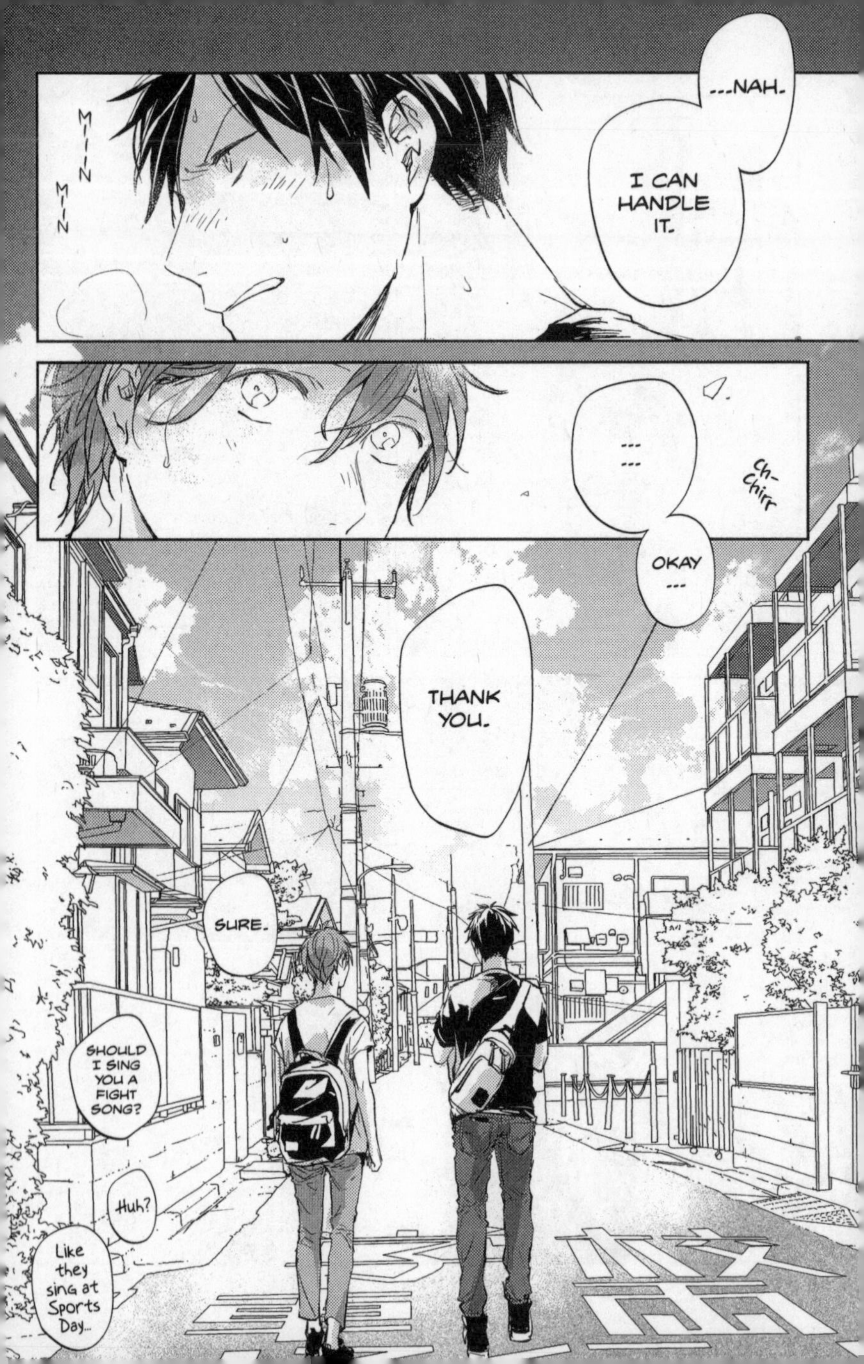
...NAH.
I CAN HANDLE IT.
MI-IN MI-IN
Ch-Chirr
... ...
OKAY ...
THANK YOU.
SURE.
SHOULD I SING YOU A FIGHT SONG?
Huh?
Like they sing at Sports Day...

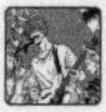

given
@given_ssn

Our bassist Haruki's hair keeps getting longer and longer...

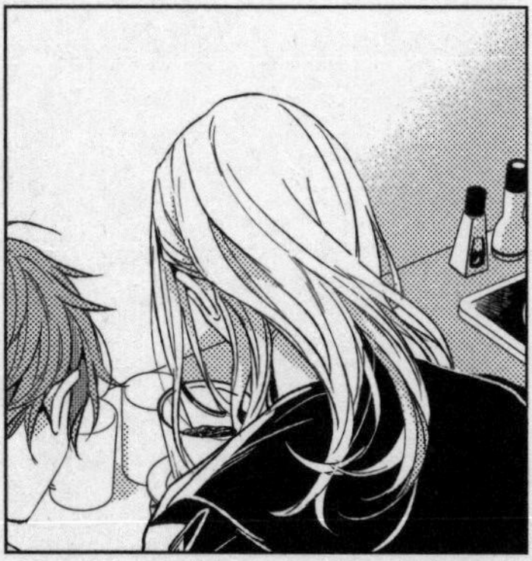

given

by Natsuki Kizu

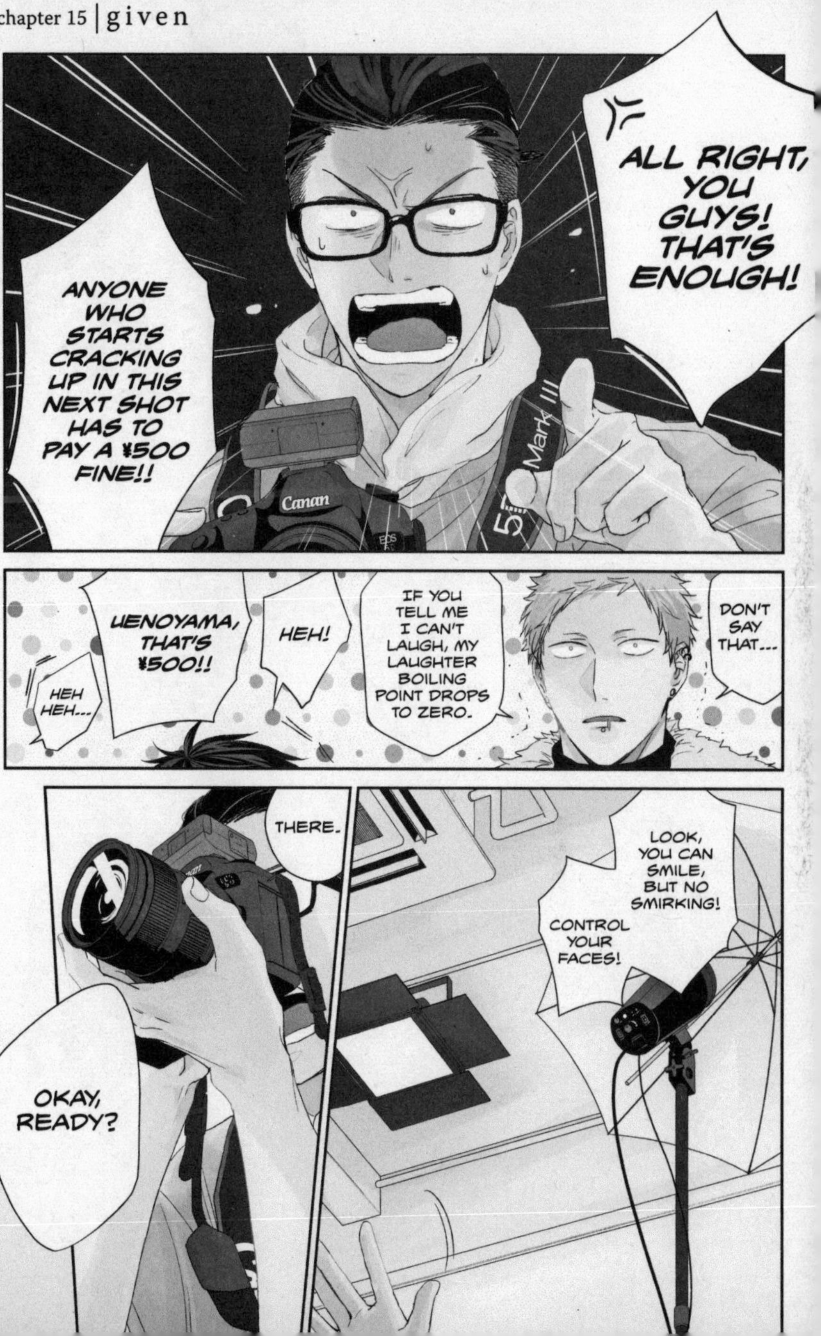
ALL RIGHT, YOU GUYS! THAT'S ENOUGH!
ANYONE WHO STARTS CRACKING UP IN THIS NEXT SHOT HAS TO PAY A ¥500 FINE!!
Mark III
Canan
DON'T SAY THAT...
IF YOU TELL ME I CAN'T LAUGH, MY LAUGHTER BOILING POINT DROPS TO ZERO.
HEH!
UENOYAMA, THAT'S ¥500!!
HEH HEH...
LOOK, YOU CAN SMILE, BUT NO SMIRKING!
CONTROL YOUR FACES!
THERE.
OKAY, READY?

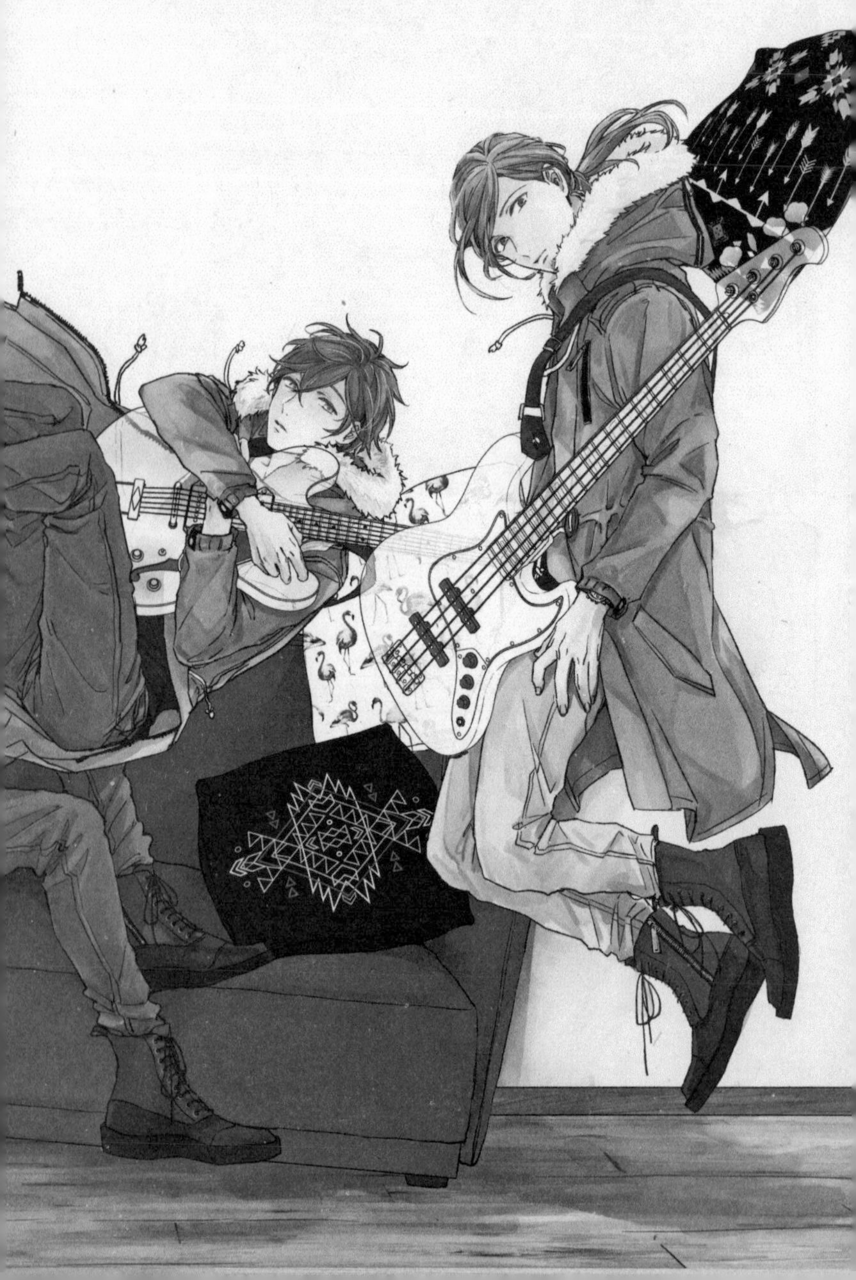

chapter 15
given

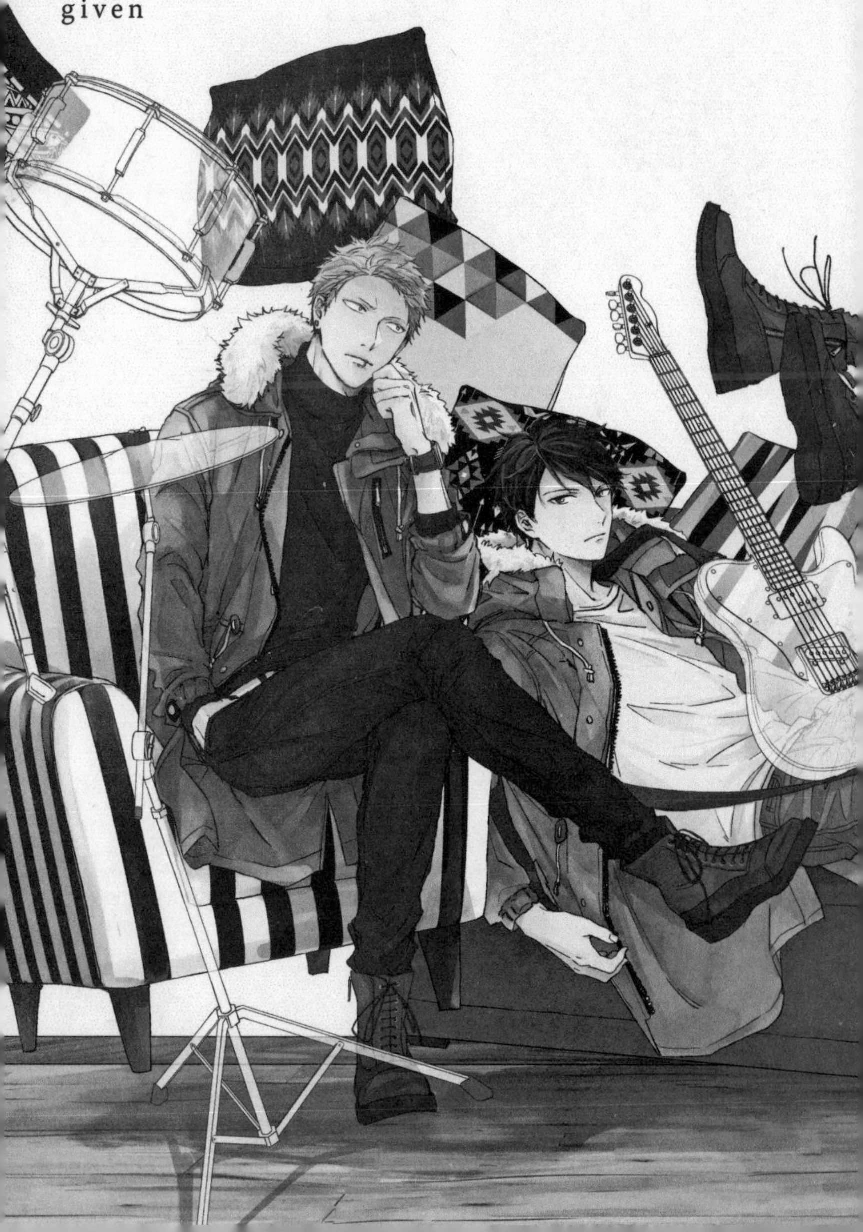

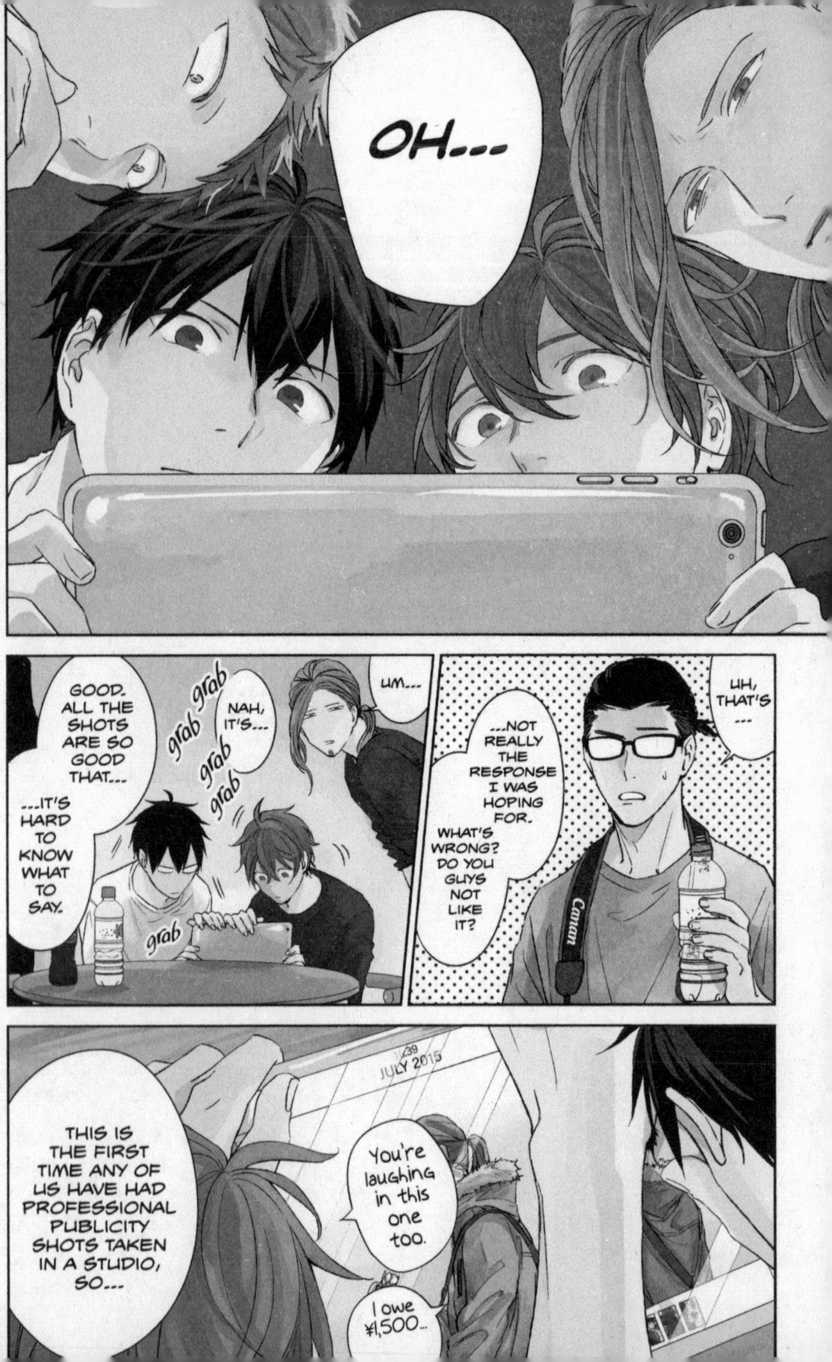
OH...
UH, THAT'S ...
...NOT REALLY THE RESPONSE I WAS HOPING FOR.
WHAT'S WRONG? DO YOU GUYS NOT LIKE IT?
Canon
UM...
NAH, IT'S...
grab grab grab grab grab
GOOD. ALL THE SHOTS ARE SO GOOD THAT...
...IT'S HARD TO KNOW WHAT TO SAY.
grab
JULY 2015
You're laughing in this one too.
THIS IS THE FIRST TIME ANY OF US HAVE HAD PROFESSIONAL PUBLICITY SHOTS TAKEN IN A STUDIO, SO...
I owe ¥1,500...

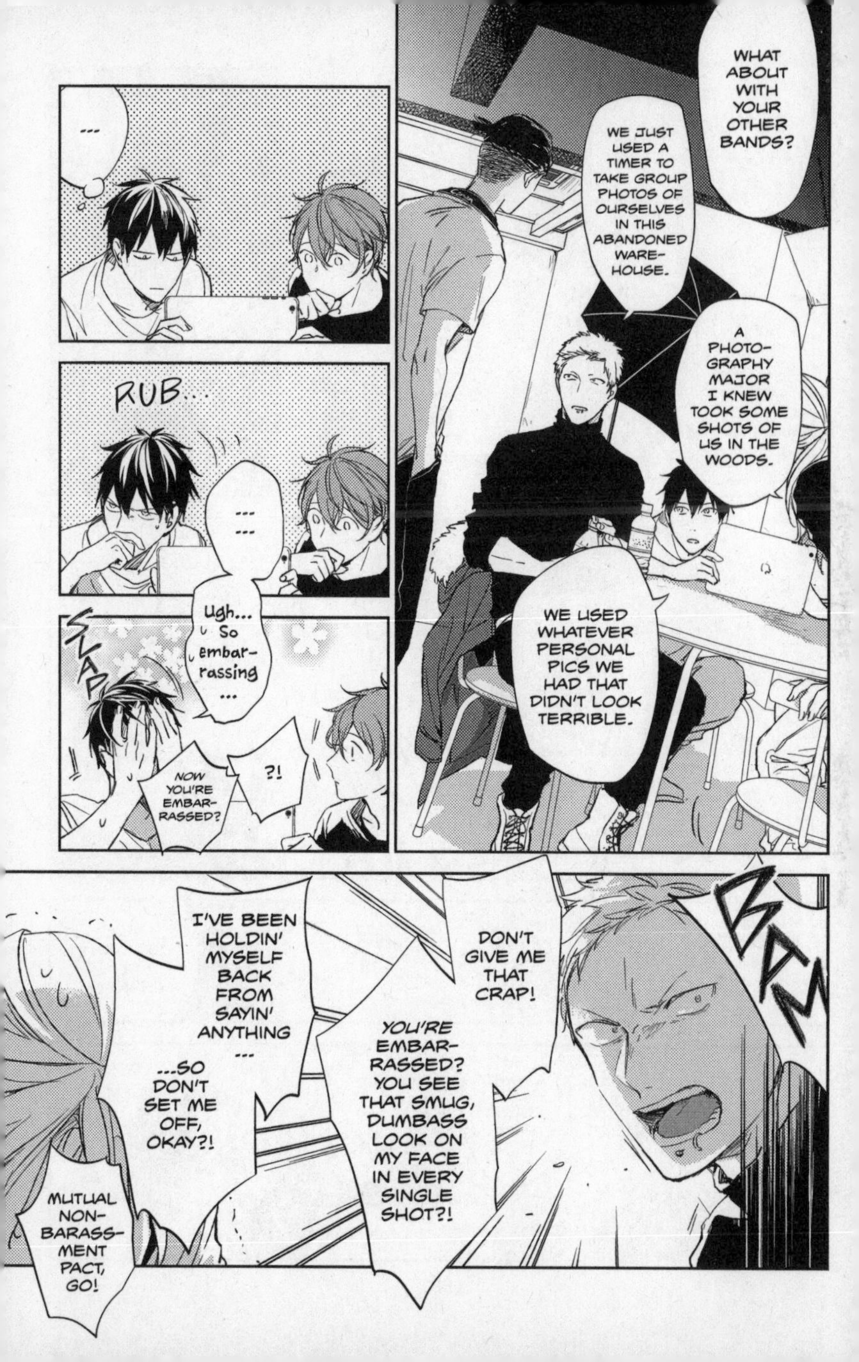
WHAT ABOUT WITH YOUR OTHER BANDS?
WE JUST USED A TIMER TO TAKE GROUP PHOTOS OF OURSELVES IN THIS ABANDONED WARE-HOUSE.
A PHOTOG-RAPHY MAJOR I KNEW TOOK SOME SHOTS OF US IN THE WOODS.
WE USED WHATEVER PERSONAL PICS WE HAD THAT DIDN'T LOOK TERRIBLE.
...
RUB...
... ...
Ugh... So embar-rassing...
SLAP
?!
NOW YOU'RE EMBAR-RASSED?
BAM
DON'T GIVE ME THAT CRAP!
YOU'RE EMBAR-RASSED? YOU SEE THAT SMUG, DUMBASS LOOK ON MY FACE IN EVERY SINGLE SHOT?!
I'VE BEEN HOLDIN' MYSELF BACK FROM SAYIN' ANYTHING...
...SO DON'T SET ME OFF, OKAY?!
MUTUAL NON-BARASS-MENT PACT, GO!

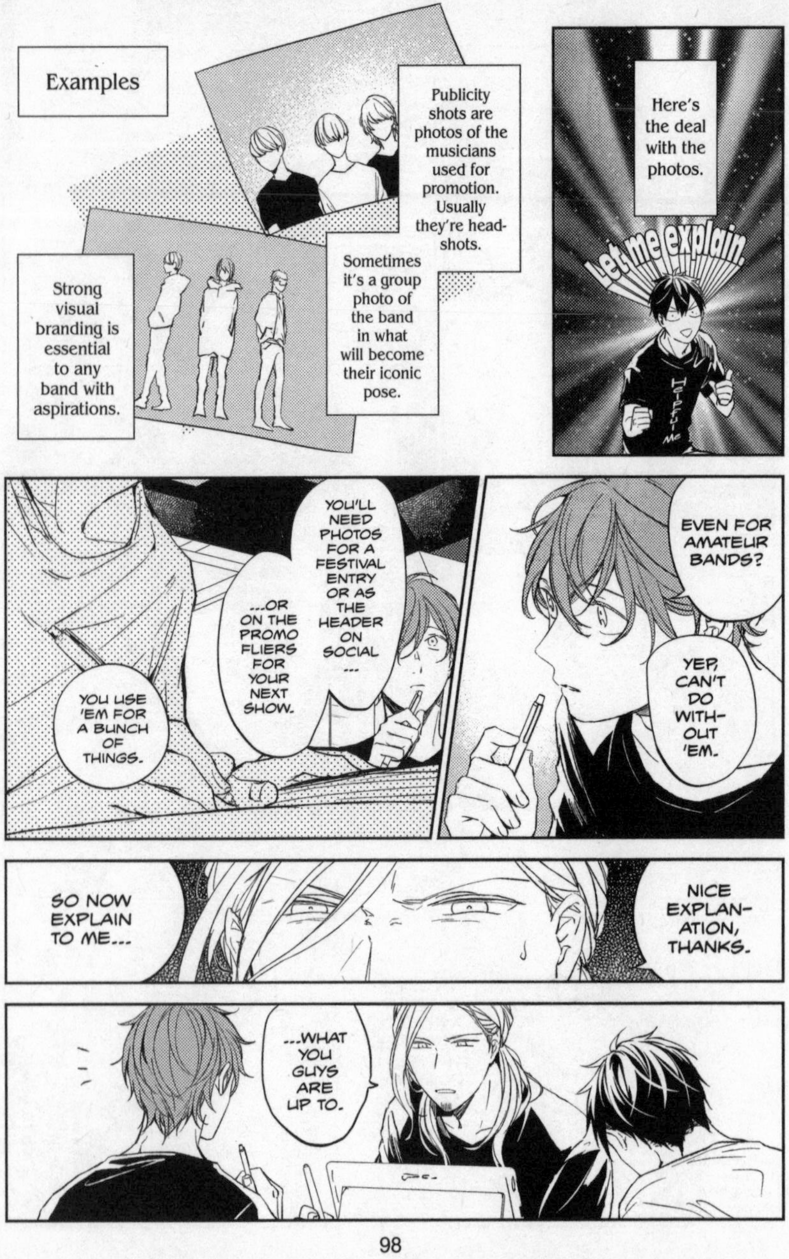
Here's the deal with the photos.
Let me explain.
Helpful Me
Examples
Publicity shots are photos of the musicians used for promotion. Usually they're head-shots.
Sometimes it's a group photo of the band in what will become their iconic pose.
Strong visual branding is essential to any band with aspirations.
EVEN FOR AMATEUR BANDS?
YEP, CAN'T DO WITHOUT 'EM.
YOU'LL NEED PHOTOS FOR A FESTIVAL ENTRY OR AS THE HEADER ON SOCIAL...
...OR ON THE PROMO FLIERS FOR YOUR NEXT SHOW.
YOU USE 'EM FOR A BUNCH OF THINGS.
NICE EXPLANATION, THANKS.
SO NOW EXPLAIN TO ME...
...WHAT YOU GUYS ARE UP TO.

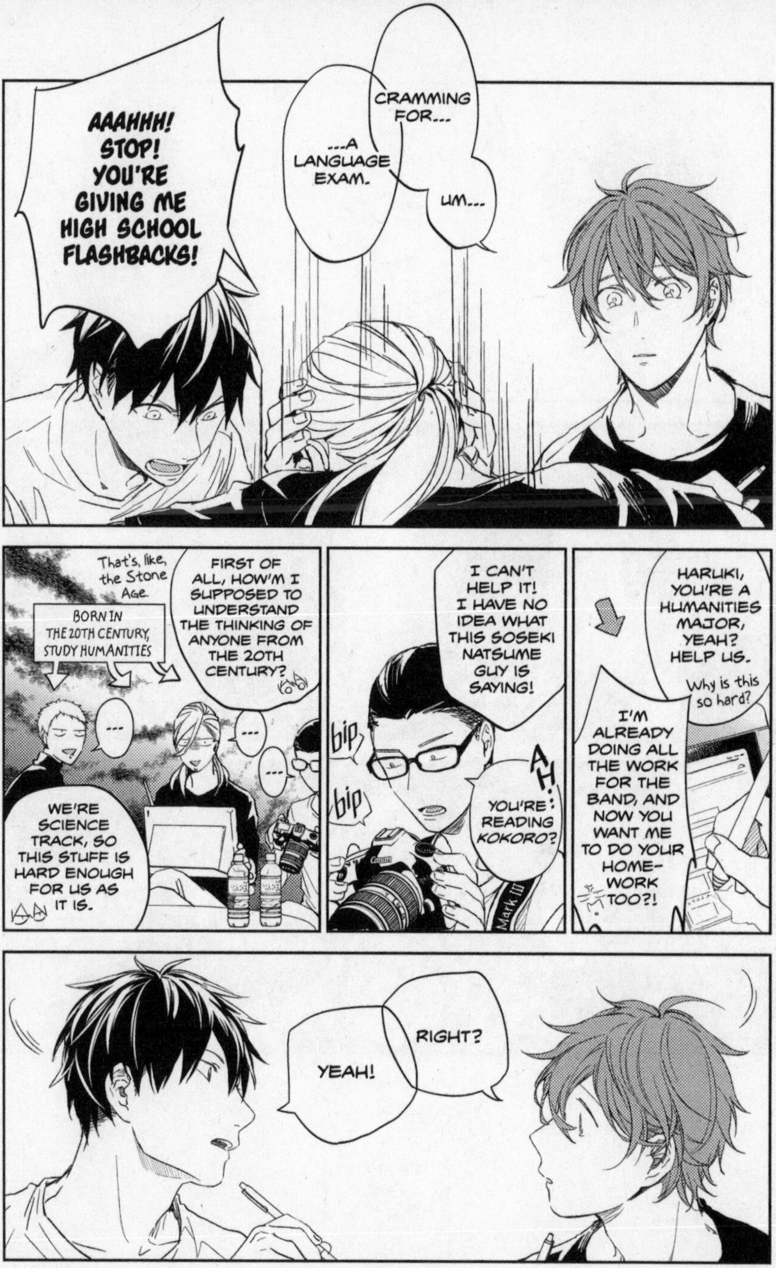
CRAMMING FOR...
UM...
...A LANGUAGE EXAM.
AAAHHH! STOP! YOU'RE GIVING ME HIGH SCHOOL FLASHBACKS!
HARUKI, YOU'RE A HUMANITIES MAJOR, YEAH? HELP US.
Why is this so hard?
I'M ALREADY DOING ALL THE WORK FOR THE BAND, AND NOW YOU WANT ME TO DO YOUR HOME-WORK TOO?!
I CAN'T HELP IT! I HAVE NO IDEA WHAT THIS SOSEKI NATSUME GUY IS SAYING!
AH!
YOU'RE READING KOKORO?
bip
bip
FIRST OF ALL, HOW'M I SUPPOSED TO UNDERSTAND THE THINKING OF ANYONE FROM THE 20TH CENTURY?
That's, like, the Stone Age.
BORN IN THE 20TH CENTURY, STUDY HUMANITIES

WE'RE SCIENCE TRACK, SO THIS STUFF IS HARD ENOUGH FOR US AS IT IS.
RIGHT?
YEAH!

beam
...
blush
...
...
Pat
...

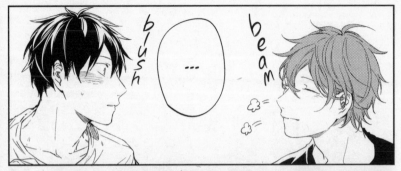

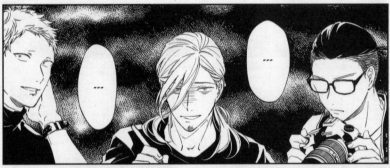

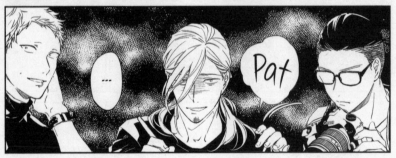

IT WAS THE HEIGHT...

...OF
SUMMER.

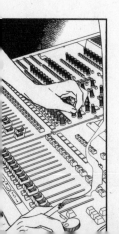

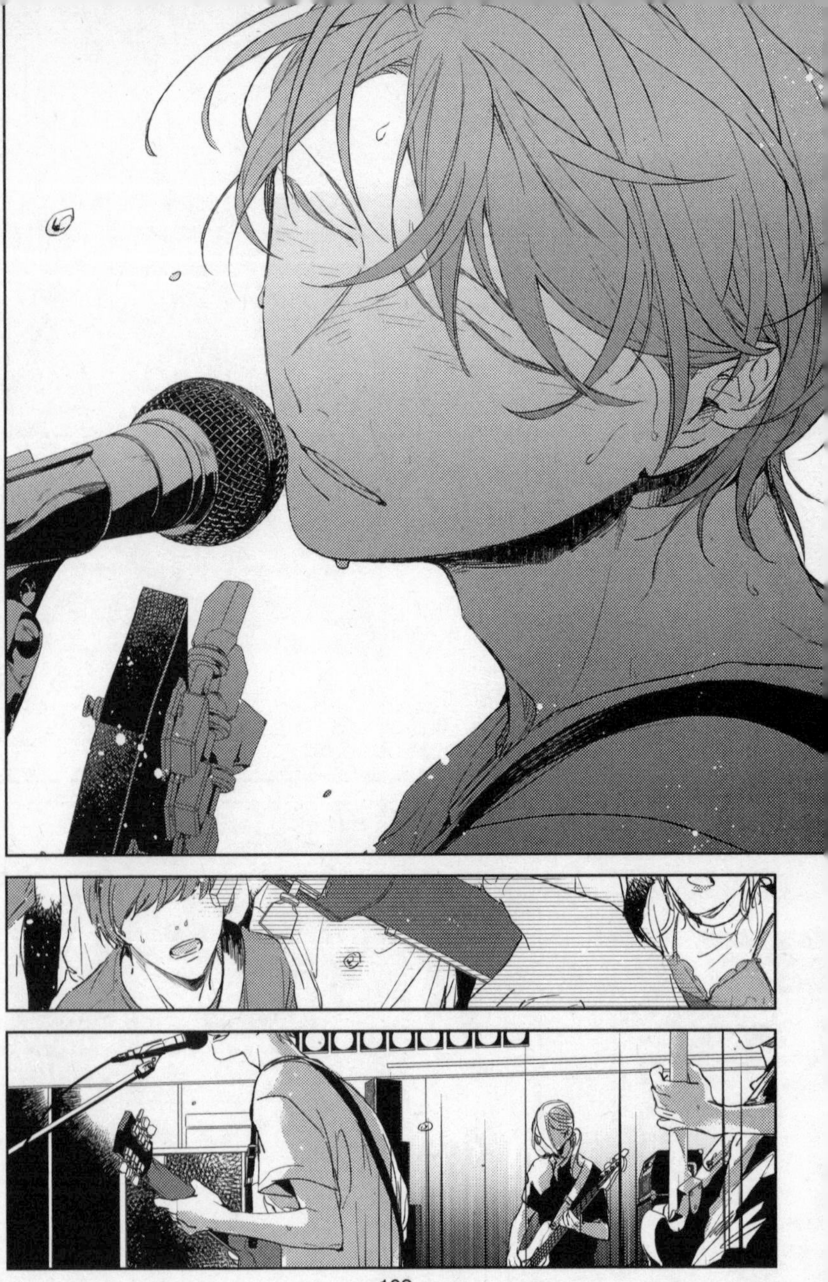

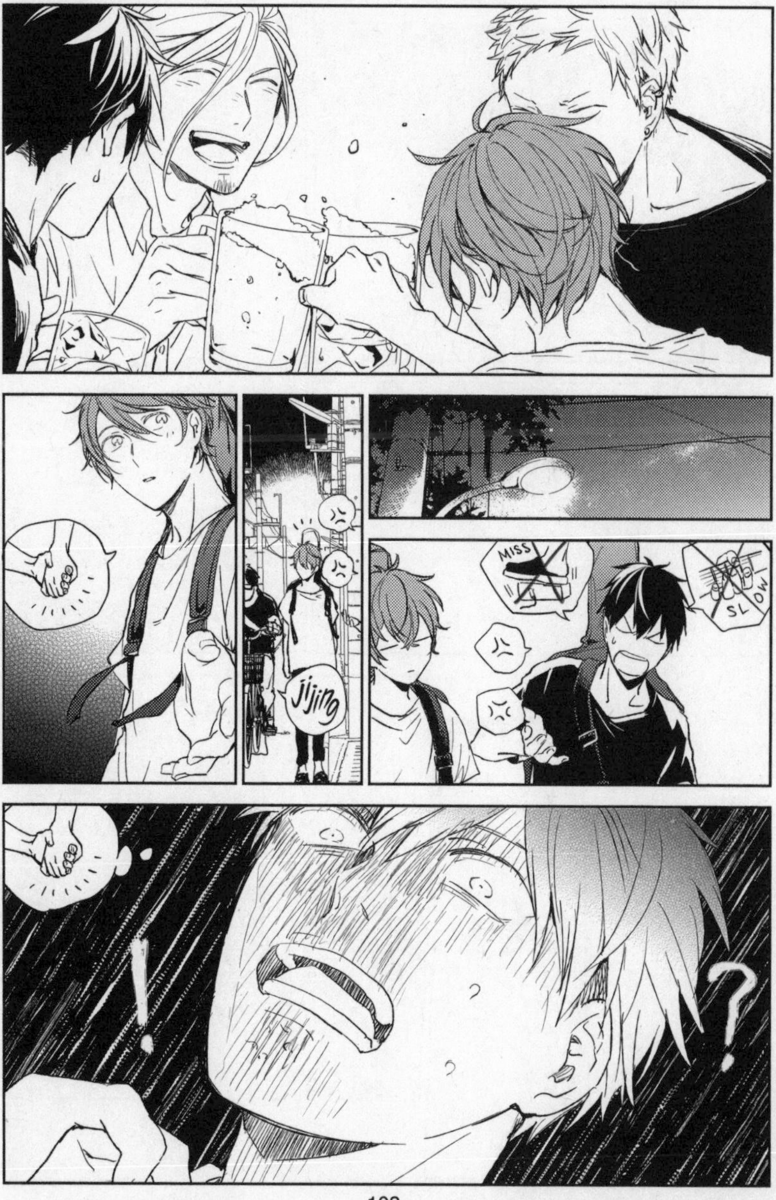
SLOW
MISS
jijing
!
?

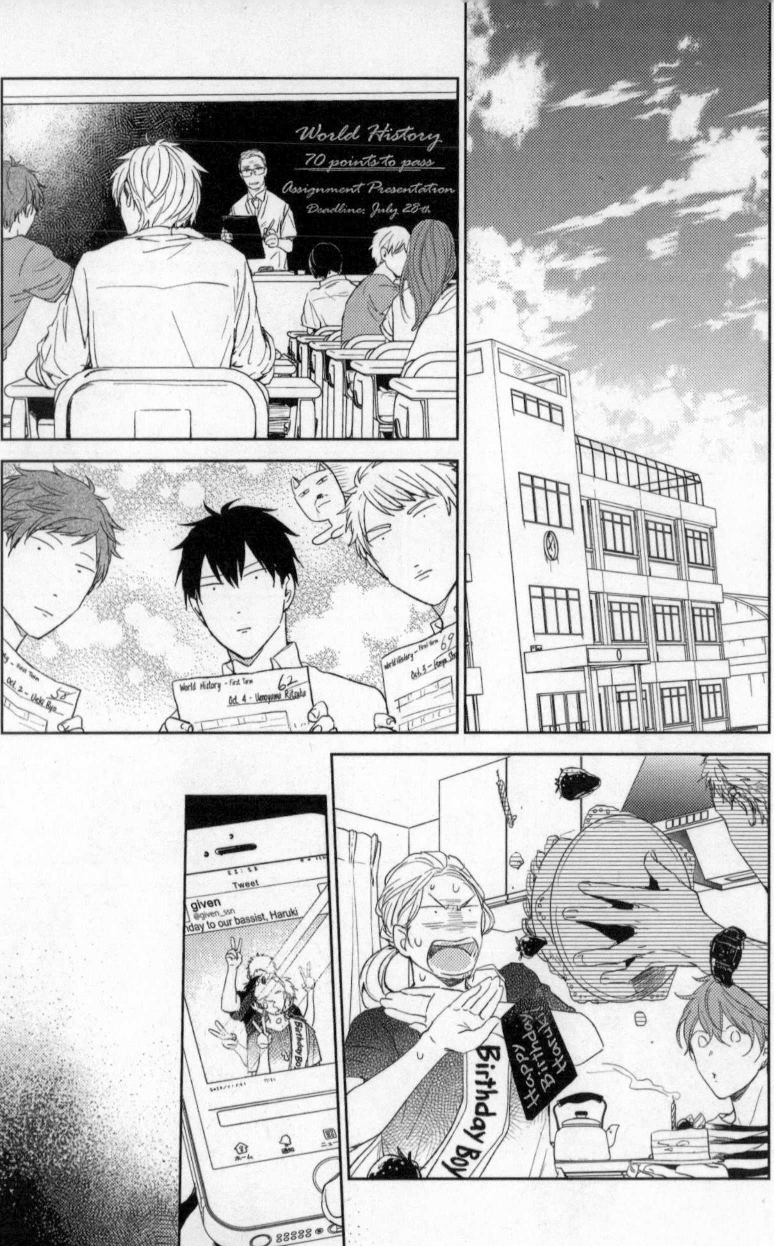
World History
70 points to pass
Assignment Presentation
Deadline: July 28th
World History - First Term
62
Oct. 4 - Uenoyama Ritsuka
Oct. 2 - Ueki Ryo
58
World History - First Term
69
Oct. 3 -
Happy Birthday Haruki
Birthday Boy
Tweet
given
@given_ssn
nday to our bassist, Haruki

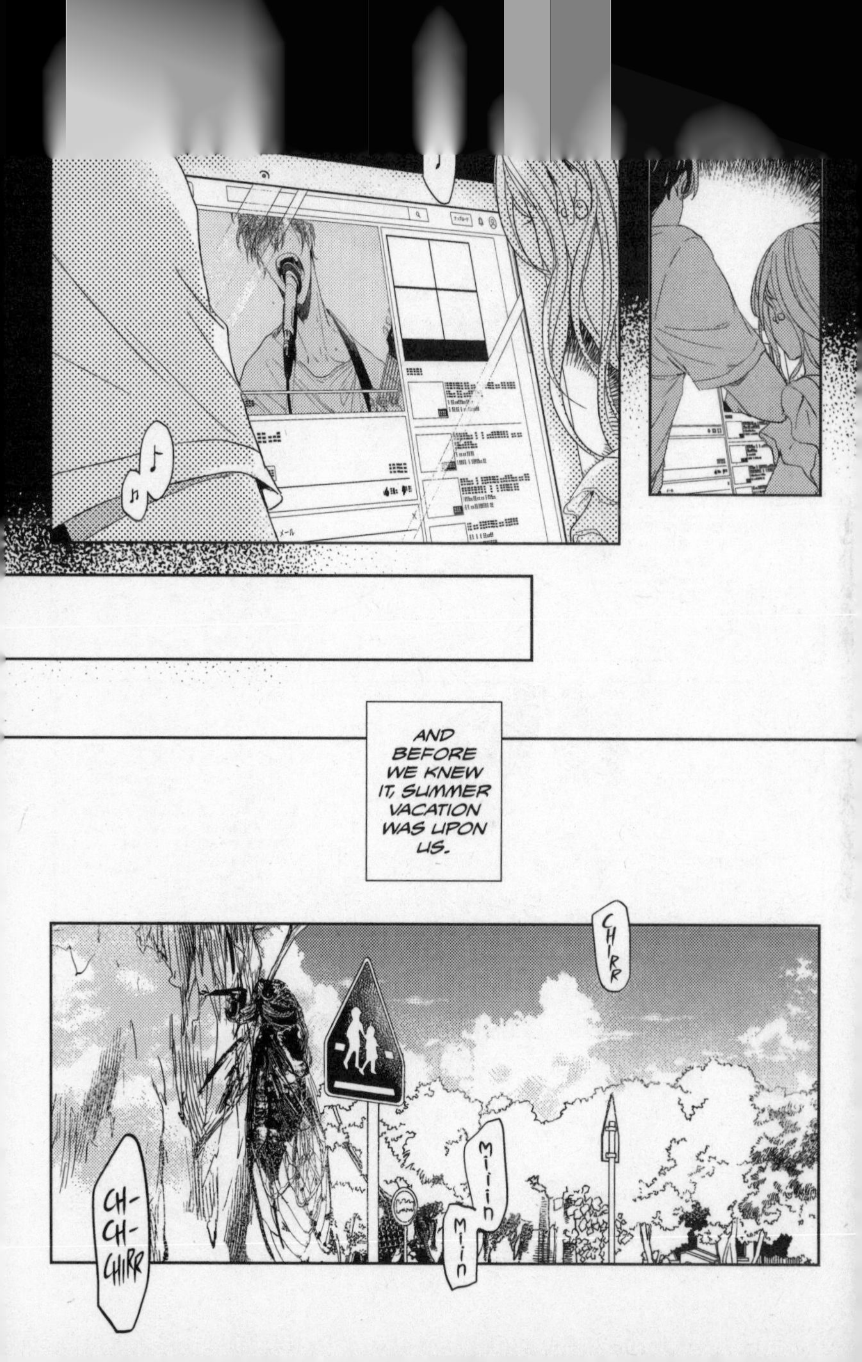
AND BEFORE WE KNEW IT, SUMMER VACATION WAS UPON US.
CHIRR
Miiin
Miin
CH-CH-CHIRR

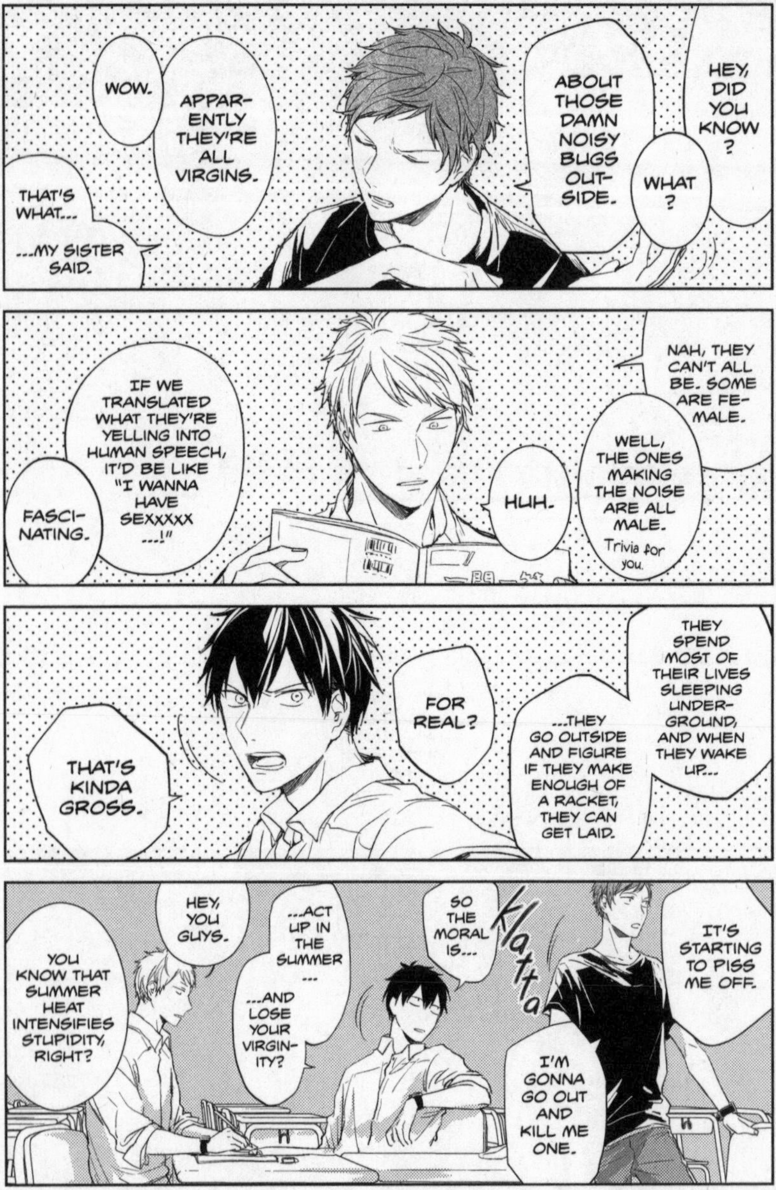
HEY, DID YOU KNOW?
WHAT?
ABOUT THOSE DAMN NOISY BUGS OUTSIDE.
APPARENTLY THEY'RE ALL VIRGINS.
WOW.
THAT'S WHAT...
...MY SISTER SAID.
NAH, THEY CAN'T ALL BE. SOME ARE FE-MALE.
WELL, THE ONES MAKING THE NOISE ARE ALL MALE.
Trivia for you.
HUH.
IF WE TRANSLATED WHAT THEY'RE YELLING INTO HUMAN SPEECH, IT'D BE LIKE "I WANNA HAVE SEXXXXX ...!"
FASCI-NATING.
THEY SPEND MOST OF THEIR LIVES SLEEPING UNDER-GROUND, AND WHEN THEY WAKE UP...
...THEY GO OUTSIDE AND FIGURE IF THEY MAKE ENOUGH OF A RACKET, THEY CAN GET LAID.
FOR REAL?
THAT'S KINDA GROSS.
IT'S STARTING TO PISS ME OFF.
I'M GONNA GO OUT AND KILL ME ONE.
Klatta
SO THE MORAL IS...
...ACT UP IN THE SUMMER...
...AND LOSE YOUR VIRGIN-ITY?
HEY, YOU GUYS.
YOU KNOW THAT SUMMER HEAT INTENSIFIES STUPIDITY, RIGHT?

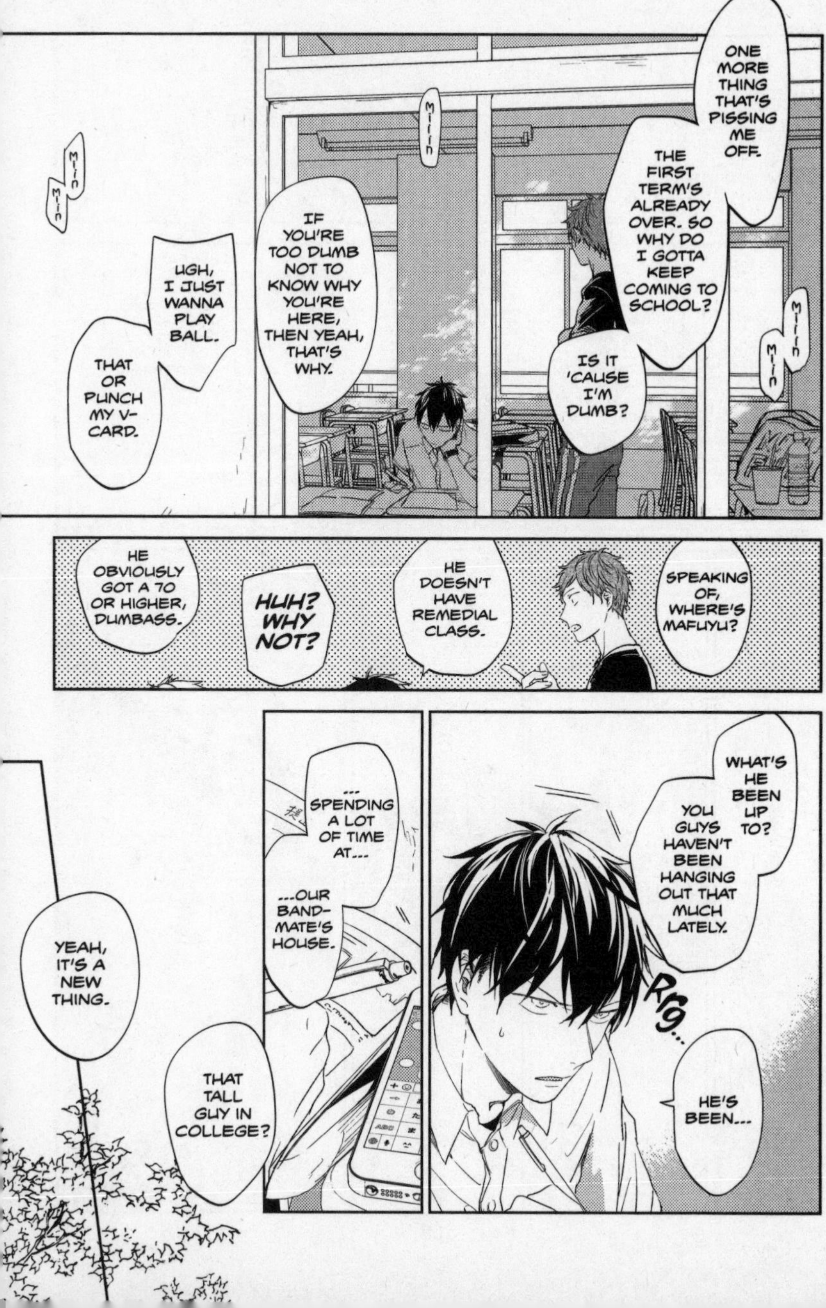
ONE MORE THING THAT'S PISSING ME OFF.
THE FIRST TERM'S ALREADY OVER. SO WHY DO I GOTTA KEEP COMING TO SCHOOL?
Miin
Miin
IS IT 'CAUSE I'M DUMB?
Miin
IF YOU'RE TOO DUMB NOT TO KNOW WHY YOU'RE HERE, THEN YEAH, THAT'S WHY.
UGH, I JUST WANNA PLAY BALL.
THAT OR PUNCH MY V-CARD.
Miin
Miin
SPEAKING OF, WHERE'S MAFUYU?
HE DOESN'T HAVE REMEDIAL CLASS.
HUH? WHY NOT?
HE OBVIOUSLY GOT A 70 OR HIGHER, DUMBASS.
WHAT'S HE BEEN UP TO?
YOU GUYS HAVEN'T BEEN HANGING OUT THAT MUCH LATELY.
Rrg...
HE'S BEEN...
...SPENDING A LOT OF TIME AT...
...OUR BAND-MATE'S HOUSE.
THAT TALL GUY IN COLLEGE?
YEAH, IT'S A NEW THING.

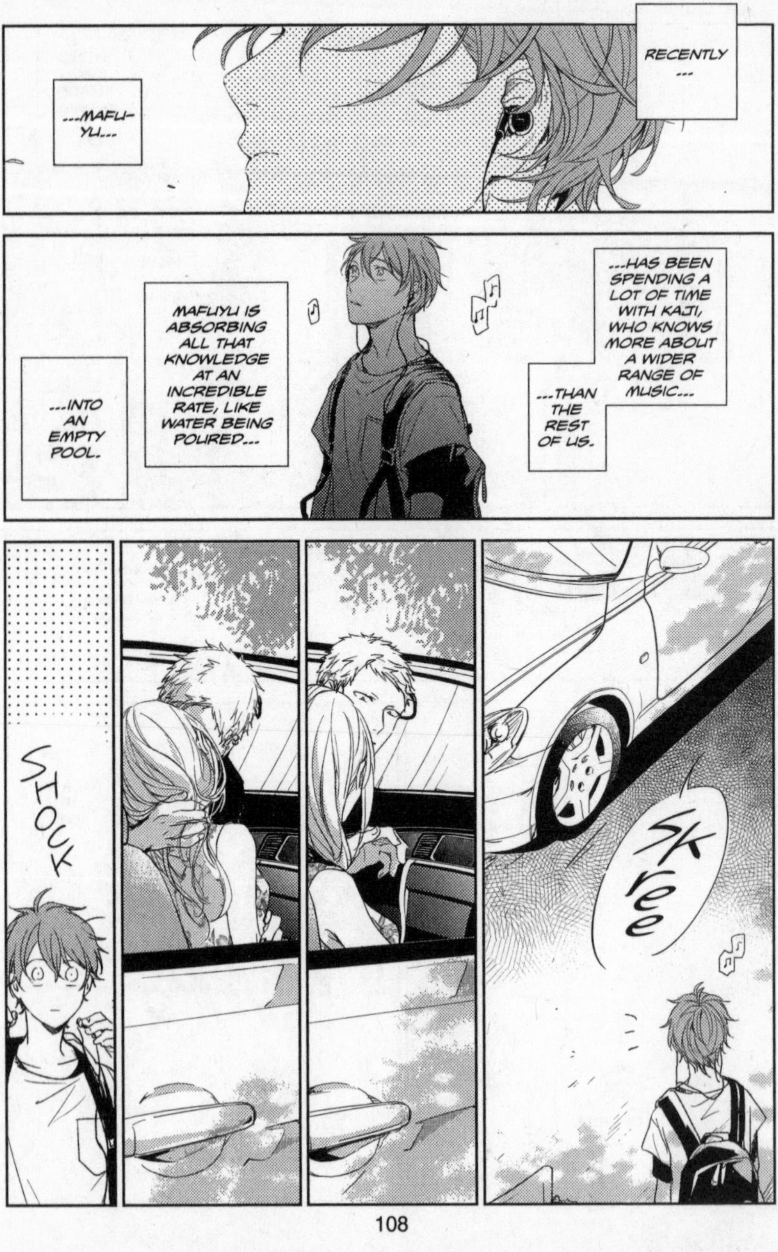
RECENTLY...
...MAFUYU...
...HAS BEEN SPENDING A LOT OF TIME WITH KAJI, WHO KNOWS MORE ABOUT A WIDER RANGE OF MUSIC...
...THAN THE REST OF US.
MAFUYU IS ABSORBING ALL THAT KNOWLEDGE AT AN INCREDIBLE RATE, LIKE WATER BEING POURED...
...INTO AN EMPTY POOL.
SKREE
SHOCK

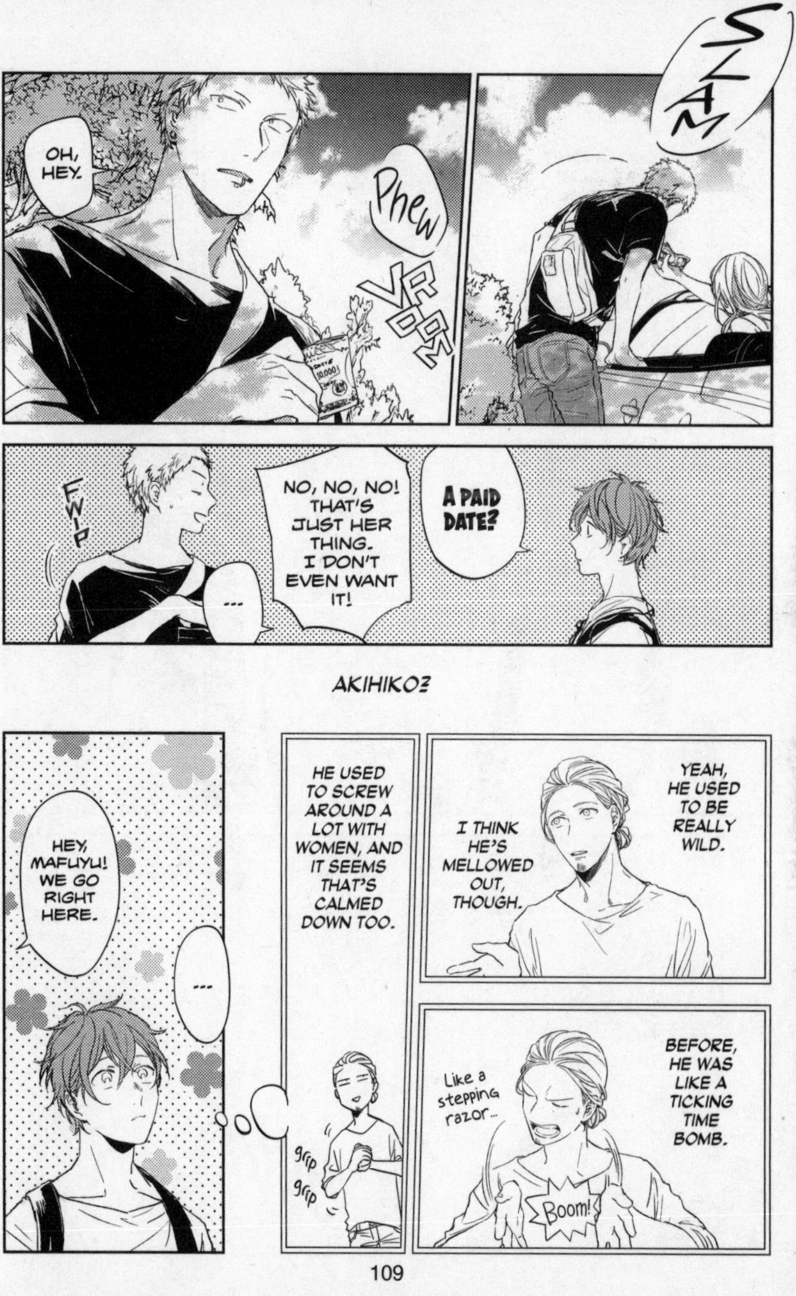
SLAM
OH, HEY.
Phew
VROOM
A PAID DATE?
NO, NO, NO! THAT'S JUST HER THING. I DON'T EVEN WANT IT!
...
FWIP
AKIHIKO?
YEAH, HE USED TO BE REALLY WILD.
I THINK HE'S MELLOWED OUT, THOUGH.
BEFORE, HE WAS LIKE A TICKING TIME BOMB.
Like a stepping razor...
Boom!
HE USED TO SCREW AROUND A LOT WITH WOMEN, AND IT SEEMS THAT'S CALMED DOWN TOO.
grip
grip
HEY, MAFUYU! WE GO RIGHT HERE.
...

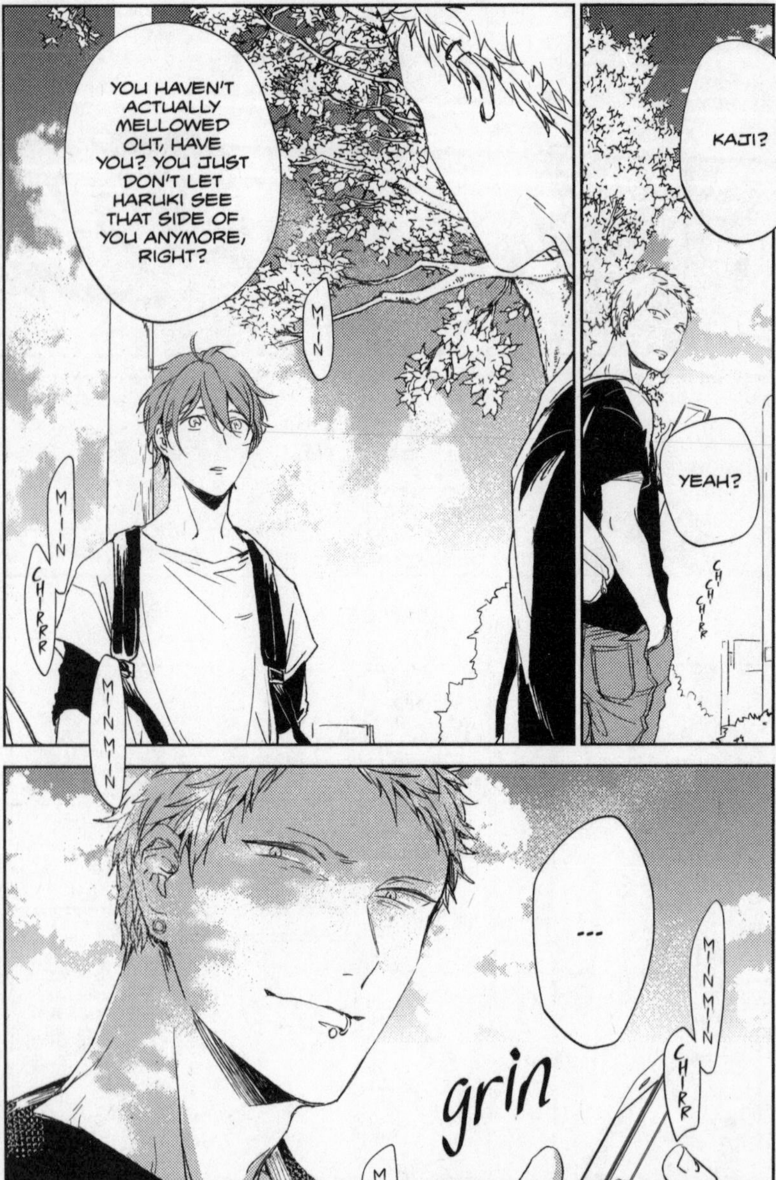
KAJI?
YEAH?
CHI CHI CHIRR
YOU HAVEN'T ACTUALLY MELLOWED OUT, HAVE YOU? YOU JUST DON'T LET HARUKI SEE THAT SIDE OF YOU ANYMORE, RIGHT?
MIIN
MIIN CHIRRR
MIINMIIN
...
MIINMIIN CHIRR
grin
MIIN

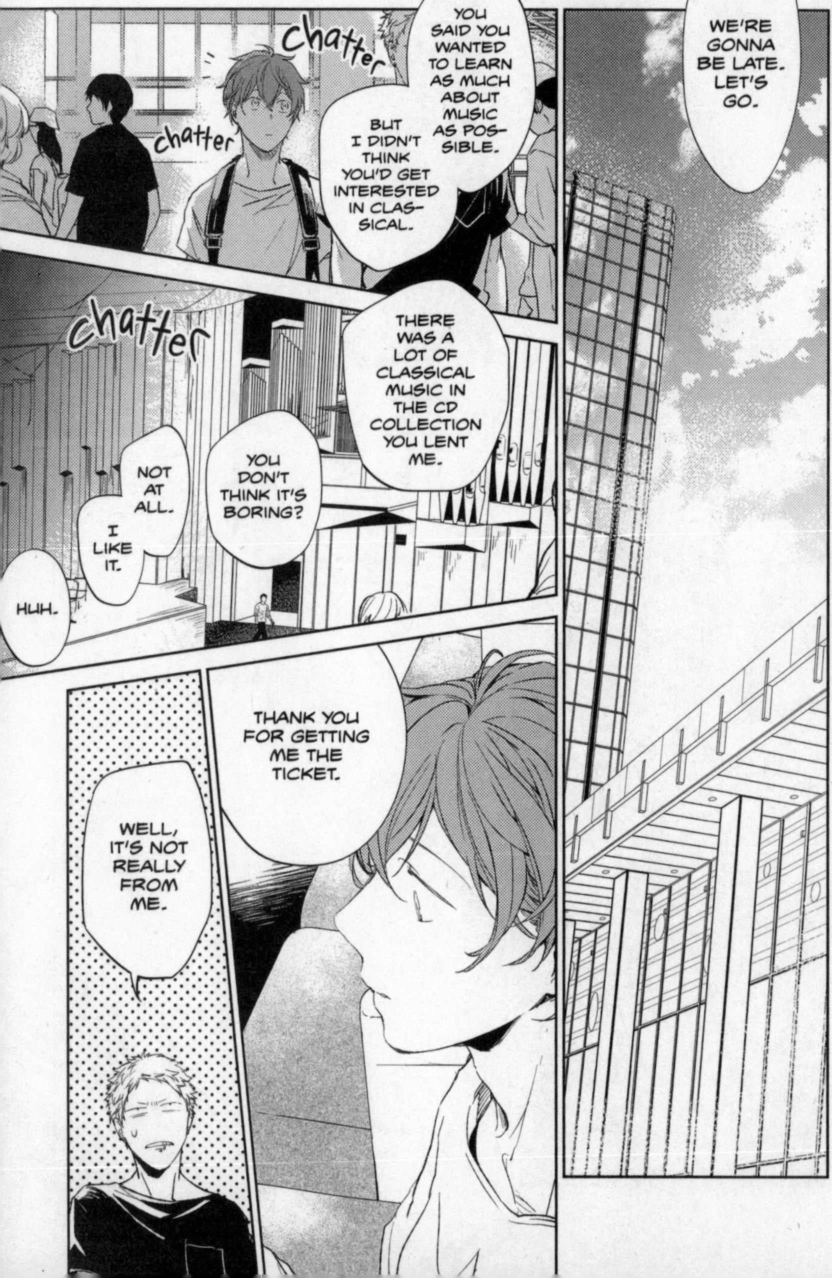
WE'RE GONNA BE LATE. LET'S GO.
YOU SAID YOU WANTED TO LEARN AS MUCH ABOUT MUSIC AS POSSIBLE.
BUT I DIDN'T THINK YOU'D GET INTERESTED IN CLASSICAL.
chatter
chatter
chatter
THERE WAS A LOT OF CLASSICAL MUSIC IN THE CD COLLECTION YOU LENT ME.
YOU DON'T THINK IT'S BORING?
NOT AT ALL.
I LIKE IT.
HUH.
THANK YOU FOR GETTING ME THE TICKET.
WELL, IT'S NOT REALLY FROM ME.

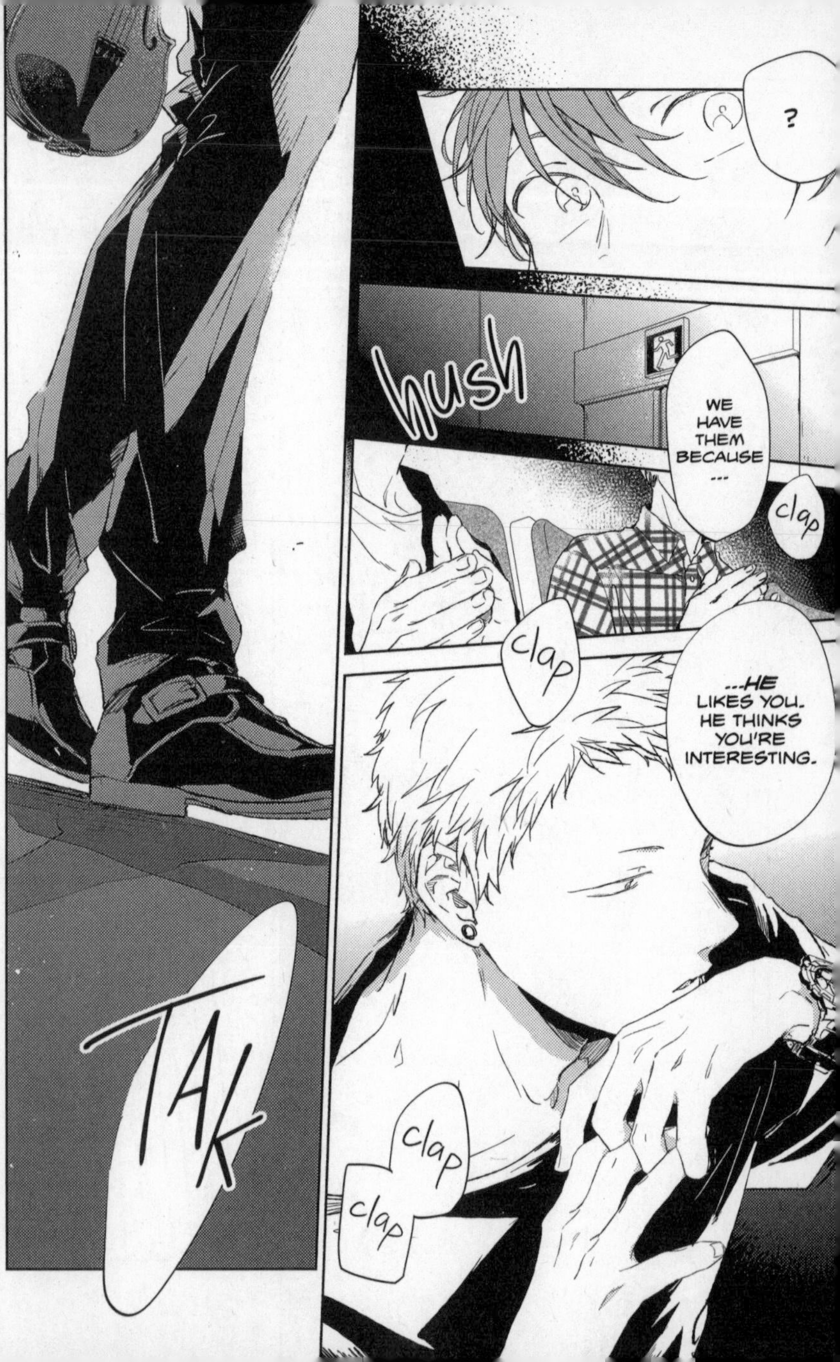
?
WE HAVE THEM BECAUSE ...
hush
clap
clap
...HE LIKES YOU. HE THINKS YOU'RE INTERESTING.
clap
clap
TAK

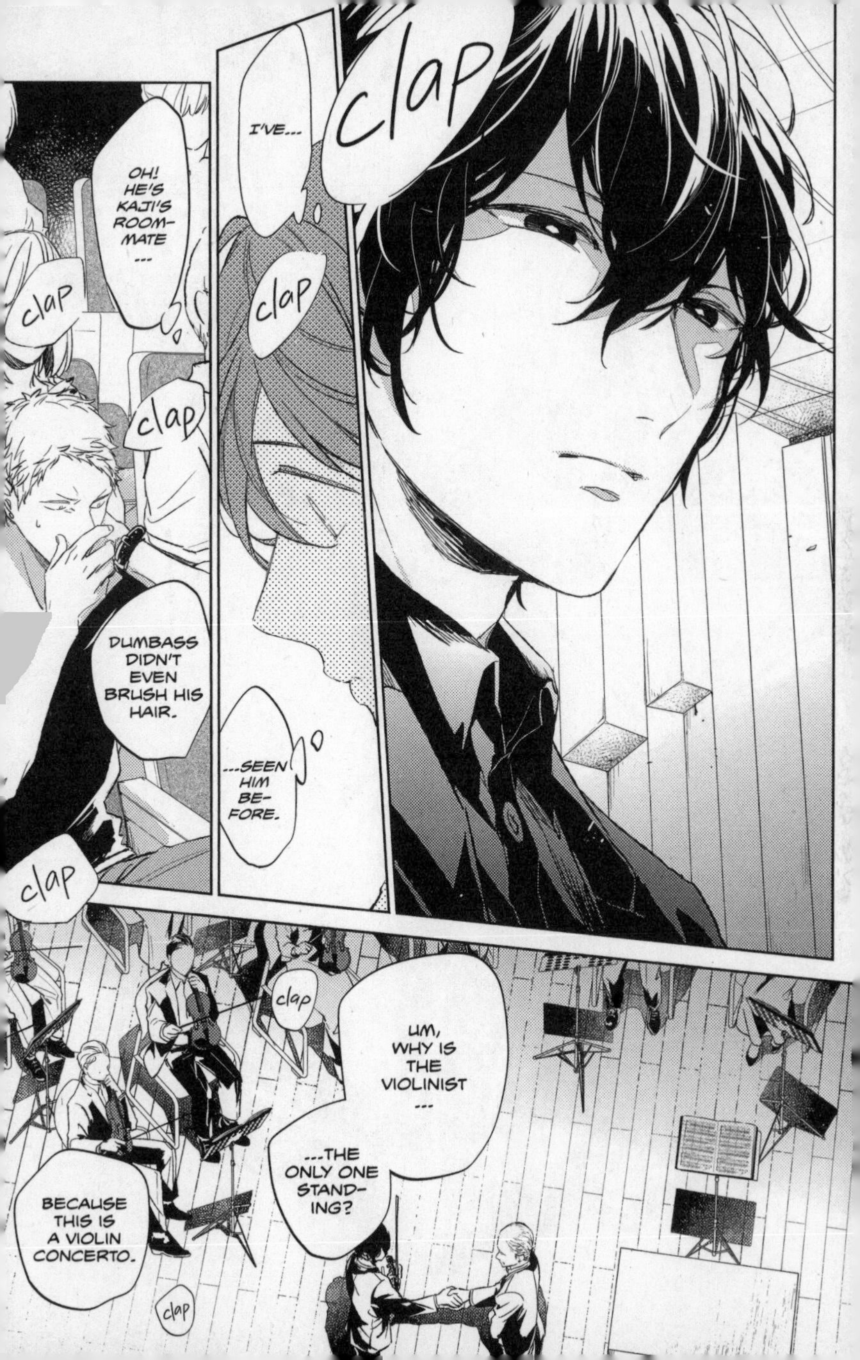
clap
I'VE...
clap
...SEEN HIM BEFORE.
OH! HE'S KAJI'S ROOMMATE...
clap
clap
DUMBASS DIDN'T EVEN BRUSH HIS HAIR.
clap
clap
UM, WHY IS THE VIOLINIST...
...THE ONLY ONE STANDING?
BECAUSE THIS IS A VIOLIN CONCERTO.
clap

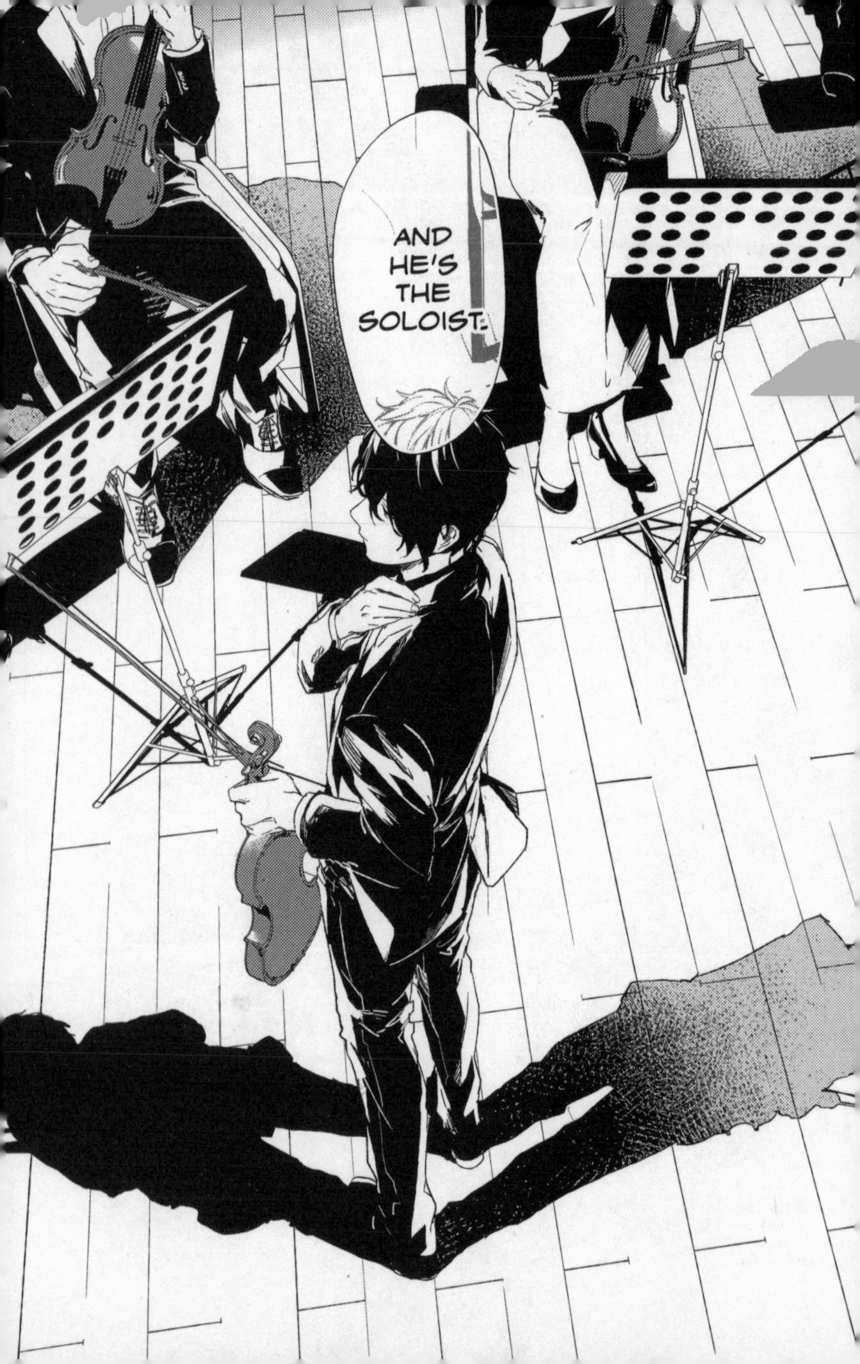
AND HE'S THE SOLOIST.

given
@given_ssn

Happy birthday to our bassist, Haruki

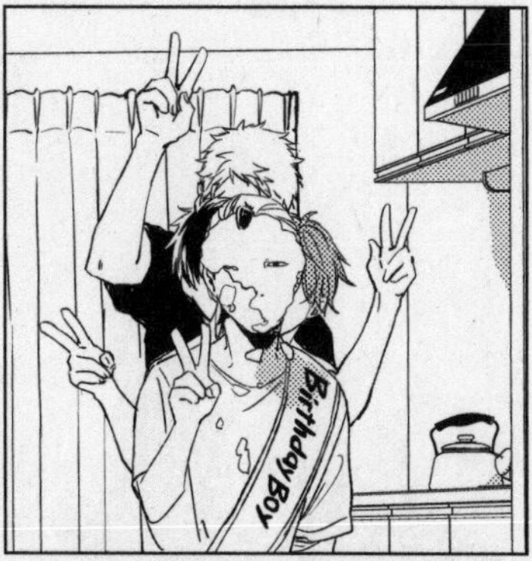
Birthday Boy

Ryo Ueki (17)

180 cm
(Second-year high school student)

Birthday: 5/31   Sign: Gemini
Blood Type: A

Basketball Club, Center

He's been in the same class as
Uenoyama and Itaya since their
first year and got into music
because of their influence.

No Fun
(When Ueki's
Gone)

RECENTLY, UEKI'S BEEN ACTING GROUCHY. EVERYTHING IS EITHER "LAME" OR "DUMB."

NO, THAT'S WAY TOO DUMB.

NOW, EVERY TIME HE SAYS ONE OF THOSE WORDS...

THAT'S LAME.

...THESE CLOWNS RESPOND BY MAKING WEIRD FACES BEHIND HIS BACK.

SOMETIMES THEY HOLD THE FACES FOR LONG ENOUGH...

...THAT OTHER PEOPLE IN THE ROOM NOTICE, BUT THEY DON'T REACT AT ALL...

...TO KEEP UEKI FROM FINDING OUT.

UEKI ISN'T COMING TODAY?

NOPE.

CH-CHEER UP, GUYS...

Lost their purpose in life.

given

by Natsuki Kizu

chapter 16

given

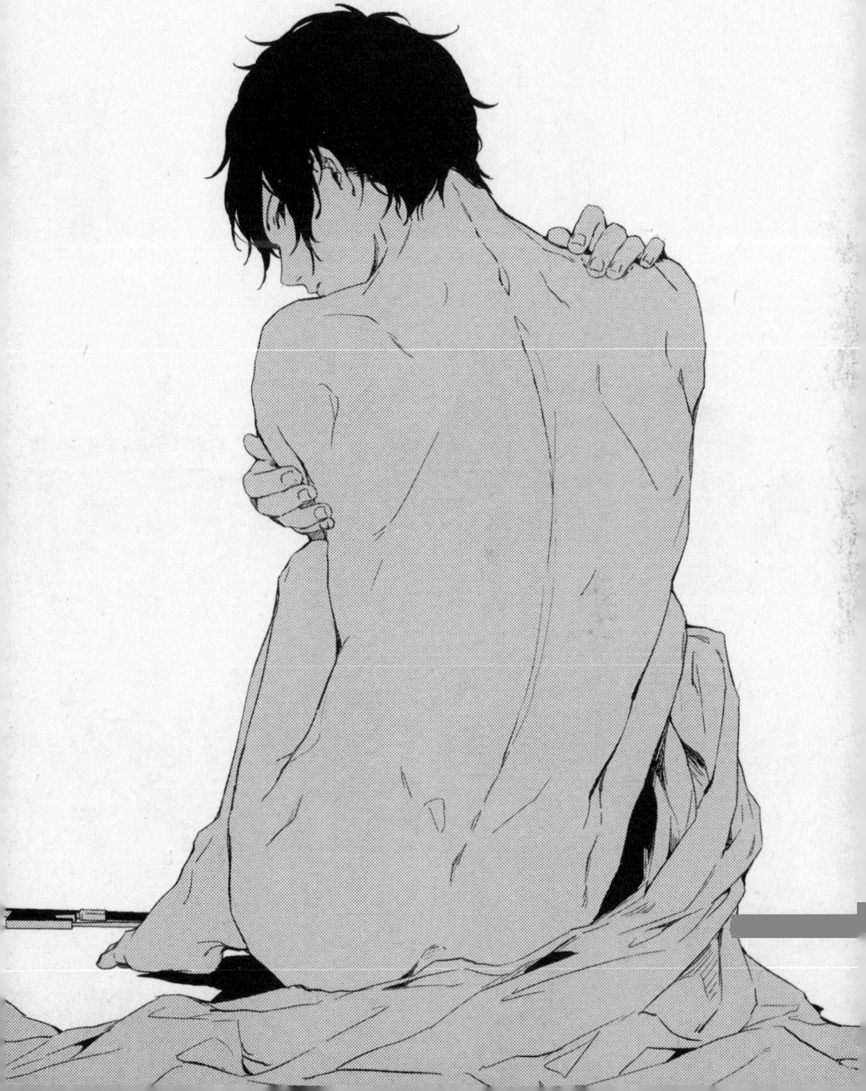

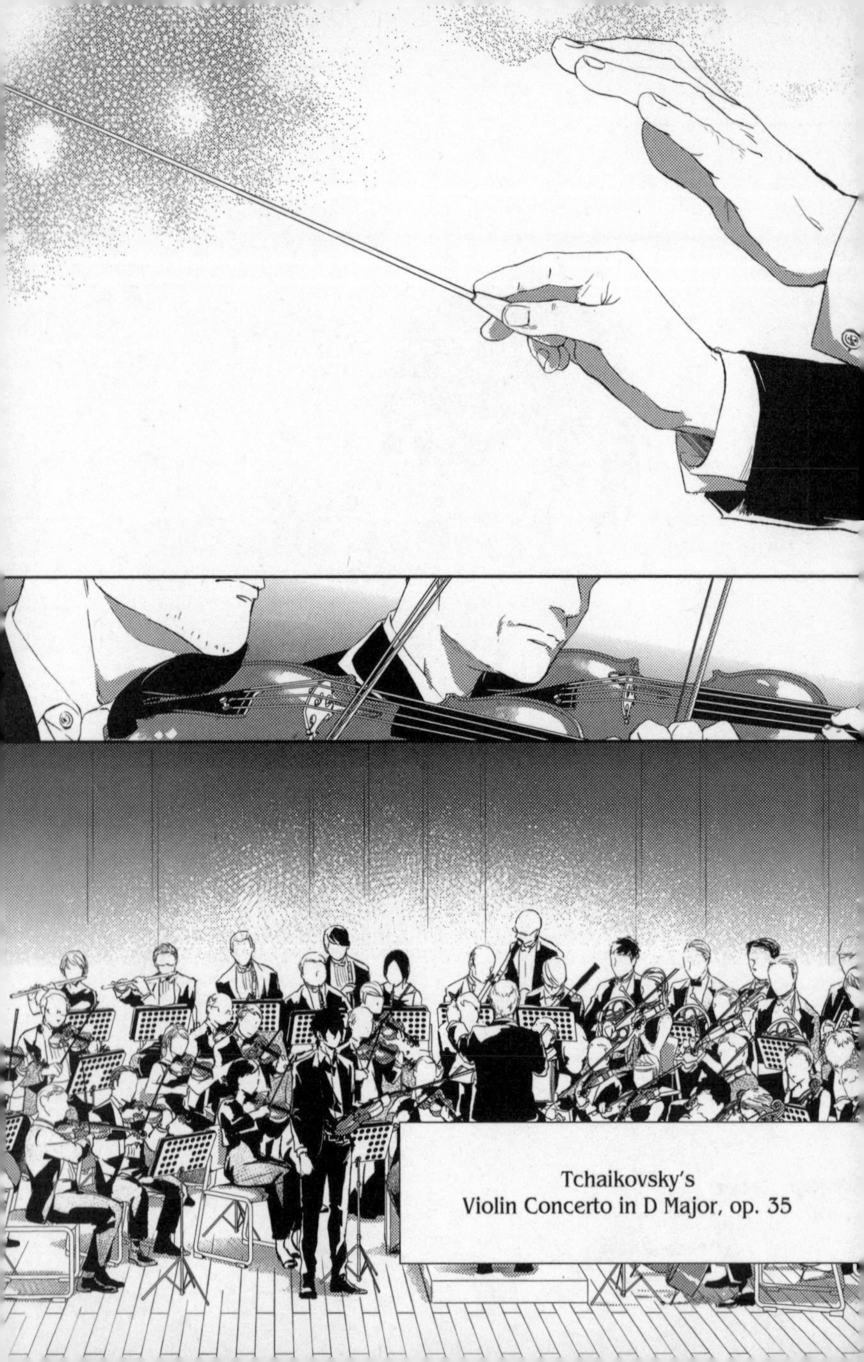
Tchaikovsky's
Violin Concerto in D Major, op. 35

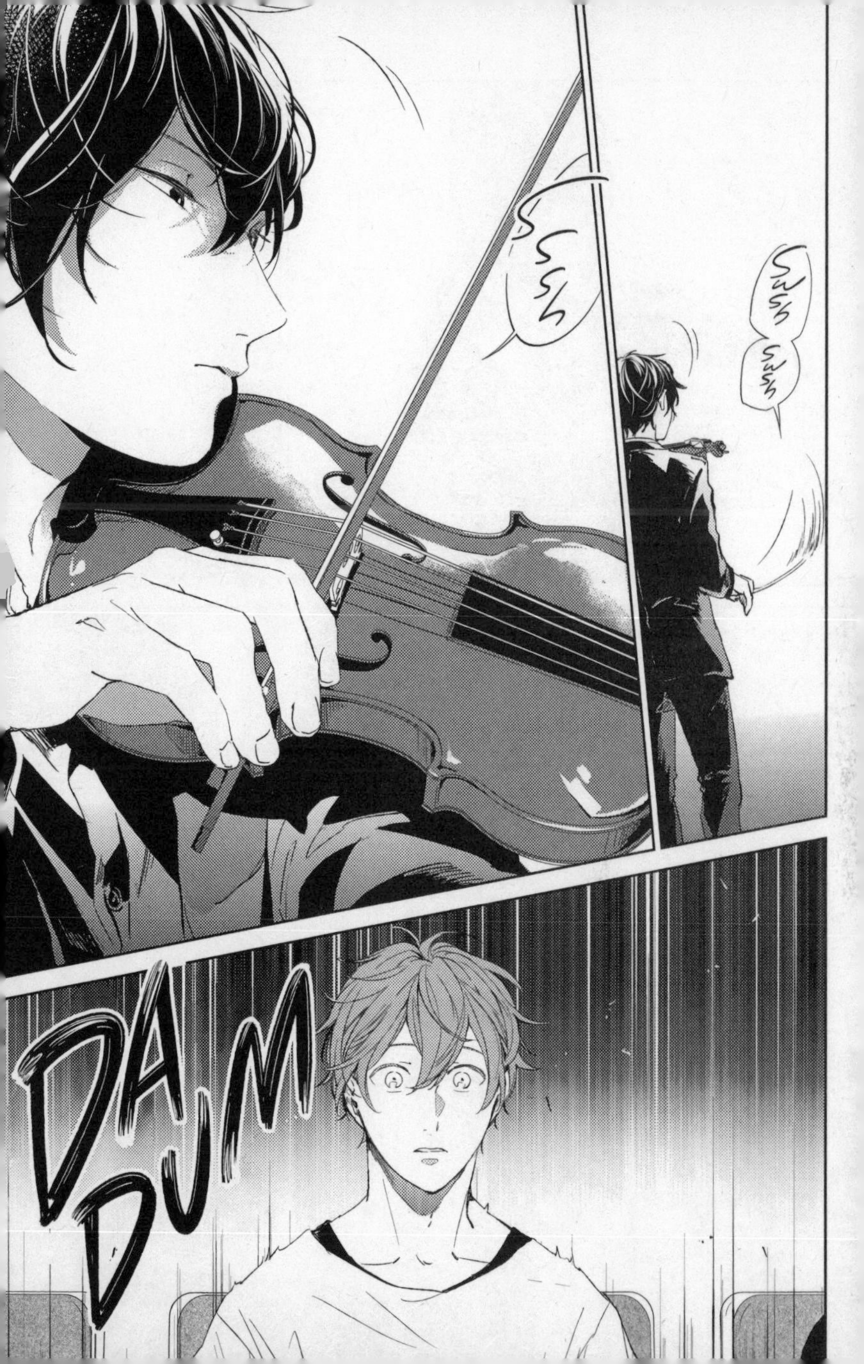
DA DUM

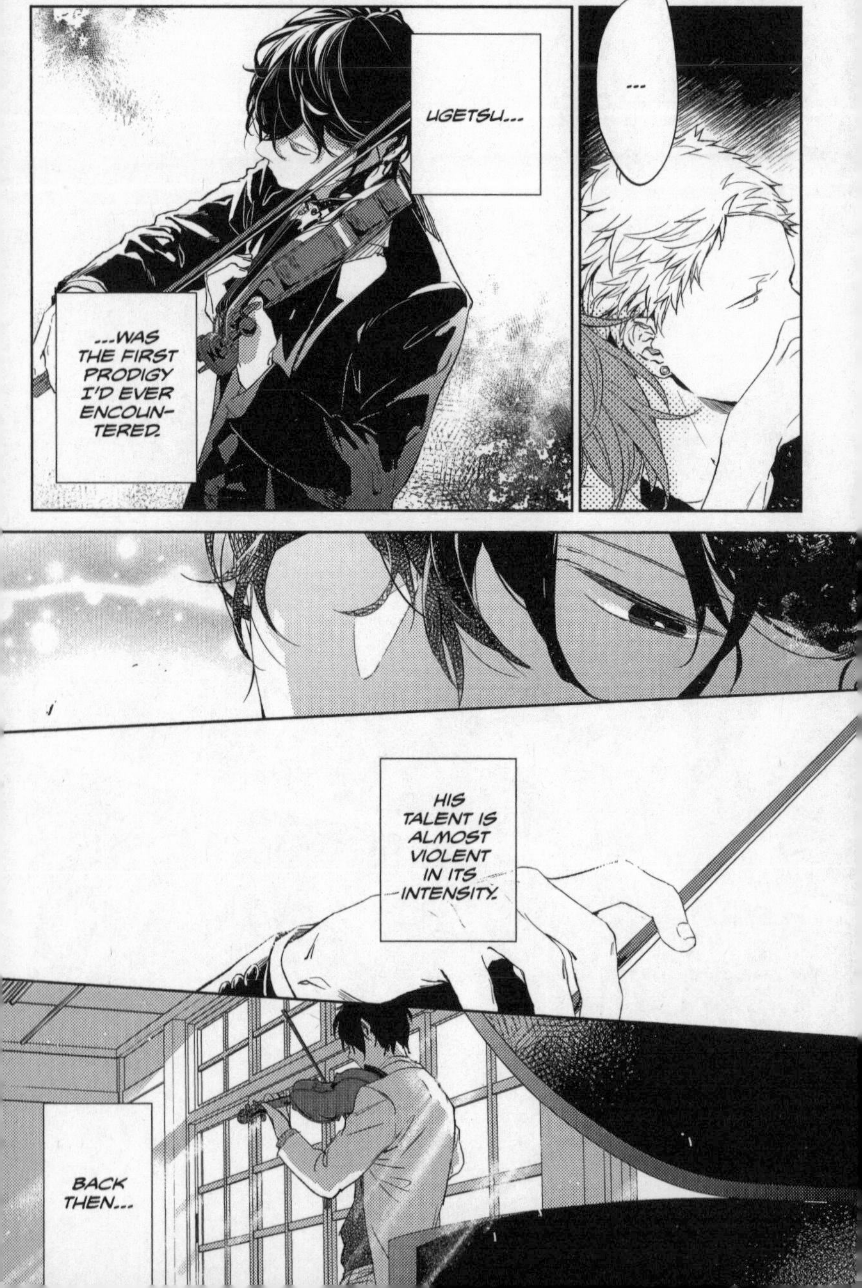
...
UGETSU...
...WAS THE FIRST PRODIGY I'D EVER ENCOUNTERED.
HIS TALENT IS ALMOST VIOLENT IN ITS INTENSITY.
BACK THEN...

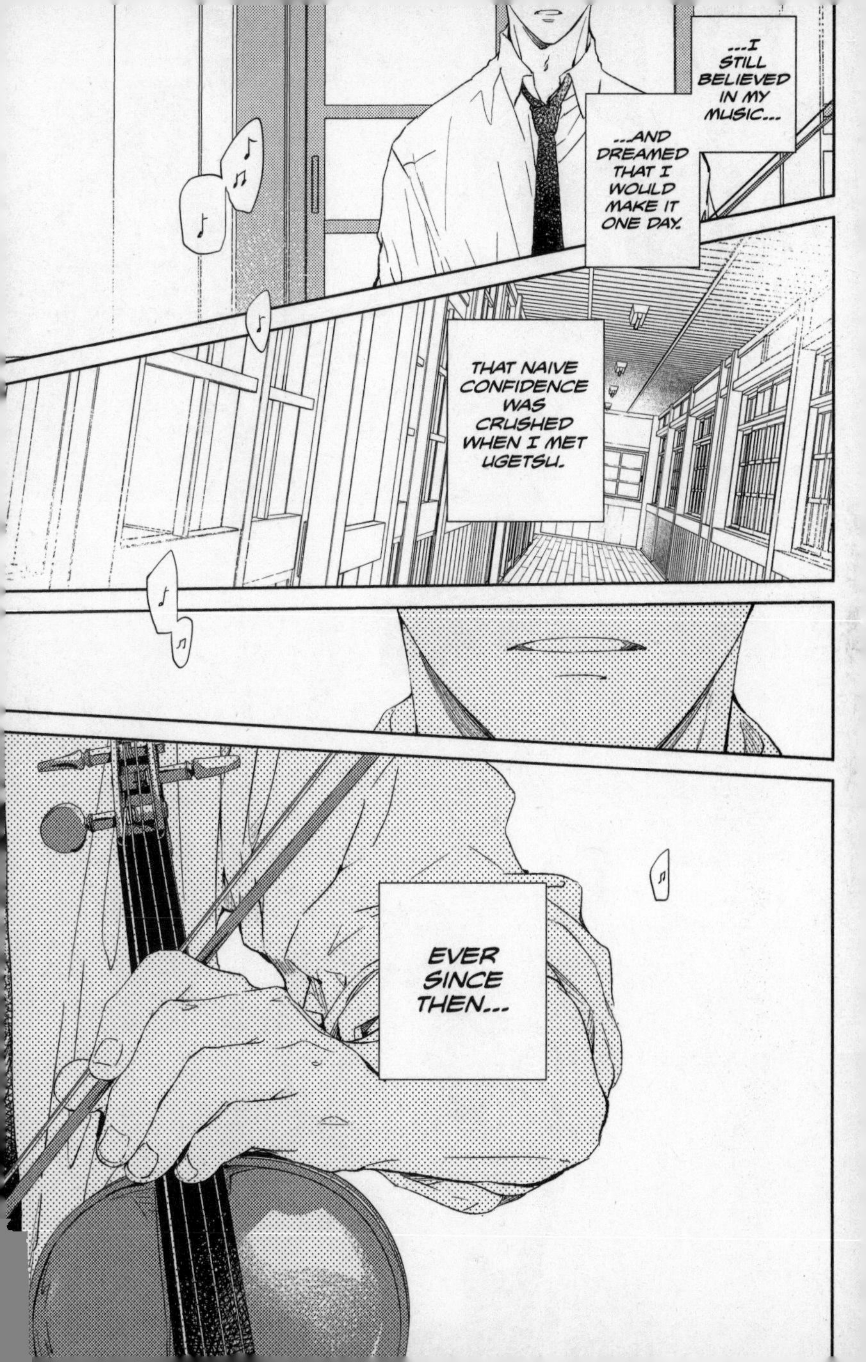
...I STILL BELIEVED IN MY MUSIC...
...AND DREAMED THAT I WOULD MAKE IT ONE DAY.
THAT NAIVE CONFIDENCE WAS CRUSHED WHEN I MET UGETSU.
EVER SINCE THEN...

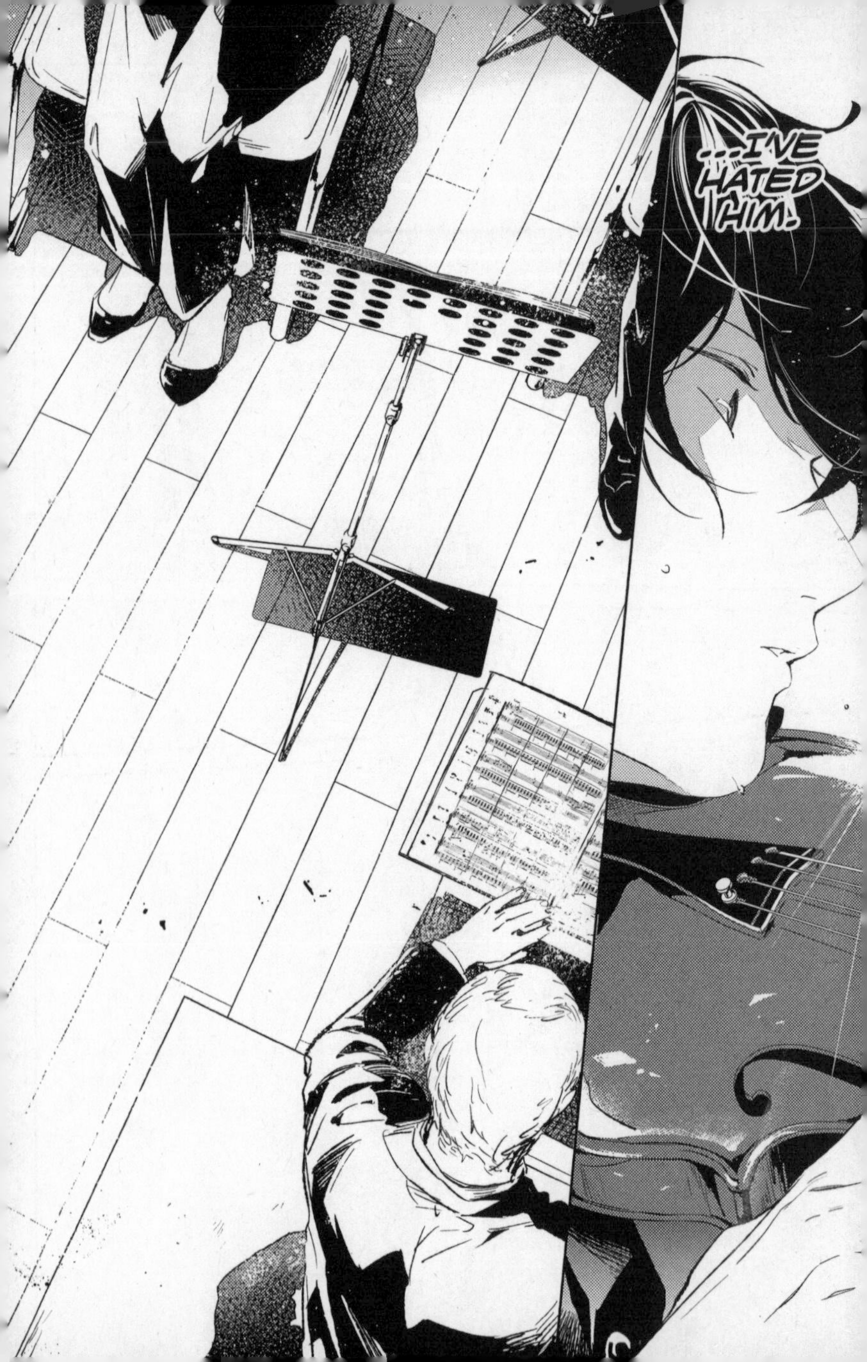
...I'VE HATED HIM.

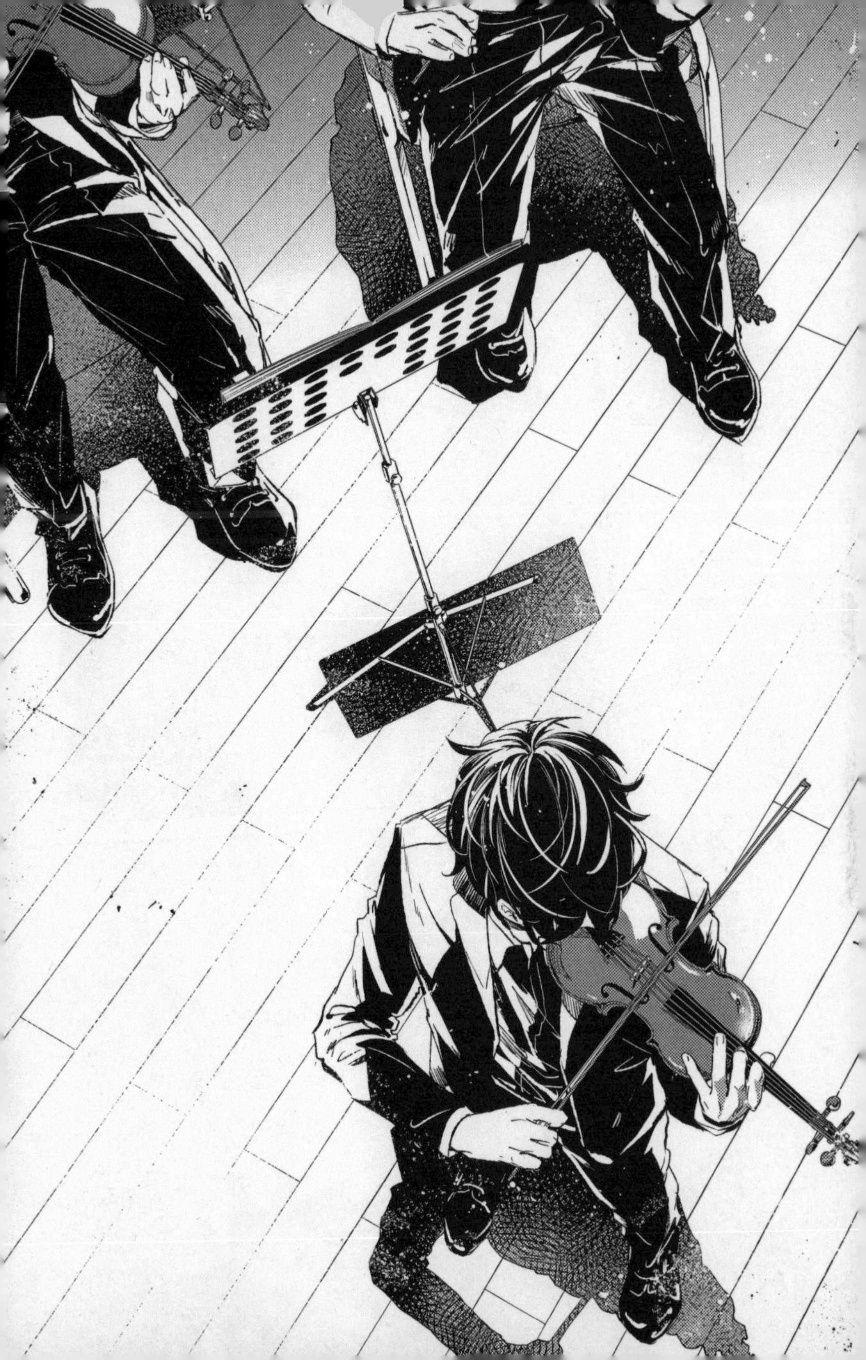

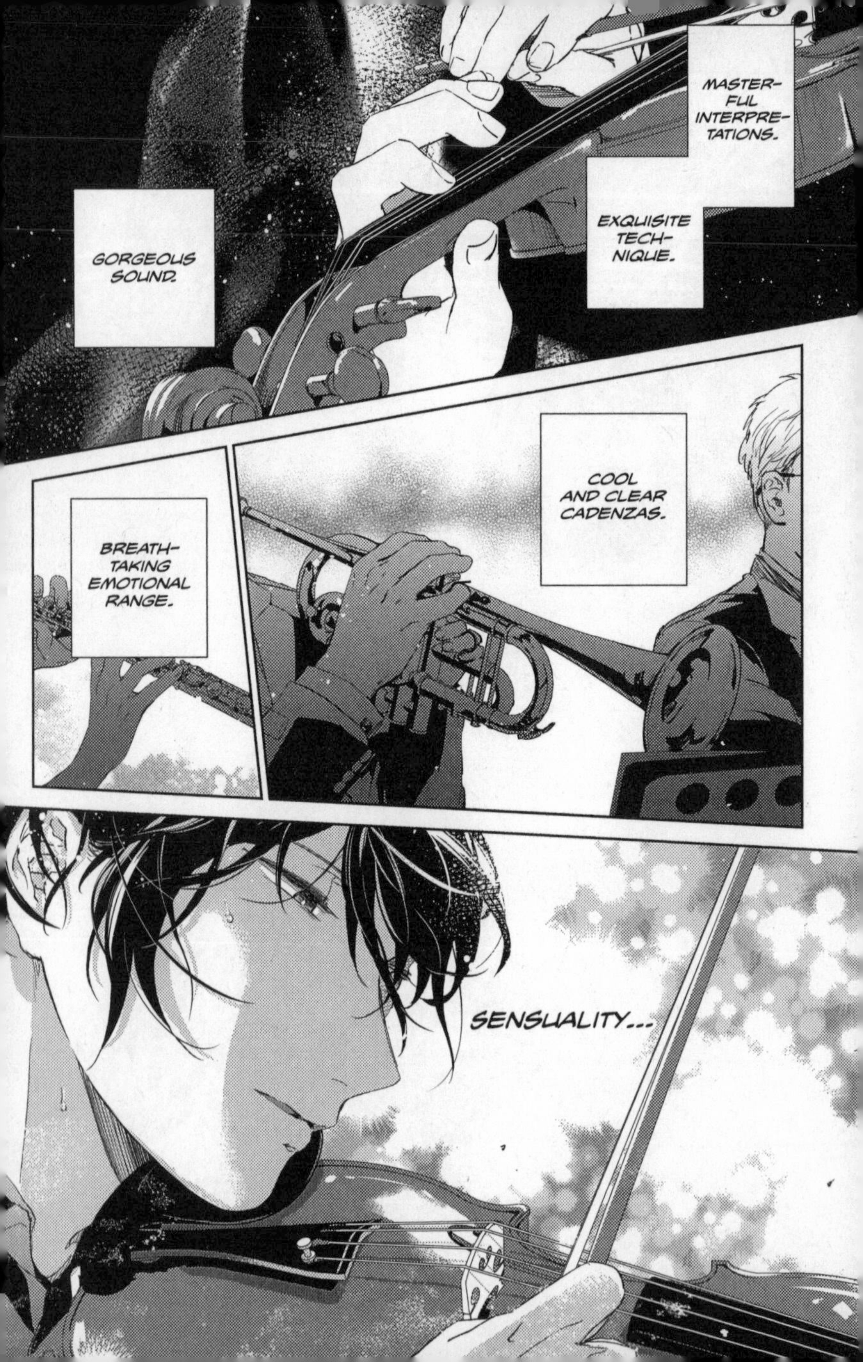
MASTERFUL INTERPRETATIONS.
EXQUISITE TECHNIQUE.
GORGEOUS SOUND.
COOL AND CLEAR CADENZAS.
BREATHTAKING EMOTIONAL RANGE.
SENSUALITY...

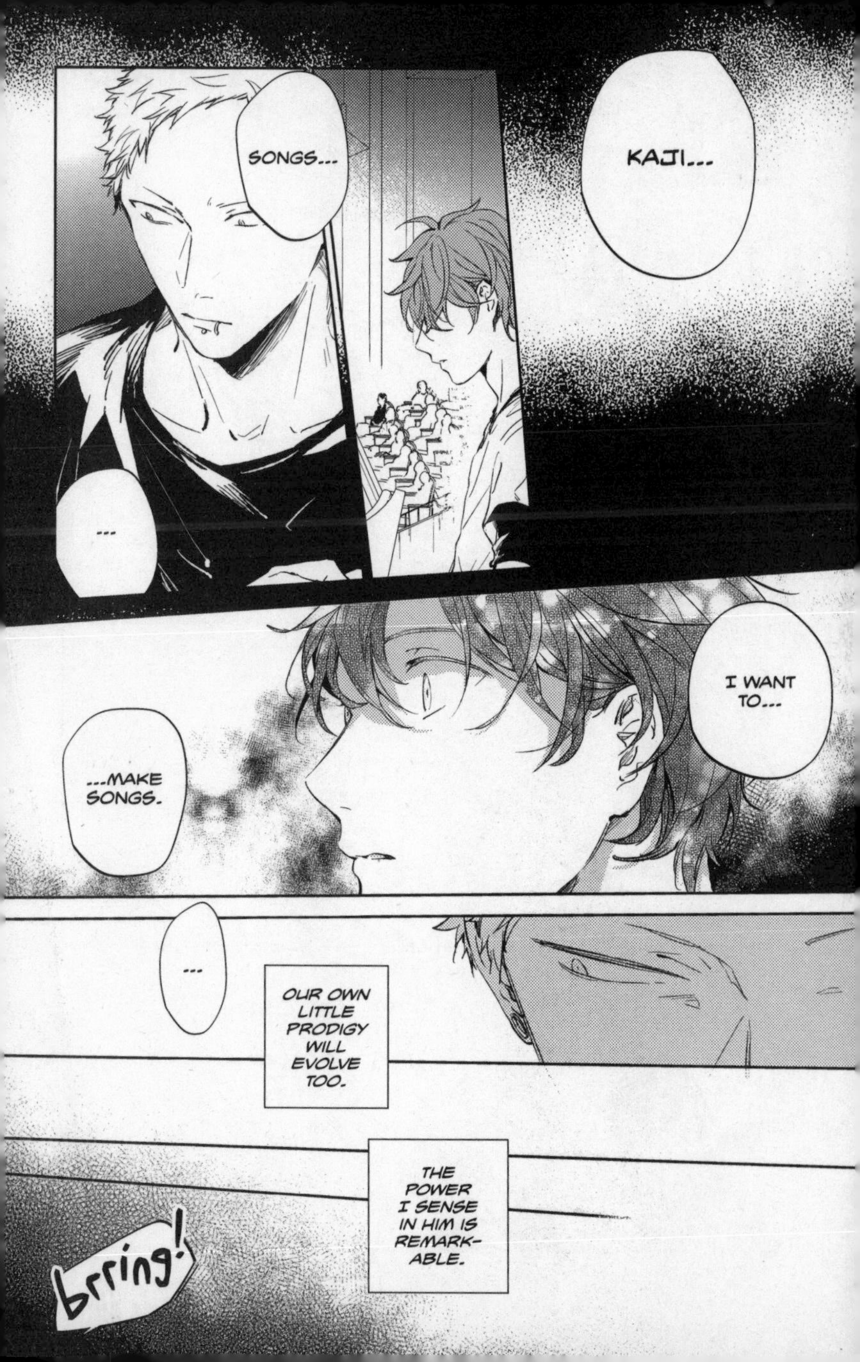
KAJI...
SONGS...
...
I WANT TO...
...MAKE SONGS.
...
OUR OWN LITTLE PRODIGY WILL EVOLVE TOO.
THE POWER I SENSE IN HIM IS REMARKABLE.
brring!

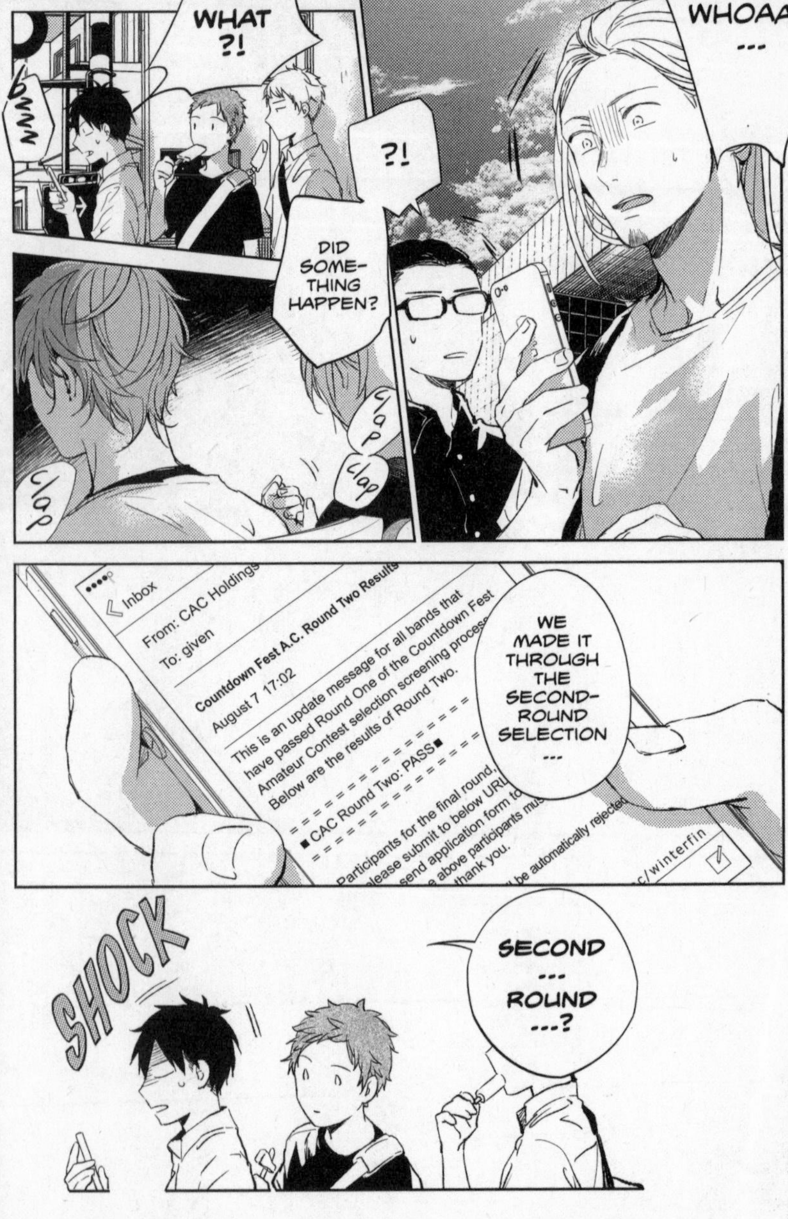
WHOAAA ---
?!
DID SOMETHING HAPPEN?
WHAT ?!
MMM
clap clap
clap clap
Inbox
From: CAC Holdings
To: given
Countdown Fest A.C. Round Two Results
August 7 17:02
This is an update message for all bands that have passed Round One of the Countdown Fest Amateur Contest selection screening process. Below are the results of Round Two.
■ CAC Round Two: PASS ■
WE MADE IT THROUGH THE SECOND-ROUND SELECTION ---
SECOND --- ROUND ---?
SHOCK

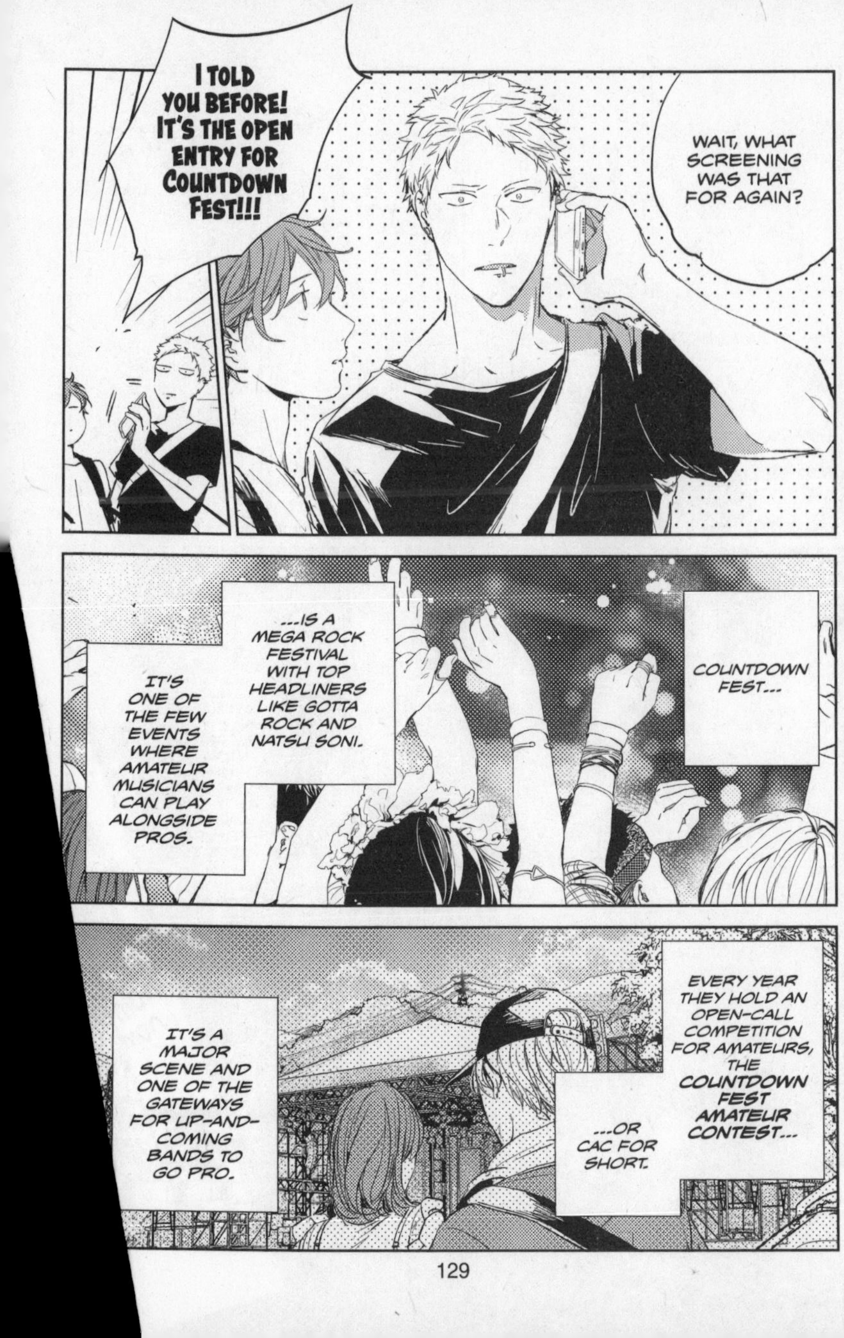
WAIT, WHAT SCREENING WAS THAT FOR AGAIN?
I TOLD YOU BEFORE! IT'S THE OPEN ENTRY FOR COUNTDOWN FEST!!!
COUNTDOWN FEST...
...IS A MEGA ROCK FESTIVAL WITH TOP HEADLINERS LIKE GOTTA ROCK AND NATSU SONI.
IT'S ONE OF THE FEW EVENTS WHERE AMATEUR MUSICIANS CAN PLAY ALONGSIDE PROS.
EVERY YEAR THEY HOLD AN OPEN-CALL COMPETITION FOR AMATEURS, THE COUNTDOWN FEST AMATEUR CONTEST...
...OR CAC FOR SHORT.
IT'S A MAJOR SCENE AND ONE OF THE GATEWAYS FOR UP-AND-COMING BANDS TO GO PRO.

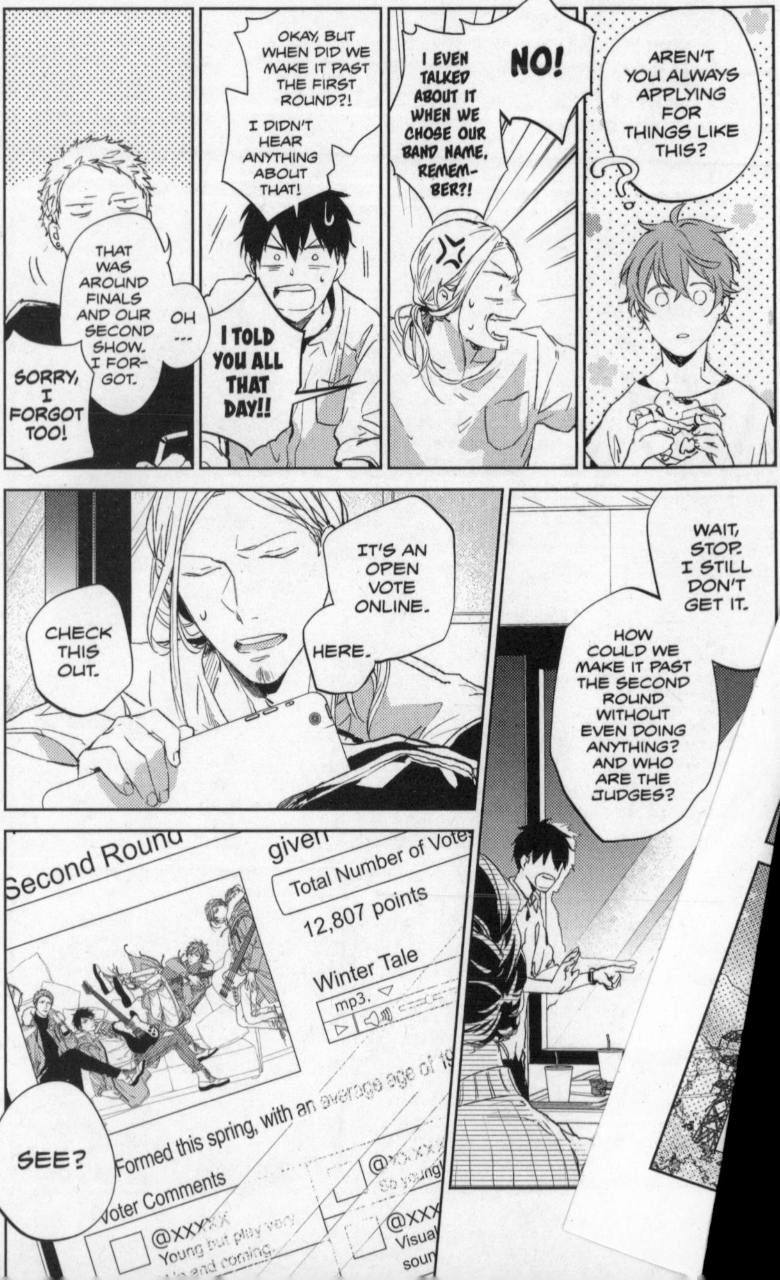
AREN'T YOU ALWAYS APPLYING FOR THINGS LIKE THIS?
NO!
I EVEN TALKED ABOUT IT WHEN WE CHOSE OUR BAND NAME, REMEMBER?!
OKAY, BUT WHEN DID WE MAKE IT PAST THE FIRST ROUND?!
I DIDN'T HEAR ANYTHING ABOUT THAT!
I TOLD YOU ALL THAT DAY!!
THAT WAS AROUND FINALS AND OUR SECOND SHOW. I FORGOT.
OH ---
SORRY, I FORGOT TOO!
WAIT, STOP. I STILL DON'T GET IT.
HOW COULD WE MAKE IT PAST THE SECOND ROUND WITHOUT EVEN DOING ANYTHING? AND WHO ARE THE JUDGES?
IT'S AN OPEN VOTE ONLINE.
HERE.
CHECK THIS OUT.
Second Round
given
Total Number of Vote
12,807 points
Winter Tale
mp3.
Formed this spring, with an average age of
Voter Comments
@XXXXX
SEE?

WE GOT TONS OF COMMENTS.
...rmed this spring, with
Voter Comments
@XXXX
So young
@XXXXX
Young but play at a high level. Up and coming.
@XX
Visual
soun
@XXXX
Their lyrics are so moving.
I THOUGHT IT'D BE GOOD PUBLICITY EVEN IF PEOPLE JUST SAW OUR NAME ON THE LIST OF BANDS.
...!
YOU ENTERED US WITH THE VIDEO FROM OUR FIRST SHOW.
WE'RE A TOTALLY UNKNOWN BAND...
...SO TO BE HONEST, WE DIDN'T GET ALL THAT MANY VOTES.
BUT WE GOT AN UNUSUALLY HIGH NUMBER OF COMMENTS, AND THAT WAS RE-FLECTED IN THE POINT SCORE.
THE COMMENT FUNCTION IS LINKED TO SOCIAL MEDIA SITES, SO ALL THE COMMENTS ABOUT US FEED TO OUR AC-COUNTS.
HAVE YOU SEEN HOW MANY FOLLOWERS WE HAVE NOW?
...
glance
THIS HAS GOTTA BE A MISTAKE!
flinch

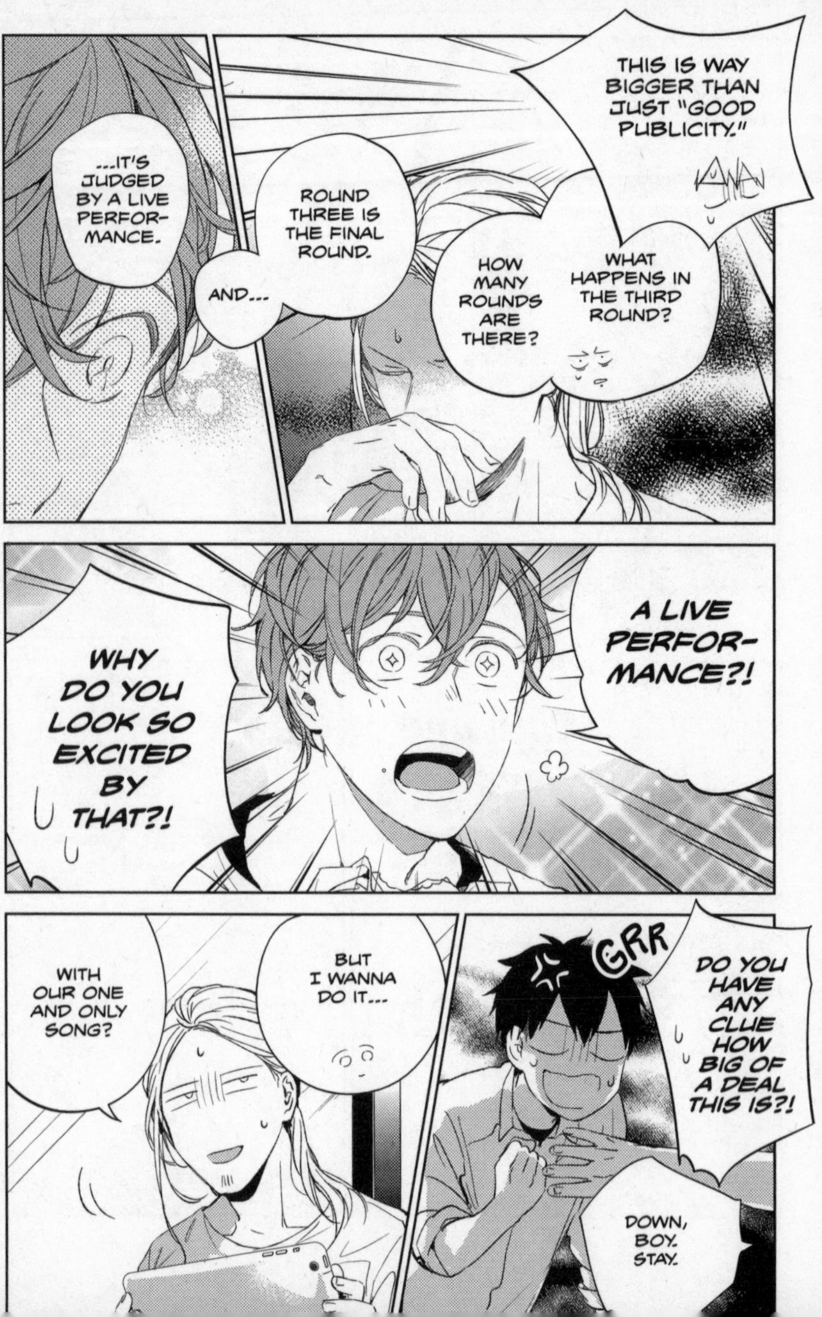
THIS IS WAY BIGGER THAN JUST "GOOD PUBLICITY."
WHAT HAPPENS IN THE THIRD ROUND?
HOW MANY ROUNDS ARE THERE?
ROUND THREE IS THE FINAL ROUND.
AND...
...IT'S JUDGED BY A LIVE PERFORMANCE.
A LIVE PERFORMANCE?!
WHY DO YOU LOOK SO EXCITED BY THAT?!
GRR
DO YOU HAVE ANY CLUE HOW BIG OF A DEAL THIS IS?!
DOWN, BOY. STAY.
BUT I WANNA DO IT...
WITH OUR ONE AND ONLY SONG?

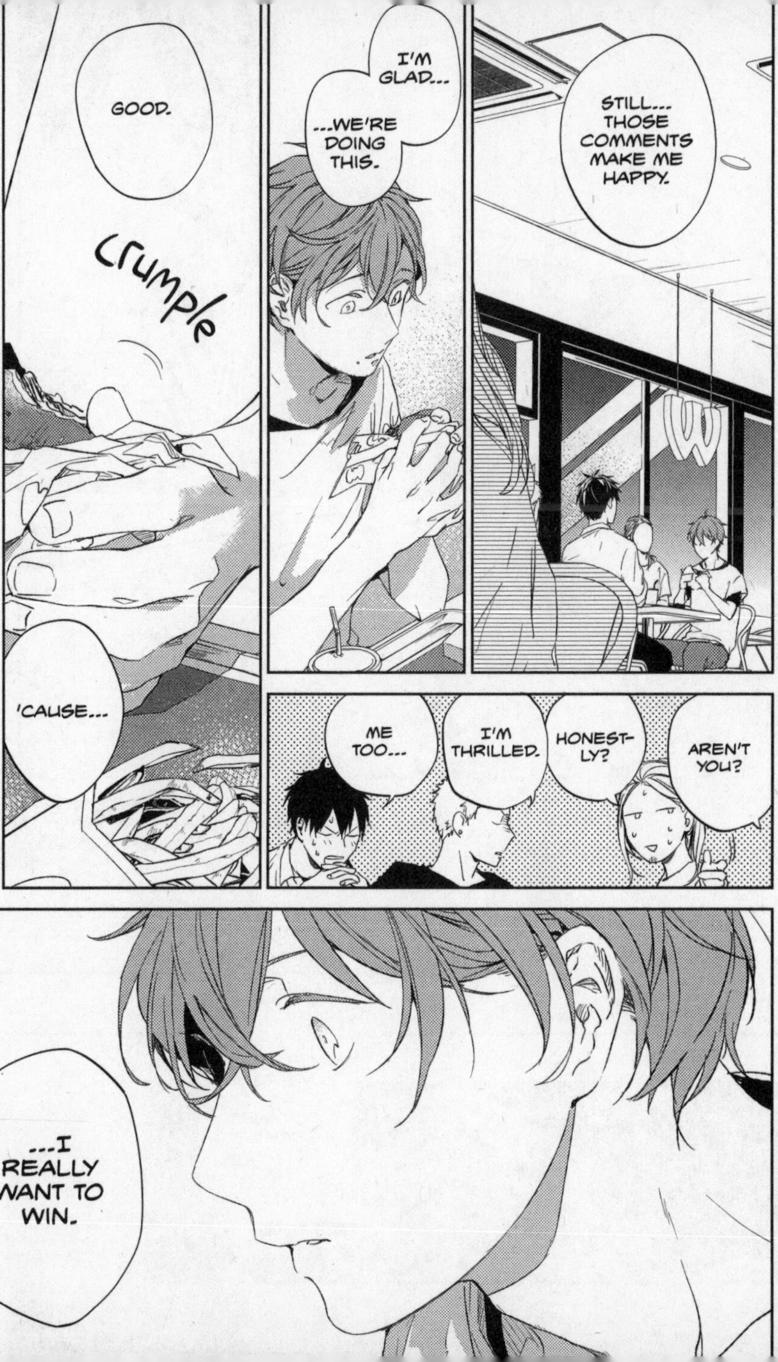
STILL... THOSE COMMENTS MAKE ME HAPPY.
I'M GLAD...
...WE'RE DOING THIS.
AREN'T YOU?
HONEST-LY?
I'M THRILLED.
ME TOO...
GOOD.
Crumple
'CAUSE...
...I REALLY WANT TO WIN.

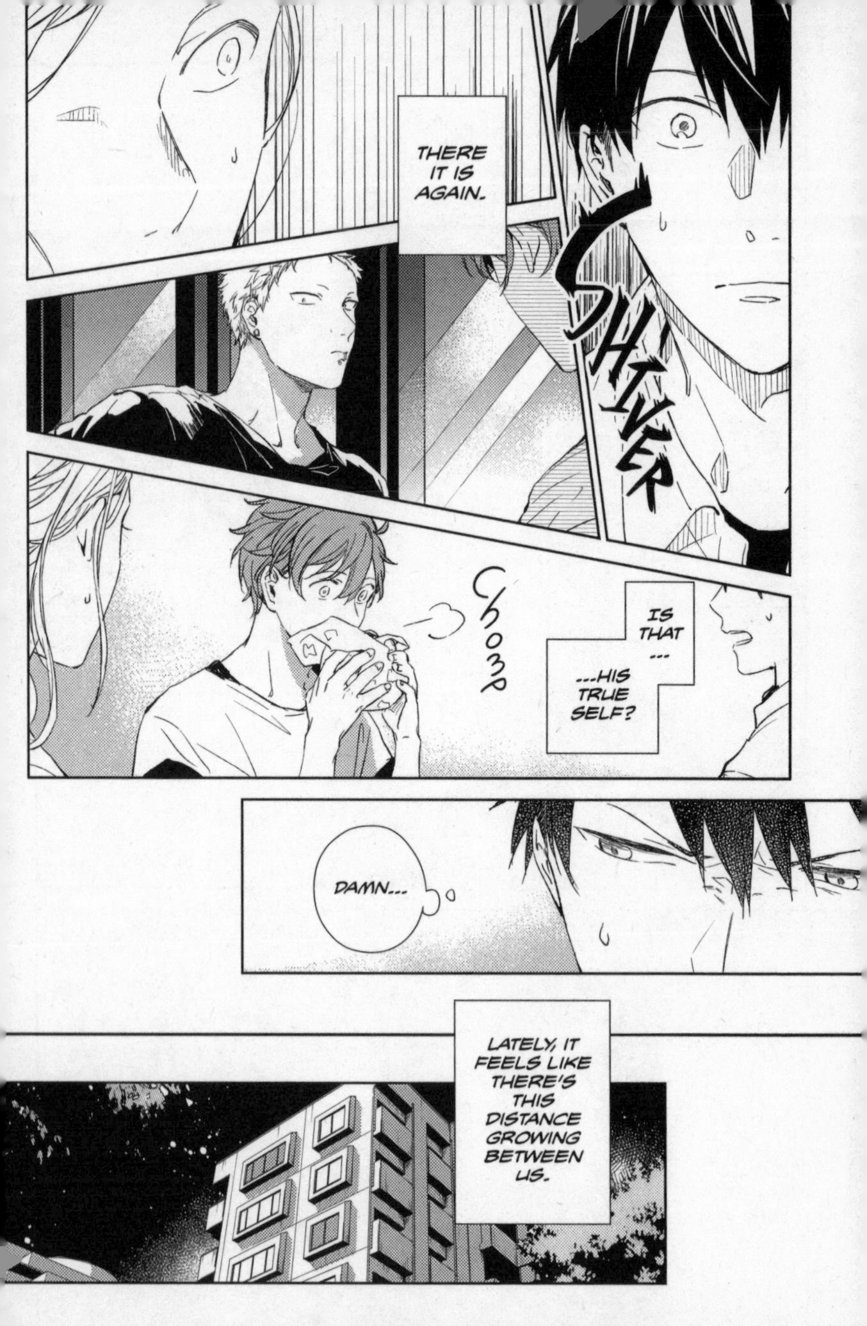
THERE IT IS AGAIN.
SHIVER
IS THAT...
...HIS TRUE SELF?
CHOMP
DAMN...
LATELY, IT FEELS LIKE THERE'S THIS DISTANCE GROWING BETWEEN US.

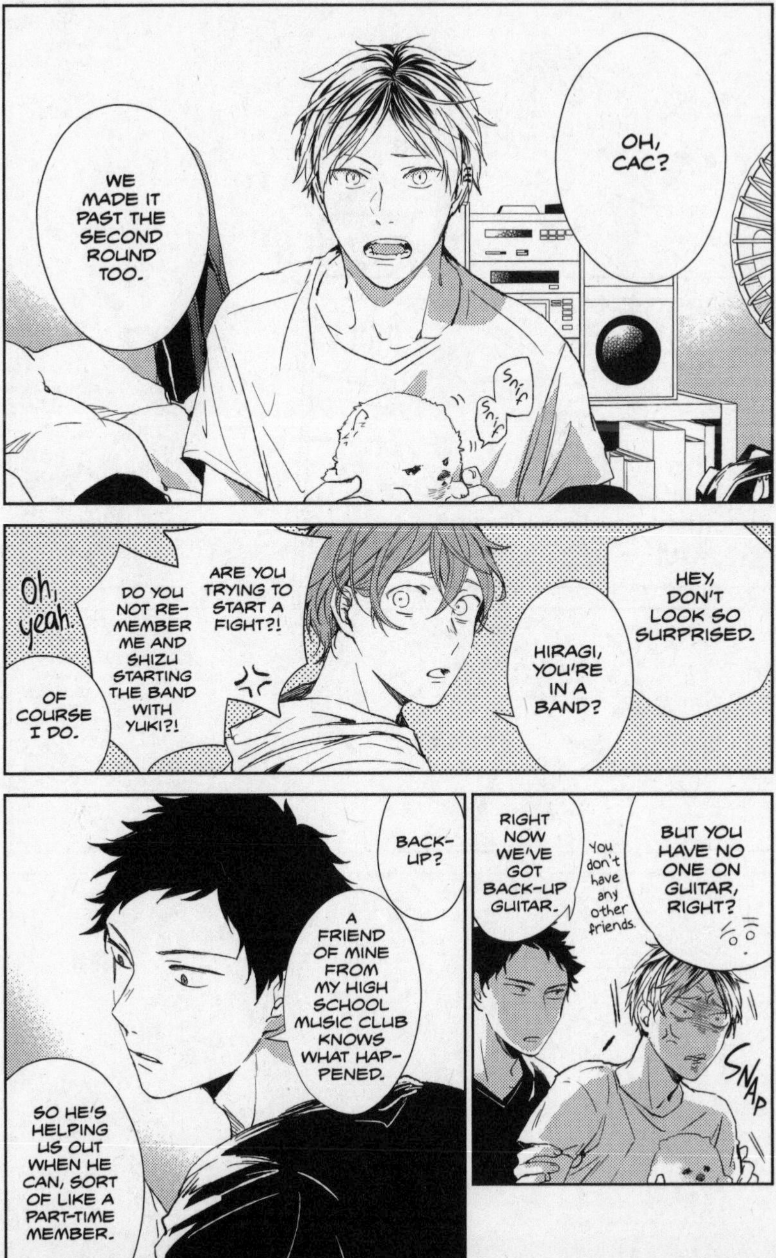
OH, CAC?
WE MADE IT PAST THE SECOND ROUND TOO.
Snif Snif
HEY, DON'T LOOK SO SURPRISED.
HIRAGI, YOU'RE IN A BAND?
ARE YOU TRYING TO START A FIGHT?!
DO YOU NOT REMEMBER ME AND SHIZU STARTING THE BAND WITH YUKI?!
Oh, yeah.
OF COURSE I DO.
BUT YOU HAVE NO ONE ON GUITAR, RIGHT?
You don't have any other friends.
RIGHT NOW WE'VE GOT BACK-UP GUITAR.
SNAP
BACK-UP?
A FRIEND OF MINE FROM MY HIGH SCHOOL MUSIC CLUB KNOWS WHAT HAPPENED.
SO HE'S HELPING US OUT WHEN HE CAN, SORT OF LIKE A PART-TIME MEMBER.

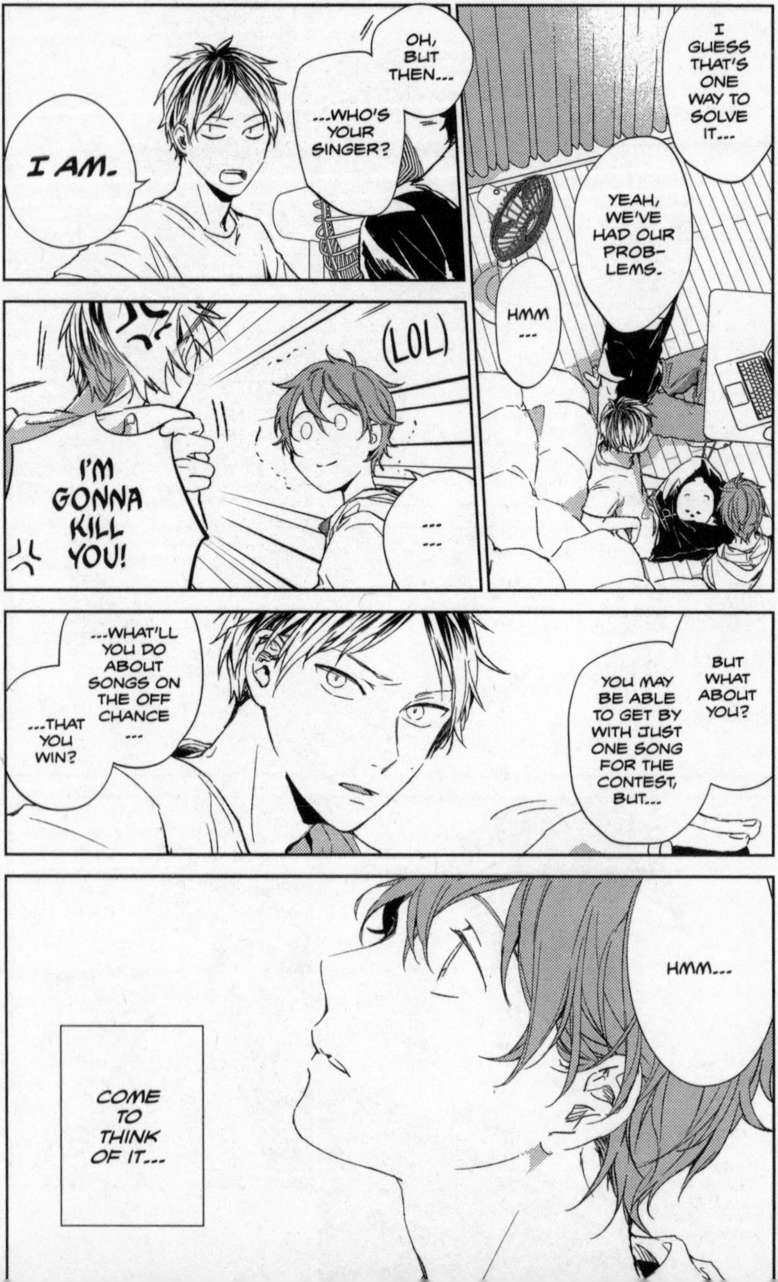
I GUESS THAT'S ONE WAY TO SOLVE IT...
YEAH, WE'VE HAD OUR PROB-LEMS.
HMM...
OH, BUT THEN...
...WHO'S YOUR SINGER?
I AM.
(LOL)
I'M GONNA KILL YOU!
......
BUT WHAT ABOUT YOU?
YOU MAY BE ABLE TO GET BY WITH JUST ONE SONG FOR THE CONTEST, BUT...
...WHAT'LL YOU DO ABOUT SONGS ON THE OFF CHANCE...
...THAT YOU WIN?
HMM...
COME TO THINK OF IT...

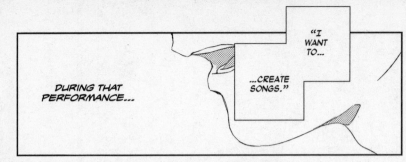

"I WANT TO...

...CREATE SONGS."

DURING THAT PERFORMANCE...

...I REALIZED...

...TWO THINGS.

FIRST...

...THAT IT'S POSSIBLE TO MAKE EMOTIONS RESONATE THROUGH SOUND.

SECOND...

...KAJI AND I ARE PROBABLY ALIKE.

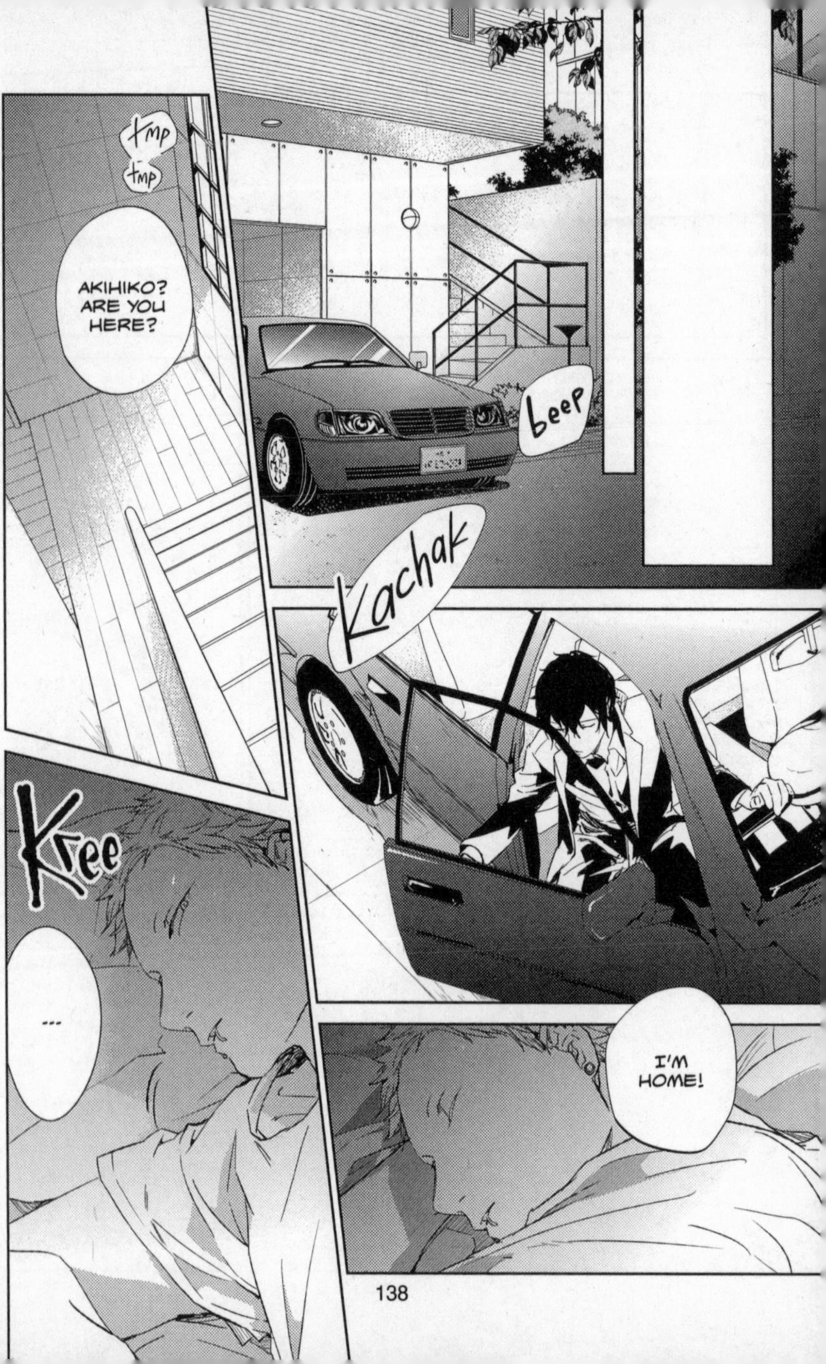

beep
Kachak
I'M HOME!
tmp
tmp
AKIHIKO? ARE YOU HERE?
Kree
...

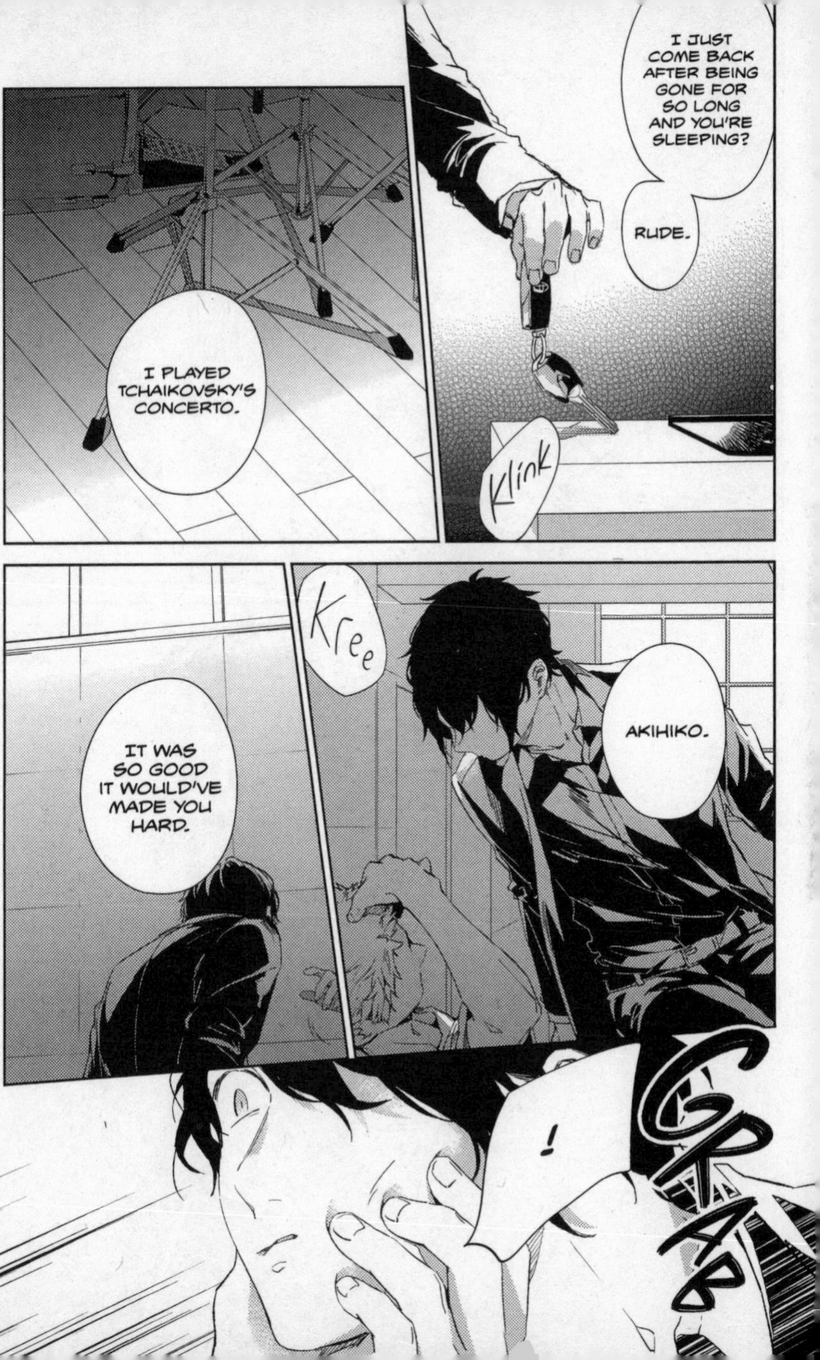
I JUST COME BACK AFTER BEING GONE FOR SO LONG AND YOU'RE SLEEPING?
RUDE.
Klink
I PLAYED TCHAIKOVSKY'S CONCERTO.
Kree
AKIHIKO.
IT WAS SO GOOD IT WOULD'VE MADE YOU HARD.
!
GRAB

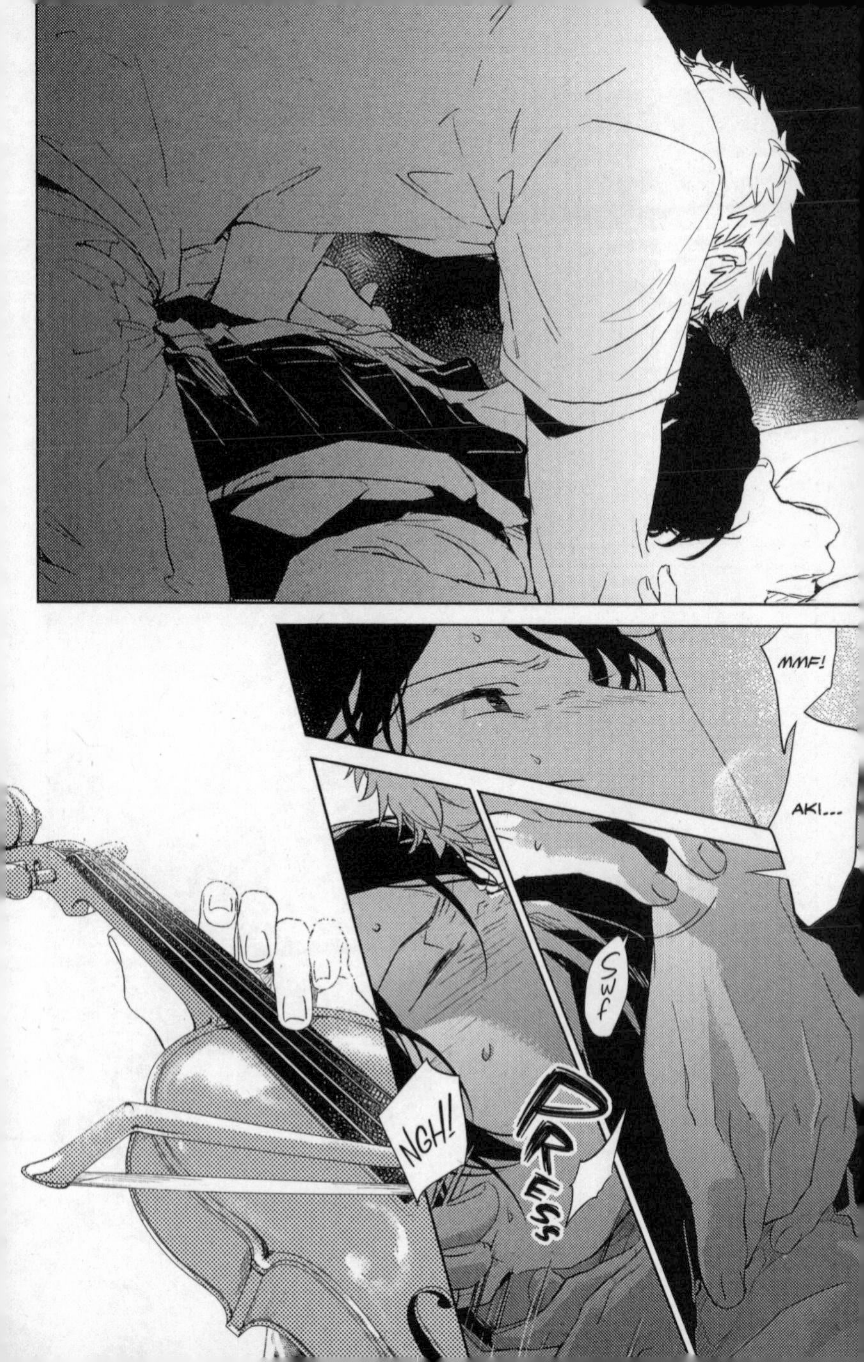
MMF!
AKI...
SWF
PRESS
NGH!

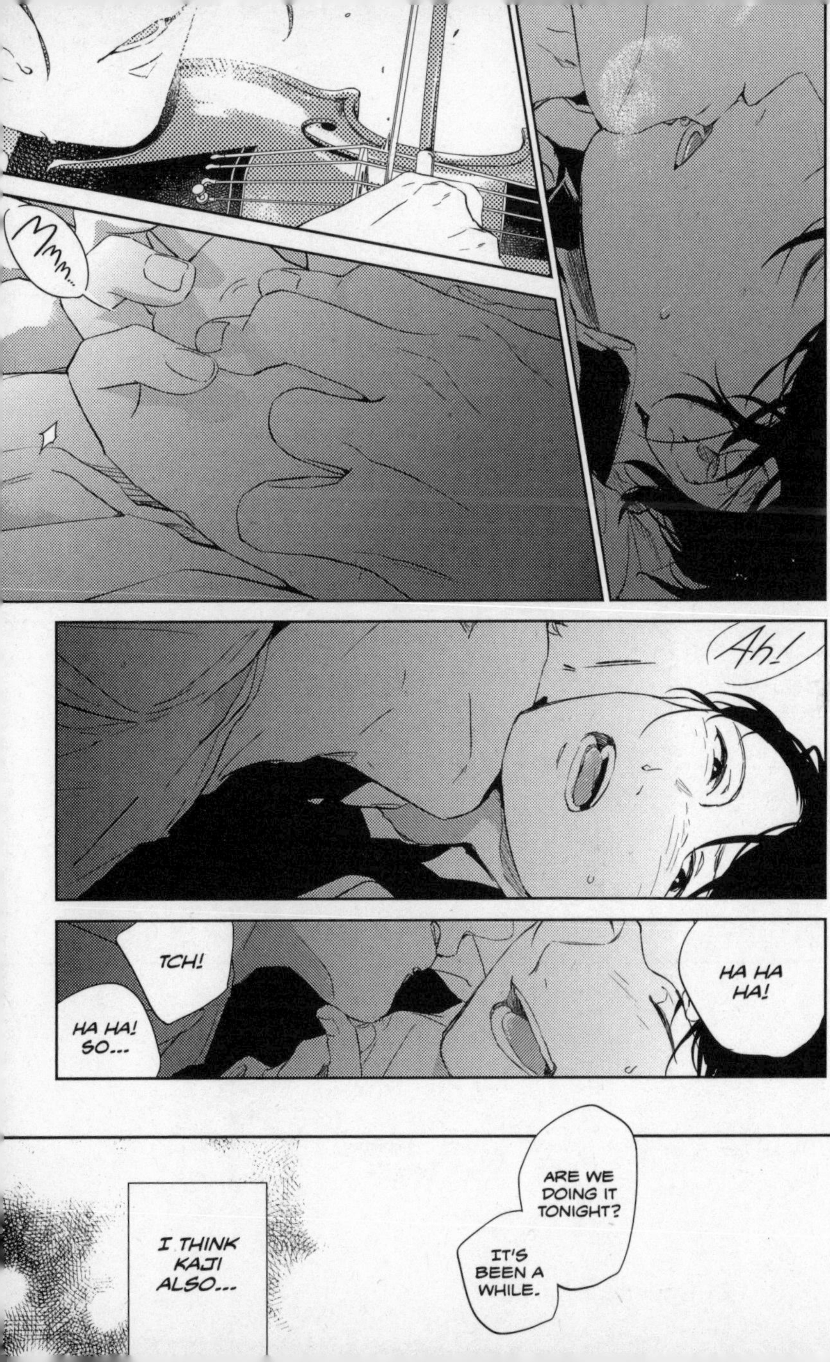
Mmm...
Ah!
HA HA HA!
TCH!
HA HA! SO...
ARE WE DOING IT TONIGHT?
IT'S BEEN A WHILE.
I THINK KAJI ALSO...

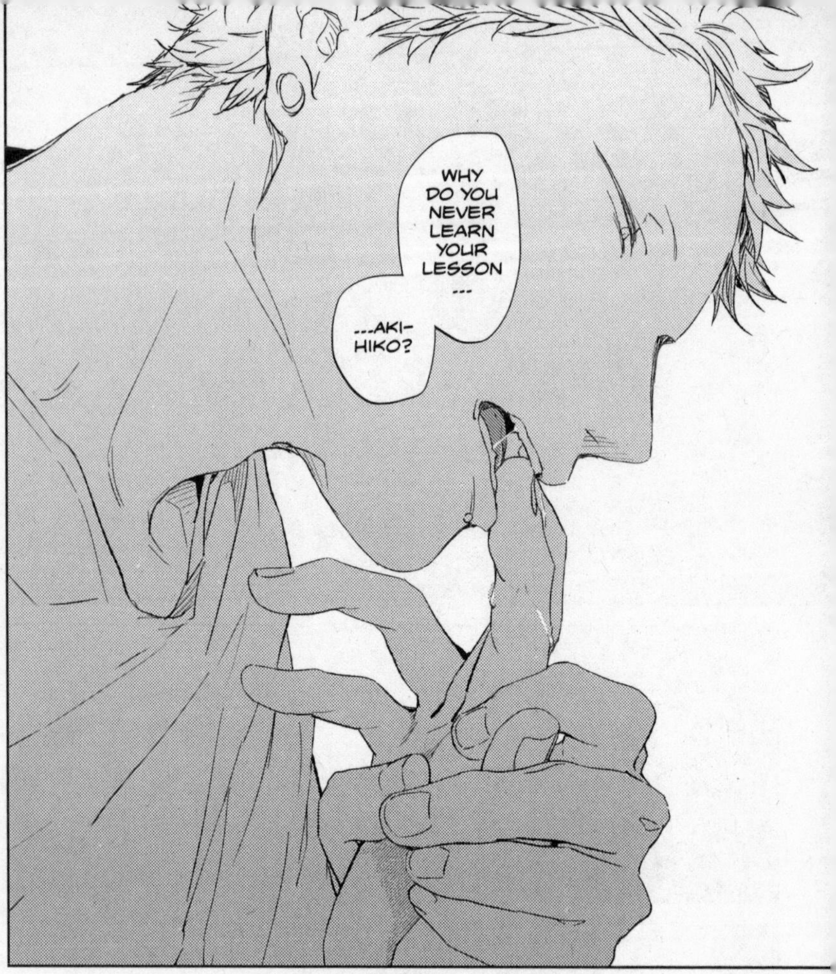
WHY DO YOU NEVER LEARN YOUR LESSON ...
...AKI-HIKO?

...FELL IN LOVE WITH SOMEONE HE'LL NEVER GET OVER...

...AND IT BROKE HIS HEART.

To Be Continued...

given
@given_ssn

Publicity shot 🐥🎸

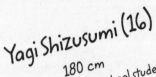

Yagi Shizusumi (16)

180 cm
(Second-year high school student)

Birthday: 11/22   Sign: Scorpio
Blood Type: B

A drummer, more or less.

Friends since childhood with Mafuyu, Hiragi, and Yuki. Formed his first band with Hiragi (bass) and Yuki (guitar).

Was in his school's handball club but then started another band.

Goes to the same high school as Hiragi.

(Princess) Hiragi

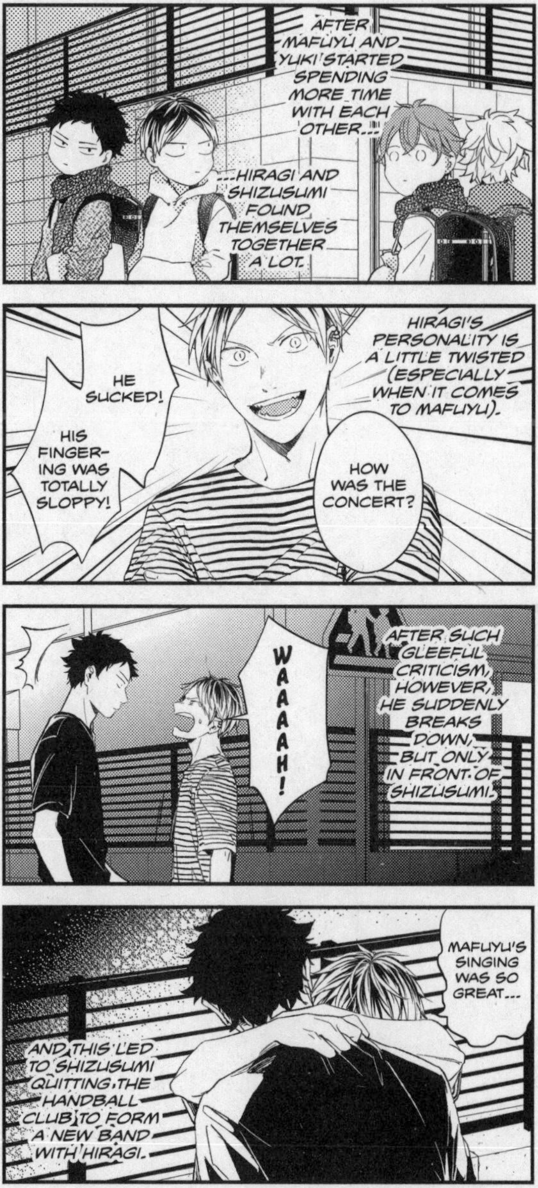
AFTER MAFUYU AND YUKI STARTED SPENDING MORE TIME WITH EACH OTHER...
...HIRAGI AND SHIZUSUMI FOUND THEMSELVES TOGETHER A LOT.
HIRAGI'S PERSONALITY IS A LITTLE TWISTED (ESPECIALLY WHEN IT COMES TO MAFUYU).
HOW WAS THE CONCERT?
HE SUCKED!
HIS FINGERING WAS TOTALLY SLOPPY!
AFTER SUCH GLEEFUL CRITICISM, HOWEVER, HE SUDDENLY BREAKS DOWN, BUT ONLY IN FRONT OF SHIZUSUMI.
WAAAAAH!
MAFUYU'S SINGING WAS SO GREAT...
AND THIS LED TO SHIZUSUMI QUITTING THE HANDBALL CLUB TO FORM A NEW BAND WITH HIRAGI.

given

by Natsuki Kizu

The First Time Itaya Deadeyed Me

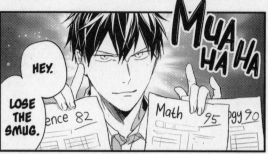

MUAHAHAHA
HEY.
LOSE THE SMUG.
Math 95
ogy 90
ence 82
YOU'RE SO OBVIOUSLY ON THE SCIENCE TRACK.
WITH THE RIGHT THEORY, I CAN SOLVE ANY PROBLEM!
THE TRADE-OFF IS A TOTAL LACK OF LINGUISTIC COMPETENCE.
HEH HEH HEH...
MATH IS SUCH A PAIN! WHY DO WE HAVE TO USE ALL THESE DUMB THEORIES?!
BUT...
...HOW CAN YOU UNDERSTAND ANYTHING WITHOUT A THEORY?
WHAT?!

The look that says "He's really, actually like this..."

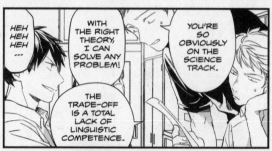

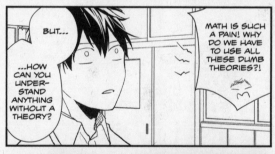

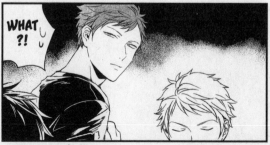

Curiosity Killed The...

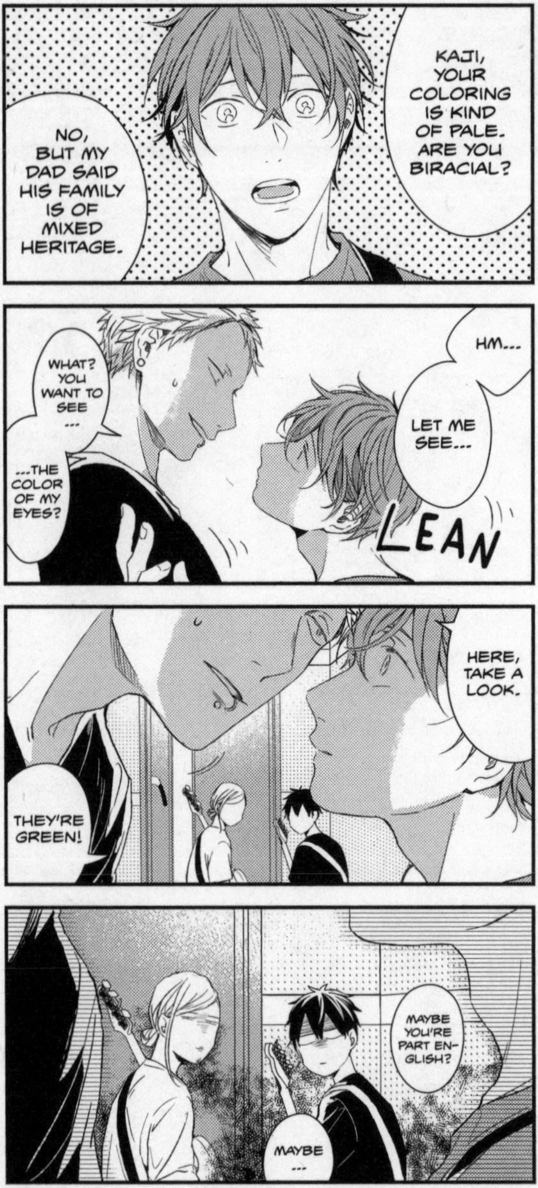
KAJI, YOUR COLORING IS KIND OF PALE. ARE YOU BIRACIAL?
NO, BUT MY DAD SAID HIS FAMILY IS OF MIXED HERITAGE.
HM...
LET ME SEE...
LEAN
WHAT? YOU WANT TO SEE ...
...THE COLOR OF MY EYES?
HERE, TAKE A LOOK.
THEY'RE GREEN!
MAYBE YOU'RE PART EN-GLISH?
MAYBE ...

Haruki: "Hey, are you okay with this?"

Seductive, Stylish Hair (Short Version)

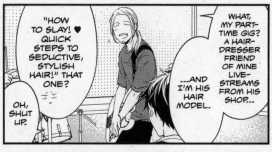

WHAT, MY PART-TIME GIG? A HAIRDRESSER FRIEND OF MINE LIVE-STREAMS FROM HIS SHOP...
...AND I'M HIS HAIR MODEL.
"HOW TO SLAY! ♥ QUICK STEPS TO SEDUCTIVE, STYLISH HAIR!" THAT ONE?
OH, SHUT UP.
Play All
How to Slay!♥Quick Steps to Seductive, Stylish Hair!
CLIK
Hair Salon Harusame In Jiyugaoka
lolololol super loool
Plays: 5,821 Comments: 689 DMs: 125
6:02
lay! ♥ Quick Ste
HI!
I'M HANAOKA FROM HAIR SALON HARUSAME.
AND THIS IS MY FRIEND HARU. WE'RE NOT SEDUCTIVE OR STYLISH, BUT WE'LL SHOW YOU HOW TO DO SOME HAIRSTYLES THAT ARE ALL THAT AND EASY TOO!
TODAY WE'LL DO A BASIC DIVIDED PONYTAIL.
Haru has really broad shoulders
Salon Harusame?
kind of persuasive
not stylish at all
OKAY, SO...
FIRST I'M LIGHTLY BLOCKING HARU'S HAIR, AND THEN I'M GOING TO CURL IT!
Haru's a guy! (♂)
wowwwww
Does he have a beard?!
lolololol
Haru is a dude (♂)
He has beautiful hair...

A moderately stylish channel.

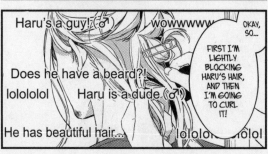

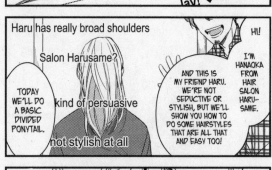

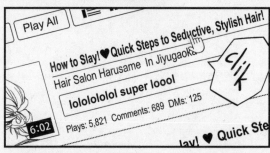

Seductive, Stylish Hair (Part Two)

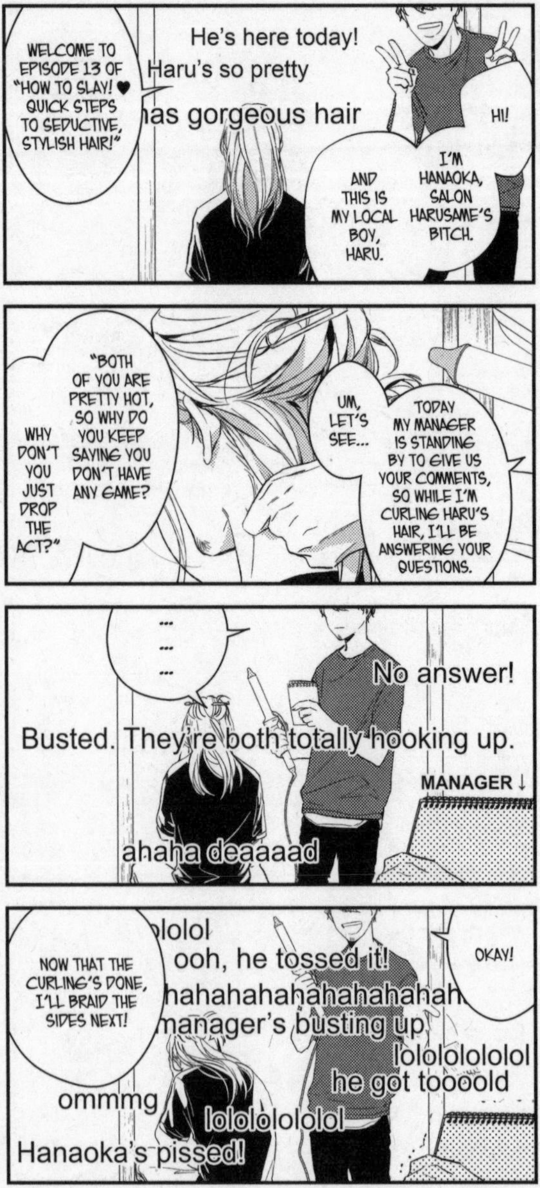
HI!
I'M HANAOKA, SALON HARUSAME'S BITCH.
AND THIS IS MY LOCAL BOY, HARU.
He's here today!
Haru's so pretty
has gorgeous hair
WELCOME TO EPISODE 13 OF "HOW TO SLAY! ♥ QUICK STEPS TO SEDUCTIVE, STYLISH HAIR!"
TODAY MY MANAGER IS STANDING BY TO GIVE US YOUR COMMENTS, SO WHILE I'M CURLING HARU'S HAIR, I'LL BE ANSWERING YOUR QUESTIONS.
UM, LET'S SEE...
"BOTH OF YOU ARE PRETTY HOT, SO WHY DO YOU KEEP SAYING YOU DON'T HAVE ANY GAME?
WHY DON'T YOU JUST DROP THE ACT?"
No answer!
...
...
...
Busted. They're both totally hooking up.
MANAGER ↓
ahaha deaaaad
OKAY!
lololol
ooh, he tossed it!
hahahahahahahahahah
manager's busting up
lolololololol
he got tooold
NOW THAT THE CURLING'S DONE, I'LL BRAID THE SIDES NEXT!
ommmg
lolololololol
Hanaoka's pissed!

His Customers Love Him

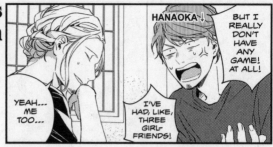

HANAOKA↓
BUT I REALLY DON'T HAVE ANY GAME! AT ALL!
I'VE HAD, LIKE, THREE GIRL-FRIENDS!
YEAH... ME TOO...
EVER SINCE I STARTED WORKING, I'VE MET TONS OF PEOPLE, BUT...IT DOESN'T LEAD TO LOVE...
THAT'S WHERE YOU HAVE ME BEAT, HARU.
HUH?
YOU'VE FOUND LOVE, RIGHT?!
THANKS TO MY GOD-LIKE STYLING, YOU CAN SEDUCE ANY WOMAN YOU WANT!!
I'M JUST KID-DING!
THAT'S NOT THE GOAL HERE.
I'll cut it off...
YO.
CUTE BRAIDS.
Serene

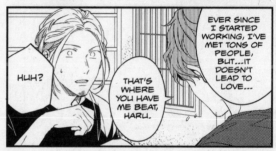

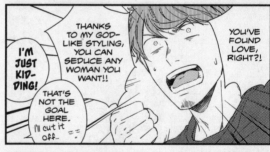

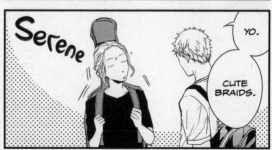

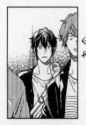

Huh?

A Cruel Death

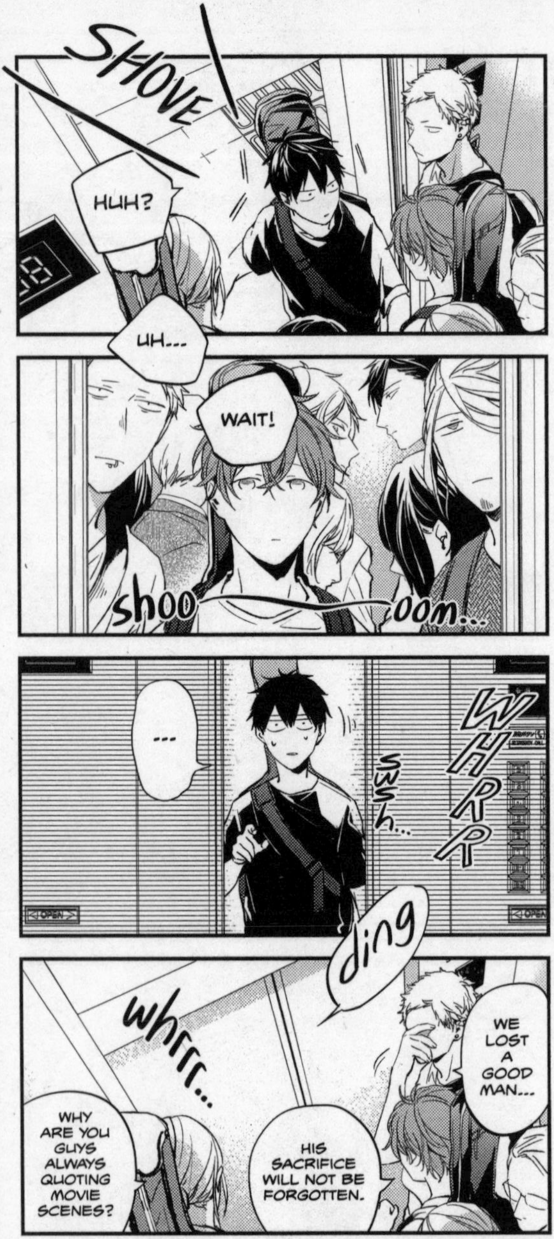
SHOVE
HUH?
UH...
WAIT!
shoo—oom...
WHRR
swsh...
...
ding
WE LOST A GOOD MAN...
whrrr...
HIS SACRIFICE WILL NOT BE FORGOTTEN.
WHY ARE YOU GUYS ALWAYS QUOTING MOVIE SCENES?

Uenoyama isn't actually dead.

I Told You Not to Post About It

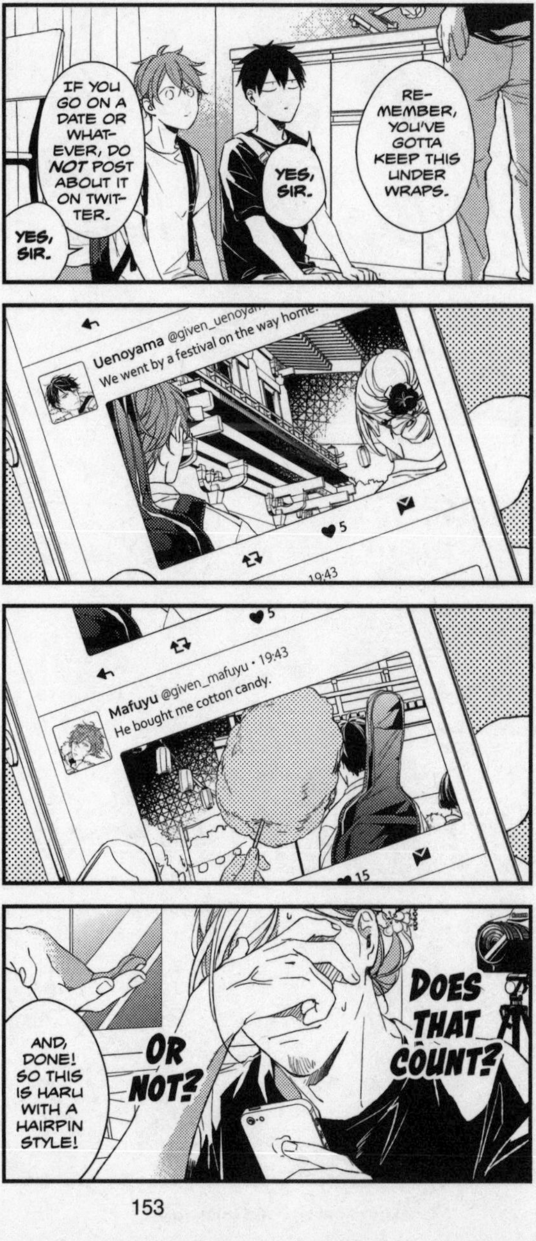
REMEMBER, YOU'VE GOTTA KEEP THIS UNDER WRAPS.
YES, SIR.
IF YOU GO ON A DATE OR WHATEVER, DO NOT POST ABOUT IT ON TWITTER.
YES, SIR.
Uenoyama @given_uenoyama
We went by a festival on the way home.
5
19:43
5
Mafuyu @given_mafuyu · 19:43
He bought me cotton candy.
15
DOES THAT COUNT?
OR NOT?
AND, DONE! SO THIS IS HARU WITH A HAIRPIN STYLE!

Furby Loves Haruki

lick
lick
lick
lick
HUH?
lick
lick
lick
lick
HEY!
GAH!
WAIT!
HELP!
FURBY REALLY LIKES YOU, HARUKI.
LICKING IS A SIGN OF AFFEC-TION.
FURBALL~!!
CONGRAT-ULATIONS. YOU'VE FOUND LOVE AT LAST.
dripping
Yeah...
Thanks...
FURBY, COME!

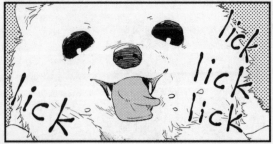

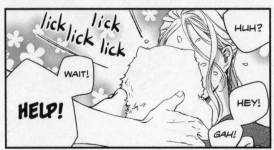

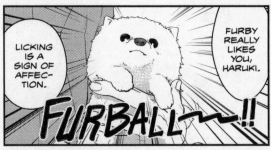

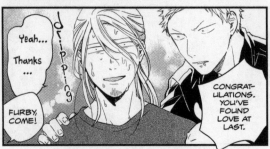

Love is moist and lukewarm.

The Dark Side of Being a Dog Owner

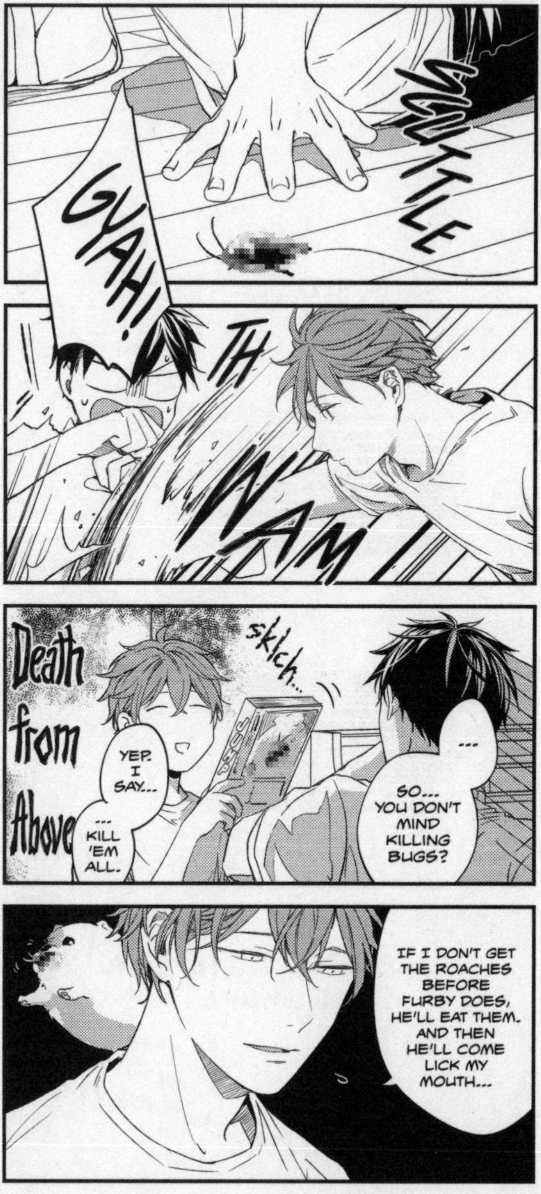
SCUTTLE
GYAH!!
THWAM
...
SO... YOU DON'T MIND KILLING BUGS?
sklch...
YEP. I SAY...
... KILL 'EM ALL.
Death from Above
IF I DON'T GET THE ROACHES BEFORE FURBY DOES, HE'LL EAT THEM. AND THEN HE'LL COME LICK MY MOUTH...

Furball (9 months)

To cheer Mafuyu up, his mother bought him a dog for his birthday. The type of dog that licks people a lot.

Bonus! Concept notes and sketches

Haruki's flat
A 15-minute walk from the station, so it's big but cheap.

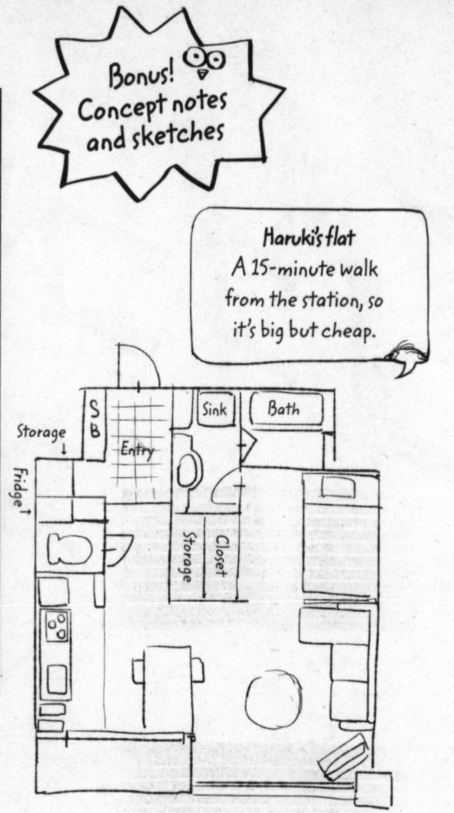

S
B
Storage
Entry
Fridge
Sink
Bath
Storage
Closet

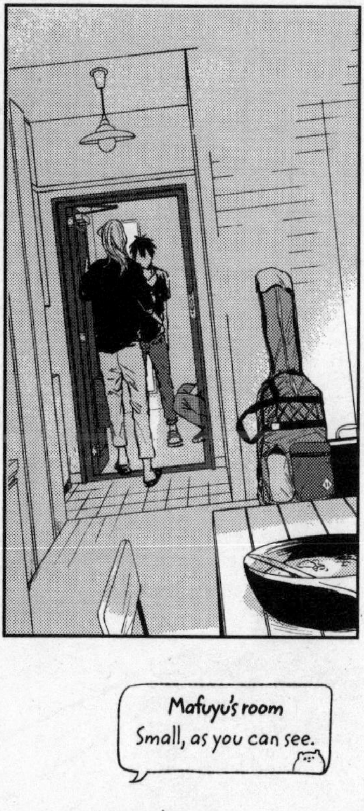

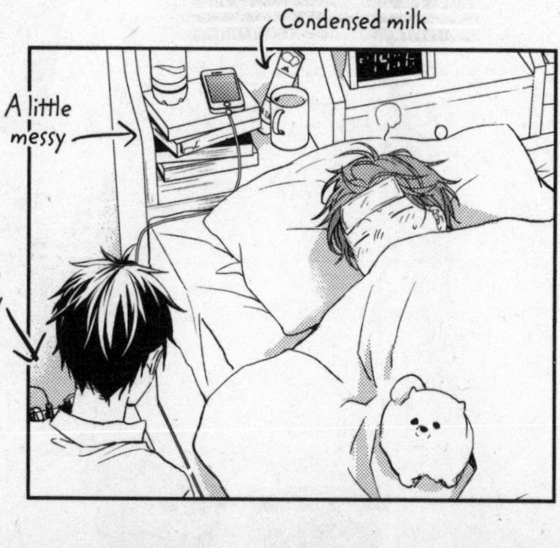

Condensed milk
A little messy
More messy

Mafuyu's room
Small, as you can see.

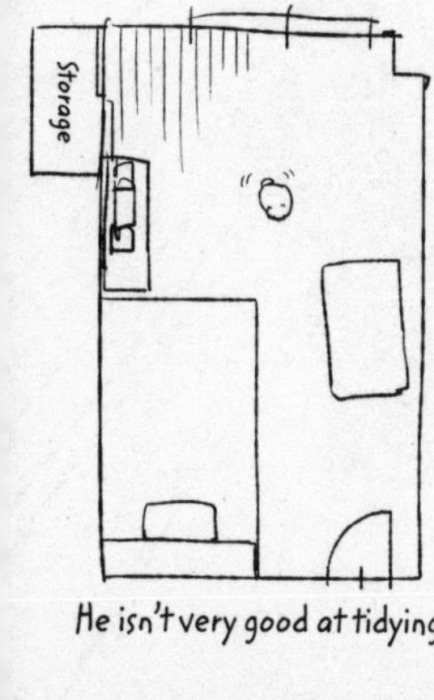

Storage

He isn't very good at tidying.

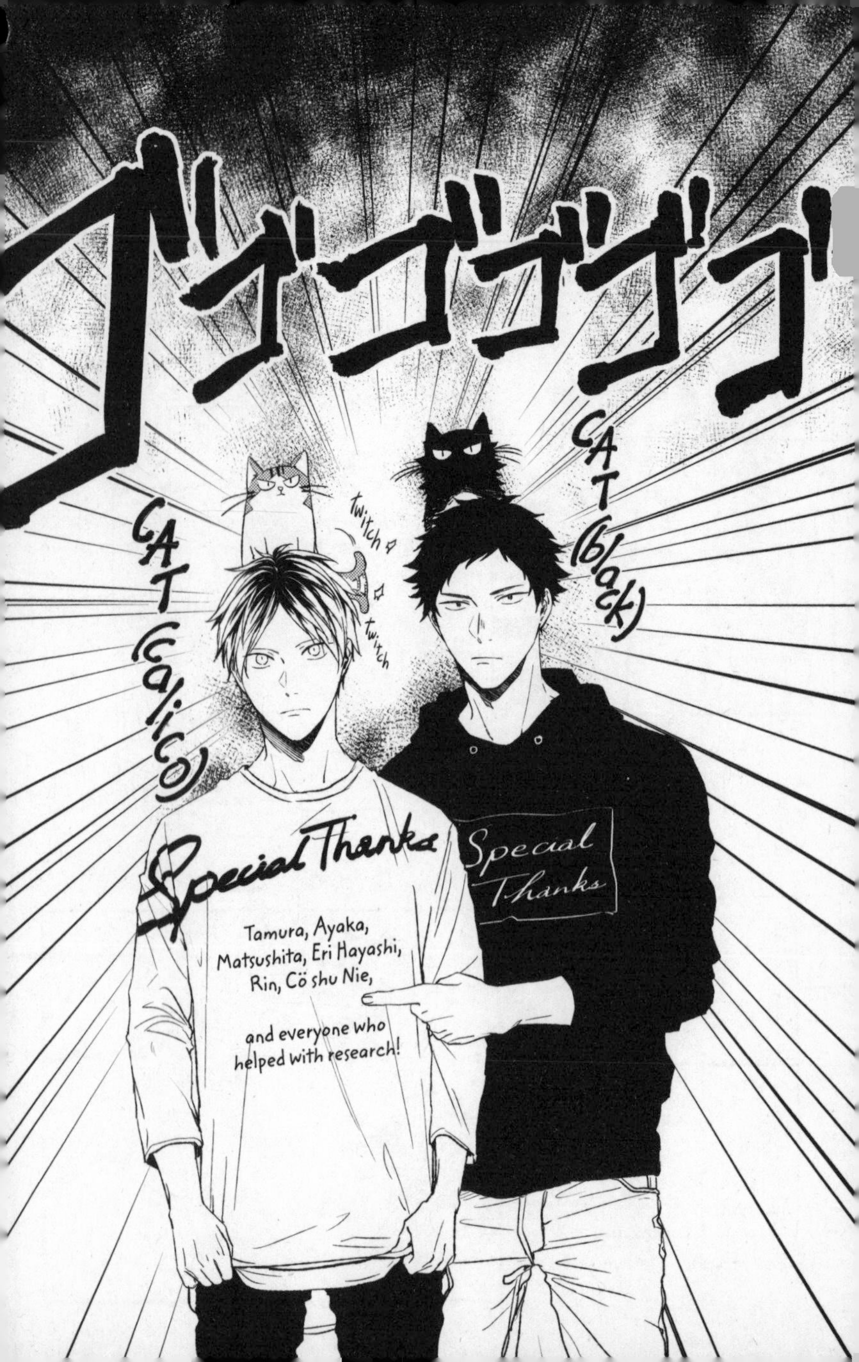
ゴゴゴゴゴ
CAT (black)
CAT (calico)
twitch
twitch
Special Thanks
Special Thanks
Tamura, Ayaka, Matsushita, Eri Hayashi, Rin, Cö shu Nie,
and everyone who helped with research!